The Blandford

ROCK AND MINERAL GUIDE

The Blandford
ROCK AND MINERAL GUIDE

James R. Tindall
Roger Thornhill

Foreword by Lord Energlyn
Head of the Department of Geology,
University of Nottingham

Blandford Press

Published by Blandford Press Limited,
167 High Holborn, London WC1V 6PH
Produced by Carter Nash Cameron Limited
25 Lloyd Baker Street, London WC1X 9AT

Copyright © 1975 by Carter Nash Cameron Limited
ISBN 0 7137 0699 6
Also published in the United States and Canada
by Van Nostrand Reinhold Company as
The Collector's Guide to Rocks and Minerals

Printed and bound by Sir Joseph Causton & Sons Ltd,
London and Eastleigh

A Carter Nash Cameron Book

Design: Tom Carter

Editor: Hamish Johnson

Picture Research: Penny Brown

Diagrams: Annabel Milne

CONTENTS

FOREWORD

The greatest breed of rock collector the world has ever known was Stone Age man. Life depended upon his ability to find and use two pieces of suitable rock with which he could fashion implements. For over a million years, *Homo sapiens* used only stone implements to hunt, carve flesh and strip skins to make clothes and boats. These stone implements were also the basis of trading. Stone Age man had a stone standard of currency which was abandoned for gold when metals were discovered. For the modern rockhound, the thrill of finding an axe is as great as that derived from unearthing a beautiful mineral. In a museum showcase, stone axes are interesting, but picking one up in a field brings home to you that you may be the first person to handle it since it was discarded thousands of years ago by Stone Age man.

Rocks have always been man's raw materials for building, but to some rocks he has accorded mythical and religious associations. Think of the effort that went into the creation of Stonehenge or the erection, block by block, of the Pyramids of Egypt. Witness, too, the mystical associations that the Scots attach to the Stone of Scone even in these allegedly enlightened times. In every country of the world there are stones that have acquired a mystical significance.

Every pebble on the sea shore has a story to tell. Like a tumbler machine, the sea has rolled angular fragments of rock torn from the cliffs by the elements into polished pebbles. Each one can be traced back to its origin. If a granite pebble is found on the sea shore of Dorset, it must have travelled from Cornwall. Suppose you were searching for gold in a river and you found some specks in your pan. The hunt would be to discover the source rock. Think back to the Klondike gold rush. Dozens of men lost their lives in a wild search for gold veins. Using this book will project your efforts into a more scientific exercise which will be more effective in a hunt for a bonanza (a word which, incidentally, comes from the name of the Indian village where gold was found in quantity in the Yukon River). In all such cases, pebbles became the sign posts—simple observation of elementary facts they contain will reveal the romance of geological stories.

The crust of the earth is changing all the time. Wind and rain devour the exposed rocks and the debris is transported by rivers into the sea. There it is swept over the continental shelf until it eventually comes to rest to form the beginning of new sedimentary rocks. Thousands of feet of such sedimentary rocks accumulate; eventually they are forced above sea level to form new lands. When the earth forces become intense, blocks of these sedimentary rocks are pushed sideways. Pile upon pile of various rock formations have accumulated in this way to end up as mountain chains like the Alps, the Rockies and the Himalayas.

All these processes are exceedingly slow. A mountain chain like the Alps would take at least fifty million years to grow to its present stature. This in itself will make the searcher of rocks realise how brief has been our time on earth. In scale it is like one day in a million years of geological time.

The crust can react violently. A sudden rupture of only a few millimetres can destroy large towns in a matter of minutes. The eruption of Krakatoa in 1883 has been called 'the loudest noise on earth'. The explosion was heard 3,000 miles away in Rodriguez Island. It created a tidal wave which drowned 36,000 people, and the dust blotted out the sun for two whole days. But these violent catastrophies are necessary evils. Earthquakes and volcanoes are natural safety valves. Without them, this planet would have exploded long ago and disappeared into outer space as meteorites and cosmic dust.

In a world which is riddled with human violence and brittle sophistication, the study of minerals and rocks fulfils a prophylactic function in our lives. It is a hobby which takes us into interesting places and usually into beautiful scenery. Hunting for geological knowledge makes seaside holidays more interesting; it creates an urge to leave houses and roads behind and to disappear into the mountains. It is an experience which can also be shared with others and it will become an infectious source of delight to share one's discoveries. To obtain full satisfaction from all this, an elementary knowledge of the principles of earth-processes is an essential. To equip you with this is the object of this book. No pretence is made at conveying encyclopedic knowledge. The object is to whet your appetite in a practical manner.

Leave aside, for a moment, the thrill of finding a rare or beautiful mineral. By picking up a pebble in the garden you can begin to reconstruct the events which led to its arrival there. It is surprising what the pebble will tell you from simple observations. It may have one side flattened and streaked with grooves. This means that at one time, it was dragged over rocks by a glacier. The pebble may be pyramidal in shape, indicating that it has been sand-blasted by the winds of the desert. Simple facts of this kind will tell you much about conditions in the place where you live long before man had evolved on earth.

If you see an outcrop of red sandstones, the probability is that they have been formed from desert sand dunes. Outcrops of limestone can only mean that they were formed in a sea or lake which contained very little suspended sediment. Limestone, which is calcium carbonate precipitated in fairly clear water, is also created by the secretion of lime by marine organisms, particularly in warm seas. Consequently, most limestones signify the earlier existence of features like the coral reefs of tropical seas to-day. The chalk of the White Cliffs of Dover testifies to the existence of tropical seas extending across Britain, and even into Russia, some 90 million years ago.

In the chalk you will find fossil sea urchins, sea anemones, starfish, shark's teeth and extinct animals called belemnites, which could only have lived in tropical waters. Hunting for fossils is all the more exciting because by chance you may be the first to find a form of life no longer extant on earth.

Rocks and minerals provide the basis of science. The chemicals discovered and used by chemists came from minerals. The laws of gravity and magnetism came from the same source. Although one is apt to think that modern science belongs entirely to this century, nothing could be further from the truth. Molecular science can be traced back to the discoveries of Father Nicalaus Steno in 1671. In his quiet monastic retreat, he studied crystalline minerals. He found that crystal faces of a mineral remained at the same angle to each other, no matter how misshapen was the crystal. This remarkable fact revealed that every mineral has a precise network of molecules. Thus, the crystal faces reflected the molecular architecture of a mineral, whether it grew straight or lop-sided. This was the basis upon which knowledge of molecules developed into the understanding of the atom.

In this Atomic Age, we should not lose sight of the fact that when a rock fractures it releases more energy than any bomb yet invented, the energy of an earthquake. Coupled with this is the eruption of a volcano. Imagine the energy required to pour out the millions of gallons of lava which we see in places like Iceland or Mount Etna. This is the gigantic scale of energy which is contained beneath the fragile crust of the earth. The source of radioactive substances is in the earth's interior. They are most likely to occur in areas which have been invaded by volcanoes or saturated with molten rock in various other ways. The material used by Madame Curie to isolate radium came from such an area in the Congo.

A grasp of the general principles lends additional zest to the hunt for minerals, fossils and rocks. The search raises important questions and reveals new standards of values. It broadens the mind and brings to human behaviour a reverence for all things natural. Roaming the countryside for pleasure and taking home specimens adds a dimension to life which money cannot buy. Locked in the rocks are the secrets of the past, and in them lies the hope for the preservation of all forms of life.

This book should stimulate the reader to do two things : in the winter months to read about geology; in the summer months to go out with a geological map, a hammer and a lens in search of minerals and rocks and maybe fossils as well.

ENERGLYN

ABOUT THIS BOOK

This book sets out to present a systematic treatment of rock and mineral collecting, covering the geological background as well as the practicalities. It is intended both for the beginner who wishes to approach the hobby methodically and for the more experienced collector who has acquired a considerable amount of knowledge in a piecemeal way and might welcome a work that provides a framework for what he has learned.

The text starts with the origins of the earth and the various theories that have been advanced to explain it. The first part of the book summarises geological history and the evidence on which our knowledge of it is based. In this context, the main types of fossil are indicated; for each period, a brief sketch is given of dominant forms of life and the main geological activity.

The second part of the book deals with minerals, working from atomic structure to crystallography and chemical classification. Minerals are also looked at in terms of the geological environments in which they occur, and the main techniques which the amateur collector can use in mineral identification are described. An appendix at the end of the book lists the basic properties of a wide range of minerals.

The third part is devoted to rocks, with sections on each of the three main classes: igneous, sedimentary and metamorphic. In this part of the book, the main geological features of the earth's surface are described in terms of the processes that produced them.

The last part looks at collecting, at equipment, at the types of location where specimens are most likely to be found and at standards of behaviour for the collector. We conclude with a brief coverage of basic lapidary techniques.

One of the objects of the book is to introduce most of the technical terminology that the collector is likely to meet. For this reason, technical terms are not avoided, but are used where they are needed; the index is combined with a glossary, and each term is defined or a reference is provided to the page where the definition may be found.

This book is intended as general background reading for the collector. Although it offers general guidance on identification, it does not attempt to rival the many field guides which deal in detail with the rocks and minerals of specific areas. We hope rather that it will be useful in complementing them by providing a more general coverage and more ample illustration than they can provide.

Part 1

The Earth

The most influential of the many early theories of the origin of the solar system was the Nebular Hypothesis put forward by the Marquis de Laplace in 1796. The hypothesis assumed the existence of a large globular mass of hot gas which was slowly rotating in space. As the gas cooled, it contracted and rotated more rapidly as it conserved its angular momentum; eventually it became flattened into a disc-like shape. When the speed of rotation increased to a point when the centrifugal force at the edge of the cloud exceeded the gravitational attraction holding it together a ring of gas was thrown off, which remained in stable orbit as the cloud continued to contract. A series of rings was formed in this way, each of which was somehow swept together to form a planet. Finally, the centre of the cloud condensed to form the sun. This theory was widely accepted until it was shown that it could not account for the distribution of energy within the solar system. Although the planets have only 0.1% of the mass of the solar system, they have 98% of the energy of movement, the angular momentum, which is calculated as the product of their mass times their velocity times their distance from the sun. For Laplace's hypothesis to be true, the sun would have to be a rapidly spinning thin disc, and the planets would have to be spinning in the opposite direction to it, which they are not.

The need to account for the distribution of rotational energy in the solar system led to the development of catastrophic theories, which treated the formation of the planets as an accident. In one version the sun was assumed to have travelled alone in space until it was disrupted by a near collision with another star. The tidal forces generated by mutual gravitational attraction drew out a stream of hot material from the surface of the sun which was pulled along in the path of the passing star. This filament of material broke up into globules which condensed to form the planets. The rotational energy of the planets was imparted by the passing star. However, it was shown that no passing star would be able to impart the proper angular momentum to the filament: the material would be drawn after the receding star rather than being sent into orbit around the sun. The theory was also unable to explain how clouds of hot gas having the temperature of the sun and the mass of the planets could condense rather than disperse. The distances between stars in our galaxy, around five light years, make the near approach of two stars highly improbable, so that planetary systems would be extremely rare, perhaps unique. Modern observations suggest otherwise: several stars have been shown to have dark, invisible companions of a planetary type which can be detected by the perturbations which they cause in the stars they accompany.

Another hypothesis suggested that the sun was originally part of a binary star, one half of a two star system which revolved about a common centre of gravity. The other star exploded, and the planets formed from the debris. Stars are known to annihilate themselves in such supernova explosions: the results of one remain visible in the Crab nebula in the constellation of Taurus. This vast cloud of rapidly expanding gas and dust covers many cubic light years, and is the result of a supernova explosion which was observed by Chinese astronomers in the eleventh century. Such explosions are far too violent to provide a mechanism for the formation of planets alone.

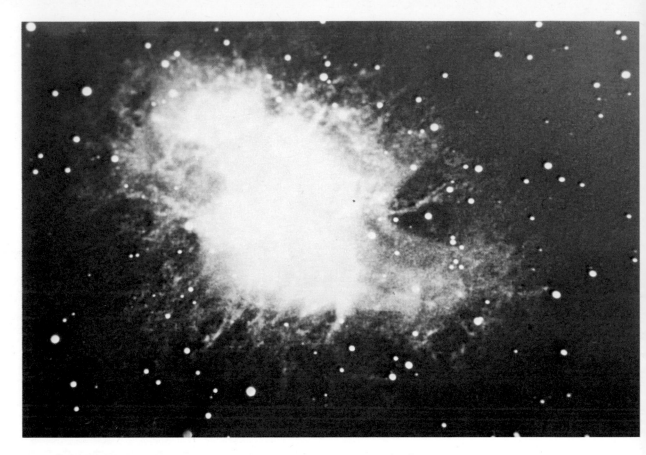

A variant of this hypothesis supposed that the sun encountered a large dust cloud during its travels through space and gathered material around it by gravitational attraction. The planets condensed from this diffuse envelope. However, the very presence of the sun in such a cloud is sufficient to ensure that planets are not formed, for a body of the sun's size would simply draw the material into itself. Modern theories are very similar to Laplace's Nebular Hypothesis, and find the source of both planetary and stellar evolution in the dust clouds alone.

The clouds of interstellar dust and gas that result when a star dies in a supernova explosion are rich in relatively heavy elements like silicon and iron; these are produced in a complex series of nuclear reactions in the star prior to the explosion. In astronomical terms, the clouds are very dense, containing around a thousand hydrogen atoms per cubic centimetre, compared with one hydrogen atom per ten cubic centimetres in normal space. Such clouds are the forming grounds of second generation stars like the sun, stars enriched in the heavier elements which predominate in dense, rocky planets like the earth.

In the initial stages, the density of the cloud slowly increases; the process is accelerated by the development of areas of random, rolling turbulence which increase the density until gravity overwhelms all other forces and the whole mass begins to collapse inwards. After ten million years, the cloud has become a thousand million times more dense, and has contracted from its original diameter of a hundred light years to a diameter of one-tenth of a light year. At this stage

The Crab Nebula in Taurus.

the cloud fragments around areas of above average density, forming smaller clouds, each capable of becoming a star. The original cloud is assumed to have been rotating : as its size reduces, its rate of rotation increases. This rotation is imparted to each of the fragments when the cloud breaks up, and produces flattening in the equatorial plane due to centrifugal force, with the result that the fragments become lens-shaped discs. Discs, in which the density of the material is relatively uniform, elongate and split to form binary stars; those with varying densities and localised concentrations of mass become denser at the centre and less dense at the edge under the influence of gravity until a mass of material consolidates at the centre to form the basis of the future star. This protosun collapses until gravitational energy released heats up its interior and causes it to radiate and become luminous. Eventually the temperature and pressure in the interior increase to a point at which a thermonuclear reaction is started, and contraction ceases. The protosun has now become a sun, a self-sustaining source of energy that is radiated in the form of sunlight.

While the protosun grew by drawing in gases from the cloud, the cloud itself cooled, and the material consolidated, with the metals and other heavy compounds near the centre, and the lighter gaseous elements and more volatile compounds on the outside. This segregation is now thought to have been the result of the interaction of the sun's magnetic field with the ionized material of the cloud. This interaction can also explain the distribution of rotational energy in the solar system : the sun was slowed down by the braking effect of its magnetic field, which transferred energy to the material of the cloud as it pushed it away. The result was an inner region of solid particles, where the dense inner planets formed, and an outer region rich in gases where the large, low density planets formed.

The way in which the planets formed is uncertain. It is possible that eddies developed within the gas cloud surrounding the protosun and that within them particles became stuck together by some form of 'cosmic glue'; this may have involved the formation of chemical bonds between the particles, or the action of ice, or of electrostatic or magnetic forces. Certainly the turbulence within the cloud would cause electric discharges which would melt and vaporise some of its constituents, making them more active physically and chemically – in effect more sticky.

The eddies increased in size as they gathered more material until they each became dense enough to generate their own gravitational fields. The cloud then broke up into a series of rotating masses which condensed into the planets as we now know them. The earth is believed to have been formed in this way about 4600 million years ago.

It seems likely that shortly after it formed, the earth consisted of a cold, homogeneous mass of material; this is suggested by an examination of certain types of meteorite which are thought to be the remains of solid material left over from the process of planetary evolution. This mass may have contained short-lived radioactive isotopes, such as Al_{26}, a highly radioactive isotope of aluminium; these could have been formed by the emission of high energy particles from magnetic flares during the interaction of the sun's magnetic field with the ionised cloud of gas and dust. Al$_{26}$ decays rapidly to become an isotope of magnesium, and in doing so it releases intense heat, enough, it is thought, to have melted the primitive earth. After this violent heating the planet settled down; heat was still produced by the decay of other isotopes, such as those of uranium, thorium, and potassium, but at a much lower level, so that it was balanced by heat losses from the surface.

A mixed mass of material will separate into its constituents when totally melted: heavy elements sink while lighter ones rise to the surface, floating on top of a molten mass like slag in a blast furnace. The materials of the earth became differentiated into layers in this way, with the crust rising to the surface as a light scum, and the heavier iron and nickel sinking to the centre. As the intense heat died away and the earth settled into thermal equilibrium, the elements began to interact chemically, forming minerals. The earth stabilised with a structure consisting of a crust containing light minerals rich in silicon, aluminium and magnesium, an intermediate mantle containing similar material but with a different physical structure, and a heavy core consisting of heavy minerals rich in iron and nickel.

THE GEOPHYSICAL STRUCTURE OF THE EARTH

At certain points on the earth's surface, huge masses of rock are being pushed together or pulled apart; when the accumulated strain becomes too great, the rock snaps at its weakest point, giving rise to the sudden

The earthquake belts.

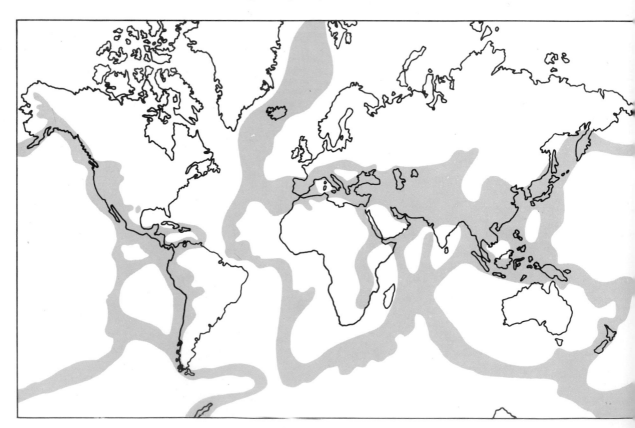

violent movement of the earth's crust known as an earthquake. There are a number of well-defined belts across the earth's surface where earthquakes are prevalent. They do not occur more than 700 kilometres from the surface, which suggests that below this depth the rocks are sufficiently elastic to absorb the strain and stress. Earthquakes happen suddenly and with no warning; they are among the most destructive of all the earth's natural phenomena, claiming an average of 14,000 lives each year. They are also the primary source of our knowledge of the earth's internal structure, since the waves they produce can be made to reveal something approximating to a crude X-ray picture of the interior.

The violent movement of rock masses in an earthquake literally shakes the earth, and produces a series of shockwaves known as seismic waves. These can be recorded and measured on a seismograph, an instrument which in its simplest form consists of a frame secured to the earth containing a freely moving spring-balanced arm. When the earth shakes, the arm remains still : by having the tip of the arm hold a pen over a revolving drum of paper the relative motion between the earth and the arm can be recorded. The result is a characteristic wavy pattern traced by the tip of the arm.

This pattern reveals three distinct types of seismic wave. The P-waves (on the left) which travel fastest are known as primary compressional waves. They consist of displacements along the direction of

A portable seismograph.

15

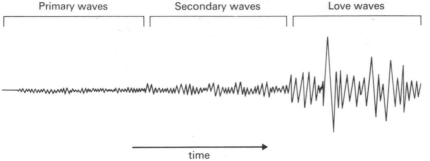

Primary waves	Secondary waves	Love waves

time

Left: A seismograph tracing.
Below left: The pattern of spread of P and S waves.
Below: The variation of the velocity of P and S waves with depth, and (below right) the corresponding levels in the earth's structure.

travel in the form of alternate compressions and expansions of the material through which they pass; in this they are like sound waves. The slower S-waves (in the centre) are known as secondary transverse shear waves. In these, the particles vibrate at right angles to the direction of travel, like light waves or the ripples in a pool of water. The slowest waves, the L-waves (on the right), are surface waves which travel round the earth in the upper twenty miles or so of rock. They are of two types: Rayleigh waves, which exhibit a rolling motion in a vertical plane like some forms of ocean waves, and Love waves, which have a similar amplitude but which travel horizontally at right angles to their direction of motion. The P and S-waves form a characteristic pattern as they spread through the earth after an earthquake.

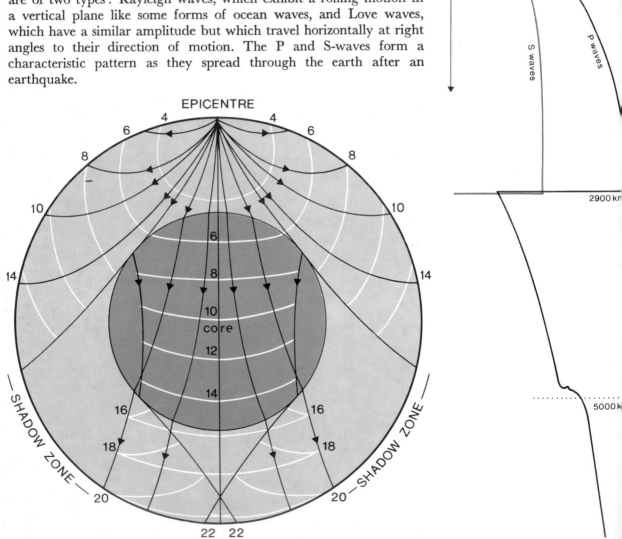

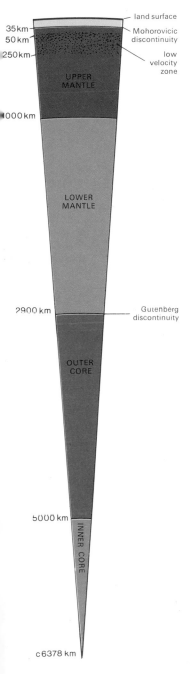

land surface

35km
50km
250km

Mohorovicic
discontinuity

low
velocity
zone

UPPER
MANTLE

1000km

LOWER
MANTLE

2900 km

Gutenberg
discontinuity

OUTER
CORE

5000 km

INNER CORE

c 6378 km

Earthquakes occur in the earth's crust, the relatively thin outer layer of light rock which extends down 35 to 50 kilometres beneath the continents and about 5 kilometres beneath the ocean floors. The crust behaves as though it is a cool and brittle layer of material resting on a hot, relatively plastic interior. It is the part of the earth we know most about, since we can easily examine and analyse rocks exposed on the surface, and deduce the geological processes that formed them. For example, it is the area where sedimentary rocks are produced: sediment derived from erosion of already existing rock formations is transported to and deposited in shallow water, either on the continental shelf or in lakes or rivers, where it settles. Over a long period, the sediment compacts and hardens, forming a layer of rock overlying the earlier rocks which had solidified from a molten state — the igneous rocks. Sedimentary rocks, which are often modified by the effects of pressure or heat, are composed of lighter elements, mainly calcium, silicon, aluminium, and magnesium.

Seismic studies and evidence from deep bore holes show that the crust is divided into two layers, although the boundary between them is variable in nature and depth, and difficult to define precisely. In the upper crust, granite rocks containing an abundance of *si*lica and *al*umina predominate; this layer is known as the SIAL or the sialic crust. The lower crust is slightly denser, and consists of basaltic rocks rich in *Si*lica and *Ma*gnesia; it is known as the SIMA or simatic crust. SIAL is generally restricted to land masses, while SIMA forms the lower layers under the continents and the whole crust under the ocean basins (apart from a thin layer of sediment).

The rocks of the two layers of the crust have been found to differ not only on composition but also in age. The age of rocks can now be accurately determined by radioactive dating, and this indicates that the SIAL of the continental areas contains rocks up to 4000 million years old, while the oldest SIMA rocks found in the ocean basins are less than 135 million years old. The lower density of the sialic crust keeps it permanently above the level at which most earth processes occur: while there is some redistribution and modification of material, it remains possible to find rocks formed relatively shortly after the formation of the earth itself. The lower crust is much younger and more geologically active; it contains many areas, including mid-ocean ridges, volcanic island arcs, and ocean trenches, where major structural processes have taken place, and are taking place even now.

In 1909, the Croatian seismologist Andrija Mohorovicic noticed that a seismograph recording an earthquake in the Balkans indicated that at a certain depth the velocity of the P-waves suddenly increased. He realised that this increase implied a change of density in the rock layers, and thus a boundary between the crust and the next layer of the earth's interior, the mantle. This transition point is known as the Mohorovicic Discontinuity, or Moho.

At the Moho, the composition of the rock changes, possibly where the temperature and pressure reach the point at which crystalline rock collapses into a denser, non-crystalline form. The Moho appears to be continuous, though this is not certain. In one or two localities, it appears that 'mantle slices' have been brought to the surface, allowing us to see what lies beneath the Moho. Mount Olympus, in the Troödos

mountains in the west of the island of Cyprus is a famous example, but though its dense rock almost certainly originates from beneath the Moho, it has been much altered by the processes that brought it to the surface.

The layer beneath the Moho, the mantle, contains 83% of the volume and 62% of the mass of the earth. It is the source of most of the earth's internal energy, and it is the prime mover in all major geological processes. Yet despite its importance, it remains physically inaccessible: it can only be studied remotely, using a variety of geological techniques. Seismology reveals variations of density which allow us to delineate different layers. Precise local measurements of gravity can reveal variations in concentrations of mass within the mantle from which variations in rock types can be inferred. Studies of magnetism, heat flow and convection give a guide to the mechanics of the processes occurring within the mantle. These methods are supplemented in the laboratory by experiments which re-create the effects on minerals of the pressures and temperatures found at great depths.

The results of these studies suggest that the mantle consists mainly of the mineral olivine, a compound of iron, magnesium, silicon, and oxygen, mixed with some less dense minerals such as pyroxene, a silicate of calcium, magnesium, and iron. These minerals, modified by high pressure and temperature, are thought to be the equivalents of the ultrabasic igneous rocks brought to the surface from great depths in volcanic pipes, and of the eclogites.

The Troodos Mountains of Cyprus.

18

Between the Moho and a depth of 1000 kilometres, a number of changes occur in the velocities of the P and S-waves which are generally taken to indicate changes in mineral composition and form as the mineral structures are subjected to an increasingly high pressure /temperature environment. Below this depth, there are no sudden changes in the velocities of P and S-waves, but rather a slow, continuous increase, which indicates a gradual increase in rock density without mineralogical change as the pressure increases. Thus the mantle has two major areas: the upper mantle, from the Moho to 1000 kilometres, a region of great changes where the rocks and their constituent minerals adjust to the conditions of increasing depth, and the lower mantle, from 1000 kilometres to 2900 kilometres, a region of gradual change. The upper mantle is active and is believed to contain convection cells, areas where the material of the earth circulates, with hot material rising towards the surface, spreading sideways, cooling, and then sinking again.

Between a depth of 50 kilometres and 250 kilometres, P and S-wave velocities are considerably reduced by a zone that absorbs an abnormally high amount of energy. This zone, the Low Velocity Zone, is probably mechanically weak and particularly hot, an area of slush where the rock is near melting point. It is the source of the mobile liquid rocks, or magmas, which rise into the earth's crust or are extruded on the earth's surface through volcanoes before solidifying as igneous rocks.

The lower boundary of the mantle was located in 1914 by Beno Gutenberg, who discovered that at a depth of 2900 kilometres below the earth's surface the velocity of P-waves is drastically reduced, while S-waves are stopped altogether. This boundary, the Gutenberg Discontinuity, is taken as evidence of a major mineralogical change, from the rock of the mantle to an area rich in iron and nickel. The absorption of S-waves at this point is evidence of a major change of state, from solid to liquid. This does not mean that at this point the earth's interior becomes a fluid as we know it. Geophysicists use the terms 'solid' and 'fluid' to describe the elastic behaviour of material under compression and stress: a 'fluid' differs from a 'solid' in that its resistance to shearing stress is much smaller than its resistance to compression. The failure to propagate S-waves, which are shear waves, thus reveals that the outer part of the earth's core is, in geophysical terms, liquid.

At a depth of 5000 kilometres, P-waves increase in velocity quite suddenly; this point is taken to mark the boundary of the inner core, where the liquid becomes solid. Calculations indicate that the inner core is at least twice as rigid as steel is at ordinary temperatures. Both the inner and outer core are thought to consist largely of iron and nickel, though it is not known in what state. Latest calculations of the density of the core suggest the presence of some other lighter element, since the density is too low for iron and nickel alone. Silicon has been tentatively put forward as the most likely candidate. The most important constituent of the core is the iron, which is the source of the currents that flow there and which produce the earth's magnetic field.

Our knowledge of the earth's inaccessible interior is largely speculative; we can examine geophysical processes directly only on or near the earth's surface. A glance at an atlas or a satellite photograph shows that the Atlantic coastlines of Africa and South America have surprisingly similar shapes, similar enough to fit neatly together and suggest the possibility that at some time in the past the two continents were joined together. The evidence for this theory was first systematised by Alfred Wegener, an Austrian meteorologist, balloonist and polar explorer, in his book *The Origin of Continents and Oceans,* published in 1915.

The real edge of the continents occurs on the continental shelf, at a point where the sea bottom falls away relatively steeply from near sea level to the deep ocean floor. When this edge is taken as the point of fit, the correlation between the coastlines of Africa and South America is even better than on an ordinary map. There is other important evidence for original continuity: mountain belts, fault trends, and glacial remains all correspond across the oceanic gap. In other areas fossil evidence is found, for example the remains of an early form of horse are found only in Florida and on the Iberian peninsula. Some of these correspondences and coincidences could be explained without invoking the idea of continental drift, but even so, an impressive body of evidence remained. Geophysicists remained sceptical, since there appeared to be no physical mechanism capable of producing the energy needed to move entire continents. Wegener suggested that the continents were originally concentrated at the South Pole and were dispersed by the earth's rotation; this was shown to be unfeasible, and the theory fell into disfavour.

The key evidence that Wegener lacked came from a relatively modern branch of geophysics – the study of paleomagnetism. Most rocks contain some iron, usually in the form of ferro-magnesian particles. In the presence of a magnetic field, these particles behave like compass needles and orient themselves in the earth's magnetic field. They can do this only when they are free to move, as when a crystal is forming in cooling liquid rock, or when a sedimentary particle settles in standing water. When this happens, the faintly magnetised particles adopt the direction of the earth's prevailing magnetic field; if the body of rock is not moved, it will contain a record of the direction of the earth's magnetic field at the time of cooling or deposition.

The magnetic record preserved in rocks revealed a long series of reversals of the earth's magnetic field; it also revealed rocks magnetised in what seemed to be the wrong direction, suggesting that the earth's magnetic pole had wandered over the surface of the earth.

However, no other evidence for this magnetic instability could be found, and the only other conclusion that could be drawn was that the continents had moved from their positions at the time the magnetic record was formed. With the pole stabilised in one position, the directions of the magnetism in the rocks may be plotted and the position of the continents in earlier geological ages can be calculated. Thus misalignments in the magnetisation of sandstone rocks in Great Britain indicated that the islands had moved, having rotated through about thirty degrees during the last 200 million years. So the continents had moved; it remained to discover the mechanism that allowed them to do so.

The answer was found not on the continents themselves, but in the

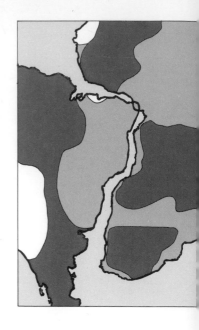

oldest rock

youngest rock

Continental fit – South America and West Africa.

North America

track of North Polar
wandering as shown by
North American rocks

Europe

track of North Polar
wandering as shown by
European rocks

Polar wandering in the Northern
Hemisphere.

depths of the oceans. Careful charting of the ocean floors during the
1950s revealed a succession of great ridges, the mid-oceanic ridges,
running through the world's oceans. Research ships discovered magnetic anomalies over these features: the magnetic polarisation was not
constant. The ocean floor on either side of the ridges was marked by
alternate bands of opposite magnetic polarity, which appeared as a
striped pattern.

The polarity of the earth's magnetic field is known to have reversed
fairly frequently during geological time: the striped pattern from the

Alternating polarity bands around
mid-oceanic ridges.

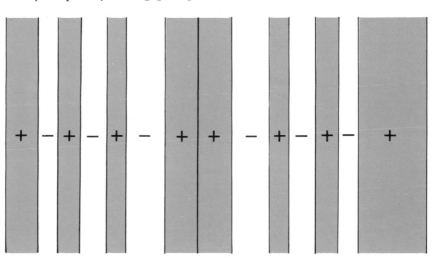

ocean floor could be accounted for as a record of reversals in the earth's magnetic field during the time that the various bands of rock were solidifying. The implication that the rocks had been formed at the mid-oceanic ridges is confirmed by the ages of the rocks, which are roughly similar on either side of each ridge.

The sea floor is now seen to be spreading out from the mid-oceanic ridges. A long crack, the median rift, runs down the centre of each ridge; through this aperture, material rises from the earth's interior and flows over the sides of the ridge. The sea bed is moving slowly away from the mid-oceanic ridges on either side, like a conveyor belt.

The Mid-Atlantic ridge appears above sea level in Iceland, which is an area of intense volcanic activity and which, like the rest of the ridge, is growing slowly from the middle outwards. The youngest rocks in Iceland occur on either side of the central rift valleys, and the rocks become progressively older the further away they are from them.

The spreading of the sea floor requires a mechanism to account for it, and the one currently suggested is convection. Convection cells are believed to exist in the upper mantle: these are areas where hot material rises to the surface, cools, and then spreads sideways before falling back into the mantle. Within the upper mantle, the rocks are at a sufficiently high temperature and pressure to move in response to thermal pressures applied over vast periods of time: rock subjected to continuous pressure over millions of years is more likely to move viscously under these conditions than to break. Thus the mid-ocean ridges are points where up-currents from the mantle reach the surface.

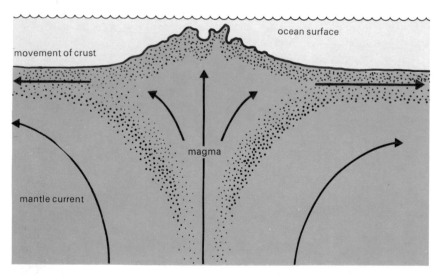

Mantle currents around a mid-ocean ridge.

The horizontal currents carry the sea floor away from the mid-oceanic ridge.

The discovery of ocean floor spreading led to a theory of the origin and construction of the earth's geological features known as plate tectonics. The earth's outer shell is seen as a number of rigid plates of cool rock which are moved about by the action of heat rising from the interior of the earth. Little change occurs in the middle of the plates: changes occur at the edges, which correspond with areas of frequent volcanic activity.

There are four types of plate boundary. The first we have already mentioned, where two plates are being manufactured at the same time at a mid-oceanic ridge and are moving away from each other. The other types of boundary are caused by the interaction of plates at their edges, and depend on the down-currents of the convection cycle.

When an oceanic plate meets a continental plate, the lighter continental material rides over the oceanic material, which returns to the mantle. The line of movement of the oceanic plate into the mantle is associated with the Benioff Zone, a narrow, inclined zone of seismic activity which is revealed when the focuses of earthquakes occurring below a depth of 200km are plotted. Those focuses fall on a nearly straight line dipping at between 45 and 60 degrees beneath the continental plate down to a maximum depth around 700km, the depth at which materials start flowing against one another without violent reactions.

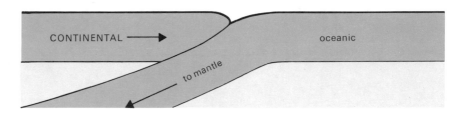

The downward movement of one plate against another causes cracks in the continental plate as a result of the shearing movement, through which material partially melted by the friction of one plate against another rises to the surface, forming volcanic island arcs. Deep sea trenches are found close to the point at which the Benioff Zone reaches the surface, and are the result of the downward pull of the oceanic plate as it moves into the mantle, producing a groove in the earth's surface. This type of boundary is found along the line of the Pacific Islands, which are volcanic and associated with deep oceanic trenches.

When the leading edges of two continental plates meet neither can return to the mantle so they collide and buckle, creating new mountain ranges from the sea floor sediments between them.

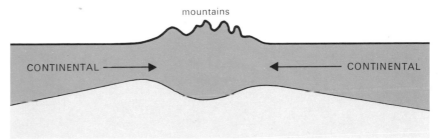

Both the Himalayan and Alpine mountain ranges were formed in this way.

When oceanic plates meet, either or both may return to the mantle, or they may be displaced sideways, so that they glide past each other creating a huge fault known as a transform fault.

Transform faults may extend on to the earth's surface, as in the notorious San Andreas fault in California where the huge American

The San Andreas fault, California.

Right:
Monterey, California, seen from Earth Resources Technology Satellite ERTS-1 in a false colour image taken to provide geological information. The main diagonal feature of the picture is the San Andreas fault. San José is at the top of the image, and the Salinas River enters the image at the bottom left, running northwest to empty into Monterey Bay.

and Pacific plates slide past each other, jostling and causing earthquakes, at a rate of $2\frac{1}{2}$ inches per year. If their present motion continued, in 20 million years Los Angeles would be as far north of San Francisco as it is now to the south.

Plate tectonics is an impressive theory because it is able to bring together all the mechanisms that shape the geological features of the earth's surface. Problems remain: some critics insist that if the earth were plastic enough to allow continents to move, then known surface irregularities would iron themselves out more rapidly than they do. There are difficulties with the operation of convection cells in the

upper mantle, since this is an area containing many discontinuities which may limit the space in which convection currents can develop and prevent them from extending laterally. Despite these problems with the mechanics of plate movement, there are now very few geologists who would deny the existence of such movement.

THE GEOPHYSICAL HISTORY OF THE EARTH

The Grand Canyon, Colorado.

Most of the striking features of the earth's surface can now be explained as the result of past plate movements. Great mountain ranges are now seen as the result of collisions between drifting continents, usually with the destruction of an ocean. Previously mountain building was explained by suggesting that the earth was contracting so that its surface wrinkled. The discovery of sea floor spreading led to a revival of the idea that the earth was expanding, but the rate of expansion required to account for tectonic effects is demonstrably not occurring. Plate tectonics is able to explain the fundamental forces involved in the process of mountain building.

Stratigraphy

Large scale theories of the earth's structural processes like plate tectonics are based on evidence from historical geology, the most important area of which is stratigraphy. This is the study of earth history in terms of the layered rocks on the earth's surface. The layering of rocks is caused either by successive flows of molten rock building up on top of each other, or, more commonly, by sedimentation, when rocks are formed from layers of sediment deposited in water. The aim of stratigraphy is to discover what conditions on the surface of the earth were like at a particular period of time. For this, a means of dating rocks is needed. Qualitative methods reveal comparative ages, indicating that one rock is older or younger than another; quantitative methods reveal the age of a rock in absolute terms. However, qualitative methods are the only ones open to most amateur geologists and rock collectors.

The most characteristic feature of sedimentary rocks is their stratification, the separation of their components into layers more or less parallel to the original surface of accumulation. The most outstanding example of this overall sedimentary structure is the Grand Canyon in the United States, which reveals a mile of rocks representing about 400

Folded strata, South Stack Lighthouse, Anglesey, Wales.

million years of the geological history of America. The relative age of rock layers can normally be determined by applying the principle of superposition, which at its simplest states that, in an undisturbed series of rock layers, the layer at the bottom is the oldest and the layer at the top is the youngest.

The term 'younging' is widely used by geologists as a shortened way of describing the direction in which the rocks become younger. Simple horizontal rock layers are comparatively rare; frequently the rocks will have been affected by the structural processes that shape the earth's surface, and they may be folded, even inverted, and they will have suffered some kind of erosion. Thus the direction of younging is not immediately obvious.

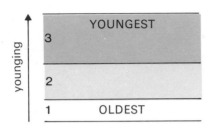

Methods of establishing the direction of younging.

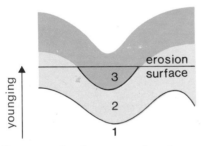 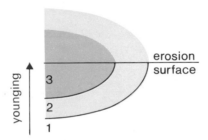

Fortunately there are often internal features within sedimentary rocks known as sedimentary structures which can be used to determine the direction of younging in the individual bed; this direction will correspond to the younging of the entire unbroken sequence of which the bed is a part.

When sedimentary rocks are deposited by a continuous current of water, as in a river or river delta, the layers are built up in a series of curved laminations.

One way in which these laminae form is by avalanching in front of a growing structure such as a sand bar.

If a storm or a flood sweeps away the upper part of the growing sandbank a truncated surface is left.

Subsequent deposition may take place on this surface. This type of composite bedding, in which bands of bedding are found inclined to each other, is common in sandstone rocks, and is known as current bedding or cross bedding.

A variant of current bedding which gives rise to layered rocks without any erosion is ripple drift bedding. This occurs when a train of ripples in the river or sea bed moves downstream with the current while sediment is being deposited. Deposition of sediment takes place on the steeper front side of the ripples, so that the ripples grow both laterally and upwards. This produces a series of small scale curved laminations.

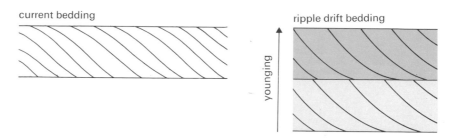

Ripple drift (false) bedding.

...ent bedding, Exmoor, Devon.

The direction of younging in current bedding and ripple drift bedding is determined by three criteria: the base of the bed is always tangential to the outer curve of laminations; the concave side of the laminations always points in the direction of the younging; any clearly truncated surface will be the upper, and thus the youngest, surface.

Some sedimentary rocks are formed deep in the oceans by turbidity currents. These are suspensions of small rocks and mud in water which occasionally flow downhill from the continental shelf like an avalanche on a mountain. They move fast enough to scour the sea bottom and collect fresh material to augment their volume. When the particles in this slurry come out of suspension, they are deposited according to size, with the coarsest at the bottom and the finest at the top.

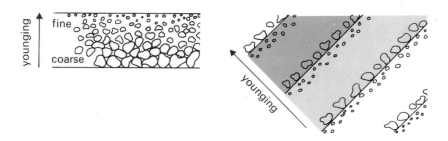

If a series of strata reveal this graded bedding, then the direction of younging can be determined reliably.

The direction of younging in a single layer of rock can sometimes be established if there is clear evidence of erosion. Erosion will only affect the upper, and thus younger, surface of a single sedimentary layer. Thus a bed of clay, which is plastic when wet and which exhibits no layered structure, may have one erosion surface, which is distinguishable by the presence of small pellets.

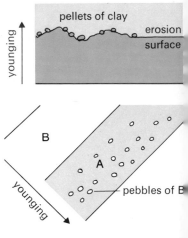

The Law of Included Pebbles can be used to determine the relative ages of the constituences of certain rock layers: when one piece of rock is included within another, the included rock is always the older. In the case of sedimentary rocks, the constituents of a sediment are always older than the sediment itself. If a sediment contains pebbles which are associated with another adjacent sediment it must be younger than that sediment.

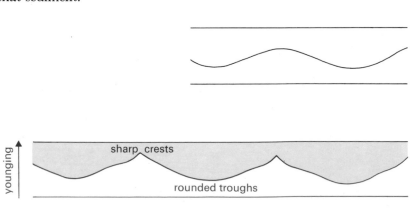

Carboniferous basal conglomerate under Carboniferous limestone; below the unconformity at the lower surface of the conglomerate layer is Lower Ordovician Slate. Thornton Force Waterfall, Ingleton, Yorkshire.

Ripple marks in Jurassic sediment, Arran, Scotland.

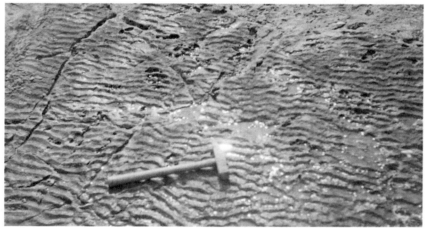

The action of moving water on a sheet of sediment produces ripple marks, like those seen on a beach after the tide recedes. These are often found preserved in ancient sandstones.

When both crests and troughs are rounded it is impossible to determine which was the upper surface; but ripples formed by the to-and-fro motion of water, known as oscillatory ripples, have sharp crests and rounded troughs, so that the direction of younging is easily recognised.

31

Suncracks develop in the mud flats of tidal reaches or flood plains when mud is baked by the sun and dries and shrinks, forming a pattern of polygonal cracks. If, as occasionally happens, the cracks become filled with a sediment such as wind blown sand before the next tide or flood, they may be preserved.

Suncracks in recent sediments.

When raindrops fall on a soft sediment (usually mud), they cause tiny crater-like pits. If these are filled in by another sediment, they may be preserved as fossil rainpits, which indicate the direction of younging.

Certain fossil remains can provide useful guides to the direction of younging. Animals with shells or hard skeletons are more likely to be preserved. Bivalve molluscs like clams and scallops are often found in

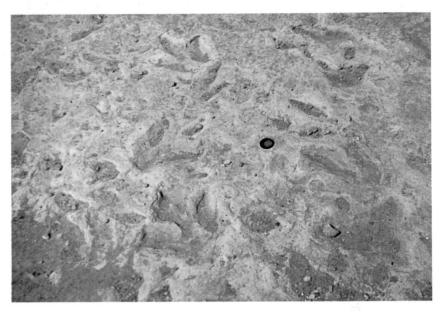

Impression of a dinosaur footprint in sandstone, from Colorado Plateau, Arizona.

beds of sediment. When the animal dies the body decays, and the two halves of the shell separate. If these are swept up as part of a sediment they will eventually be deposited with it. The orientation of the shell is important : normally it will be found with its convex surface upwards when deposited, because when it is the other way up it is unstable and liable to be moved with the current. Thus a bed containing a series of such shells orientated in a similar way can be dated in relation to its surroundings.

Animals may leave behind evidence other than their fossilised remains. These trace fossils include burrows, tracks, and footprints. For example, the impression of a dinosaur's footprint is a clear guide to younging.

Some marine worms produce U-shaped burrows, which, if preserved in rocks, can be used to determine the direction of younging since the U is always open to the upper surface.

The principle of superposition does not apply to intrusive igneous rocks, which form when molten rock is forced up from the earth's interior into existing rock layers. An intrusive igneous rock must obviously be younger than the rocks it intrudes. Igneous rocks change the rock surfaces they come into contact with when they are molten in a process known as contact metamorphosis, which results in the formation of a layer of changed rock around the intruded rock. This metamorphic aureole is a guide to the direction of younging, as in these sequences.

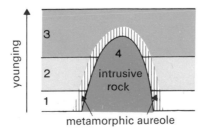

33

However all this tells us is that the intrusion is younger than the rocks it intrudes – it doesn't give us any idea how much younger it is. Sometimes the law of included pebbles can be used to set limits to the age of the intrusive rock.

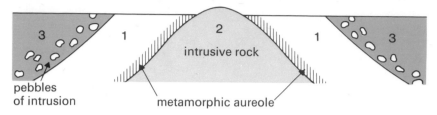

order of younging : 1, 2, 3.

1 is older than 2; 3, which has pebbles from 1 included in it, is younger than 1; thus the direction of younging is 1, 2, 3, and the upper and lower limits of the age of the intrusive rock lie between those of layers 1 and 3.

In the case of extrusive igneous rocks, molten rocks which have flowed out on to the earth's surface, usually in the form of lava, there is less of a problem. A lava flow can only metamorphose the rocks over which it flows, so that a layer of metamorphosed rock adjacent to a lava flow is always younger than the flow. The direction of younging can often be further confirmed by the fact that a lava flow frequently has a distinctive ropy, pillowy upper surface.

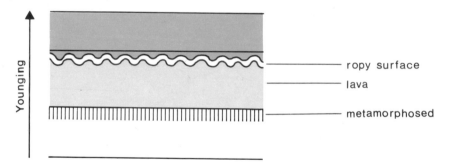

Molten lava flowing over the earth's surface, Mount Etna, Italy.

Qualitative methods give only relative ages, and are really useful only in combination with some method of determining the absolute age of rocks. The statement of the general law of radioactivity by Rutherford in 1904 opened the way to a quantitative method for dating rocks. A practical technique was first demonstrated in 1907, when Boltwood used it to date early rocks in Canada. Detailed analysis of a wide range of rocks was carried out from 1939 onwards, but laboratory methods were too imprecise to give accurate results; it was not until the mass spectrometer was developed in the 1950s that rock dating by radioactivity became commonplace.

Some elements have isotopes that are radioactive because of their unstable atomic structures: these break down spontaneously by emitting particles from their nuclei, and in the process become changed into other elements. The rate at which an unstable 'parent' element decays to become a stable 'daughter' element is constant. No external energy is required to initiate or sustain the process, which is independent of pressure, temperature, or chemical environment, and which takes place at the same rate in the laboratory as it does in nature.

The principle of absolute age determination by radioactive dating is quite simple. To determine the age of a rock which contains element A, which is known to decay at a certain rate to form element B, the total amount of each present must be measured. Assuming that all of B was derived from A by decay, the ratio of B to A is an index of the time that has passed since the decay process began. For example, when igneous rocks are formed by solidification from a molten state, the process involves a change from an open system, out of which the products of radioactive decay can escape, to a closed one, in which they are trapped. Thus the radioactive age of the rock indicates the time that has elapsed since it solidified. This date is acceptable as the age of the rock, even though it is unlikely that all portions of the lava cooled at the same time.

The rate of decay of a radioactive substance is expressed in terms of its half-life, the time it takes for half of a given amount of the substance to decay and change into its end product. For one of the isotopes of uranium, $Uranium_{238}$, this period is 4507 million years. Thus, after 4507 million years, 500 grams of $Uranium_{238}$ would be reduced to 250 grams; after another 4507 million years, only 125 grams would remain. Each radioactive substance has a different half-life, ranging from a few millionths of a second to 10,000 million years. The radioactive elements that occur naturally in minerals, and which can thus be used for dating, include $Uranium_{235}$ and $Uranium_{238}$, $Thorium_{232}$, $Rubidium_{87}$, and $Potassium_{40}$. These can be used to calculate the age of a rock sample from the measured parent/daughter ratio and the appropriate half-life only if certain conditions apply. There must have been no gains or losses of either parent or daughter element by any process other than radioactive decay. The half-life of the parent element must be accurately known, and the concentrations of both parent and daughter elements must be accurately measured. It must also be possible to make a precise correction for any amount of daughter element that is already present in the mineral or rock at the time of crystallisation. Most important, the half-life of the element must be comparable to the age of the rock which is to be determined. For example, $Carbon_{14}$, which has a half-life of 5568 years would be of no use in dating a 100 million year old rock, since the minute quantity of undecayed $Carbon_{14}$ remaining in the rock would be impossible to measure accurately.

Uranium occurs naturally as three isotopes: $Uranium_{238}$, $Uranium_{235}$, and $Uranium_{234}$. Of these the commonest is $Uranium_{238}$, which forms 99.3% of all naturally occurring uranium. Both $Uranium_{238}$ and $Uranium_{235}$ are used for radioactive dating. $Uranium_{238}$ decays through a series of transformations to a stable isotope of lead, Pb_{206}; $Uranium_{235}$ decays to another isotope of lead, Pb_{207}. The half-life of the decay sequence U_{238} — Pb_{206} is 4507 million years; for the sequence U_{235} — Pb_{207}, it is 713 million years. Uranium dating can thus be used for rocks more than 10 million years old. The most suitable materials for analysis are the minerals uraninite, a uranium ore, and zircon, both of which occur in igneous rocks and mineral veins.

Naturally occurring thorium has a half-life of 13,900 million years; it decays to another isotope of lead, Pb_{208}. There are many intermediate transformations in the decay process, and attempts to use thorium for dating purposes have led to inconsistent results. However it is used in conjunction with uranium, since most radioactive minerals contain both uranium and thorium, with the result that all three isotopes of lead are being produced in such minerals.

$Rubidium_{87}$ decays to $Strontium_{87}$; it has a half-life of 48,800 million years. Rubidium is a rare element which forms no minerals of its own, but is found in the more common potassium minerals as it will easily substitute for potassium in chemical compounds. It is thus used to date igneous and metamorphic rocks that are rich in potassium, such as some micas and feldspars. It is particularly useful for dating metamorphic rocks and is used to date rocks that are more than 10 million years old.

Potassium, an element that is common in many rocks and minerals, has one radioactive isotope, $Potassium_{40}$ which decays by two entirely distinct processes, each with its own half-life. In any given amount of $Potassium_{40}$, 11% will decay to form the gas $Argon_{40}$; this process has a half-life of 11,850 million years. The remaining 89% decays to form $Calcium_{40}$, a process with a half-life of 1470 million years. The breakdown of $Potassium_{40}$ to $Calcium_{40}$ is of little use for dating purposes, because of the abundance of ordinary calcium in most common rocks and minerals : it is not possible to measure the minute concentrations of radioactive $Calcium_{40}$ accurately enough. The Potassium – Argon decay process is useful in dating rocks over a wide range of ages, from the oldest known terrestrial rocks, about 3800 million years old, to rocks as young as 30,000 years old. Problems arise because $Argon_{40}$ is a gas and may be lost from rocks or minerals during metamorphosis, with the result that the age calculated will be an underestimate. Careful techniques and the selection of the right type of rock for this kind of analysis make it possible to minimise this kind of error.

The radioactive elements considered so far have had half-lives suitable for measuring long intervals of geological time. For measuring shorter intervals, $Carbon_{14}$ is used. Minute amounts of this radioactive isotope exist alongside ordinary carbon in the air, natural waters, and living organisms. $Carbon_{14}$ is constantly produced in the atmosphere by the action of cosmic rays; it is rapidly oxidised to form a radioactive version of carbon dioxide, and is absorbed into the carbon cycle of the earth.

$Carbon_{14}$ decays to $Nitrogen_{14}$, with a half-life of 5,568 years. It is used for dating substances up to 50,000 years old, mainly in archaeology and paleontology, but also to obtain geological information from organic remains. The remains of an animal found in a sediment indicate that the sediment was laid down at the time the animal died; the length of time since then and hence the age of the sediment is indicated by the amount of $Carbon_{14}$ left in its remains.

FOSSILS

Radioactive dating has made it possible to date later fossils with great accuracy, and the accurate dating of rocks by the same method has enabled earlier fossils to be used to date rock strata. There are a number of ways in which the remains of a living organism can be preserved as a fossil. In rare cases, the whole organism may be preserved, as with the Woolly Mammoths that have been found in the permanently frozen Alaskan and Siberian tundras. The Berezovka mammoth was found almost intact, with undigested food in its mouth and stomach. Broken bones in its body suggest that it was killed by a sudden collapse of a riverbank or some similar subsidence.

Normally, only the hard parts of an animal have a chance of being preserved, and even these undergo slow chemical changes. The shells of molluscs or the teeth and bones of vertebrates become mineralised as every pore and fissure in them becomes filled with mineral salts. A similar process can produce a cast of a soft organism, for example when a shell cavity becomes filled with mineralising salts which harden to form an internal cast. External casts, or impressions, of whole organisms may be formed when the organism

A fossil fly preserved in amber. An example of preservation of the whole organism.

Fossil ammonite with the shell preserved in iridescent pyrite. *Opposite page.* Top: Carboniferous freshwater bivalves (left); Tertiary gastropods (*Turritella*) (right). Centre: Jurassic ammonite (left); Cretaceous echinoid preserved in chalk (right). Bottom: brachiopods in Carboniferous limestone (left); trilobites in Cambrian Slate from Porth y Rhaw, Wales (right).

imprints its outline on a soft sediment which subsequently hardens. Casts and moulds also appear in the form of trace fossils, including burrows and excavations, tracks, footprints, and resting marks.

Fossils are normally found in sedimentary rocks, though a few occur in some kinds of volcanic rock, and even in some kinds of moderately metamorphosed rock; but in general, rocks which have

39

been subjected to high temperatures will not contain fossil remains. The chance of a dead organism becoming fossilised is best in a marine environment; marine fossils are much more common than those of terrestrial organisms. Although fossils seem quite numerous and are easily found, it has been calculated that only 1% of all the plant and animal species can have left remains. Measured against the vast populations of organisms that have successively inhabited the earth, the preservation of a fossil is a very rare event indeed.

The fossils of the following groups are important in the study of stratigraphy:

Coelenterates

These include the geologically important corals. Corals are well suited to fossilisation because they secrete a hard exterior cup of calcium carbonate. There are two kinds: colonial corals, which live on the bottom of warm shallow seas, and solitary corals, which often live in deep cold waters.

Lower palaeozoic graptolites

Molluscs

Bivalves are a group of marine, brackish or freshwater molluscs with two-part shells. They are generally found in shallow water, where they may lie on the bed, burrow into it, or attach themselves to plant life. They vary in size from $\frac{1}{2}$ centimetre to 10 centimetres, with exceptional examples reaching 150 centimetres.

Gastropods are marine animals with univalve shells, which are formed in one piece. The shell is usually coiled in a helical spiral. They live in fresh or sea water, and on land. A modern example is the snail.

Cephalopods are marine molluscs which have adapted so that they can swim freely. They may have univalve shells, which fill with gas to make the animal buoyant, or internal shells. Included in this group are squids, octopuses, and the important fossil nautiloids and ammonoids.

Brachiopods

Shelled marine animals which attach themselves to the sea bottom by a flexible stalk. They have bivalve shells, which open to release two coiled appendages for collecting food.

Arthropods

Animals with an external shell and jointed limbs. Modern examples are insects, crustaceans and spiders. The most important members of the group to the geologist are the extinct Trilobites, which existed in both free-swimming and burrowing forms.

Echinoderms

This group of marine animals includes starfish and sea urchins. Free-living fossil forms are known as Echinoids; Crinoids are fixed shallow water forms which generally consist of a stem bearing a cup with arms attached.

Chordates

Animals that at some stage in their lives have an internal skeleton. The now extinct Graptolites are important stratigraphically: they were branched organisms that lived in colonial clusters attached to the sea bed, often in fairly deep unaerated water. The Chordates also include the Vertebrates – fish, reptiles, birds, and mammals.

THE GEOLOGICAL TIME SCALE

The layering of the rocks on the earth's surface suggests that a series of geological changes have taken place during the earth's history. These changes form a basis for dividing the history of the earth into a series of chronological divisions.

A major change recorded in rock formations, such as in the pattern of sediment deposition, can reasonably be taken to indicate a change in the conditions on the surface of the earth. If similar changes at the same point in the rock succession can be traced in other parts of the world it can be assumed that these changes indicate the initiation of a new geological era in earth's history.

One such change which provides a natural division in the chronology of the earth is a marine transgression. This is the invasion of a large area of previously dry land by the sea; it is caused either by a rise in sea level or by the subsidence of the land. Frequently the land itself has been raised out of the sea some time previously (in what is known as a marine regression), often by a folding or fault movement. Thus we may get a succession like this.

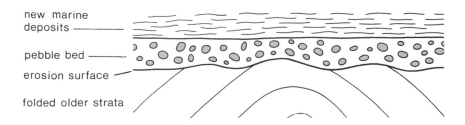

new marine deposits ———
pebble bed ———
erosion surface ⌐
folded older strata

An unconformity, Argyllshire.

When the sea invades the area, all the debris produced by erosion on the land becomes incorporated in the lowest bed of the new

41

sedimentary deposits. Even when there is no obvious differentiation between beds, the presence of such a pebble bed indicates a change of conditions on the surface. A change in deposition like this, when one layer of rock does not follow another in an immediate chronological sequence, is known as an unconformity.

The sudden appearance of a new type of fossil at a particular rock layer also indicates a change of surface conditions. Organisms whose fossils show a pattern of fairly rapid evolution can be used to date any thickness of rock, down to individual beds. Such organisms have to be widespread throughout the world: free swimming molluscs like the Ammonites and the Goniatites which display rapid evolutionary changes provide the most useful fossils for dating rock layers.

The divisions of geological time may be defined by three methods, using rock types, fossils, or radioactive dating. The use of rock types is subject to error, since different rocks may have been laid down at the same time. A marine transgression may take millions of years as the land gradually submerges; although it may result in a clearly defined sequence of beds, for example pebbles, sandstone, clay, it is quite possible that the clay was being deposited on the original coastal plain at the same time as the pebble bed was being deposited further inland. Fossils are more reliable guides to the relative age of rocks, provided that the species used is widely dispersed so that beds from a variety of areas can be correlated. Radioactive dating, in combination with stratigraphy, gives an absolute time scale, the units of which are called 'time-rock units'. The other widely used units of geological time division are 'time units'. 'Time units' refer to intervals of time, and 'time-rock units' to the strata that were deposited during those intervals. The two sets of units are related thus:

Time-rock units	Time units
Erathem	Era
System	Period
Series	Epoch
Stage	Age
Zone	'times'

The era/erathem represents the division of geological time into four major sections:

The Pre-Cambrian, covers a vast stretch of geological time from the beginning of decipherable earth history, about 4,500 million years ago, until the earliest fossilised Cambrian sediments were deposited, about 600 million years ago. During this period, vast thicknesses of rock were laid down which have subsequently undergone much deformation and change. Very little evidence of life in this period is preserved.

The Paleozoic, the 'age of the invertebrates and fishes' lasted from 600 million years ago until 225 million years ago.

The Mesozoic, the 'age of the reptiles' lasted from 225 million years ago until 70 million years ago.

The Cainozoic (or Cenozoic) covers from 70 million years ago until the present day. It is the period during which mammals became the dominant life-form on the earth.

Approx age in million years	Eras	Periods	Maximum thickness in feet	Dominant life	Systems and events
1	CAINOZOIC	QUATERNARY	6000+	Man	
11		PLIOCENE	15000	Mammals and Modern Flora	Alpine mountain building
25		MIOCENE	21000		
40		OLIGOCENE	26000		
70		EOCENE	42000		
135	MESOZOIC	CRETACEOUS	51000	Reptiles and Ammonites	
180		JURASSIC	44000		
225		TRIASSIC	30000		New Red Sandstone
270	PALEOZOIC	PERMIAN	19000	Amphibians and Coal Flora	Hercynian mountain building
350		CARBONIFEROUS	46000		
400		DEVONIAN	38000	Fishes	Old Red Sandstone
440		SILURIAN	34000	Invertebrates e.g. Trilobites and Graptolites	Caledonian mountain building
500		ORDOVICIAN	40000		
600		CAMBRIAN	4000		
	PRE-CAMBRIAN	PROTEROZOIC	Unknown	Primitive Organisms	
4500		AZOIC	Unknown		

The period/system is a subdivision of the major units of geological time; this classification is generally used by geologists. The names and relationships of the various periods are shown in the chart.

The smaller units – series, stages, zones, – are successively smaller divisions of the periods; most of the names given to them have only limited application and vary from country to country. The smallest unit, a zone, frequently corresponds to only a few beds of rock or less which can be defined chronologically by a specific assemblage of fossils.

In the remainder of this chapter, the history of the earth through the geological time scale will be considered mainly in terms of the stratigraphy of the British Isles and adjoining parts of Europe. This is not done out of patriotic prejudice: the British Isles have the advantage of containing strata from every geological period within a small area. The names given to several periods, Cambrian, Ordovician, Silurian, and Devonian, derive from British localities. Although in some cases the specific rocks mentioned do not apply to the rest of the world, the associated concepts do. In a sense, the location we study is not too important, for the configuration of land and sea that we know today bears no relation to the position of the continents in the past.

The Pre-Cambrian

About 600 million years ago, a marine transgression took place which submerged large parts of northern Europe and eastern and western North America beneath a shallow sea. The thick sedimentary deposits laid down by this sea were first studied in Wales ('Cambria'), and were named Cambrian. The rocks which underlie such sediments are known as Pre-Cambrian, and the period which they belong to spans over 80% of the total life of the earth. Until recently, this vast period of time was hardly known or investigated at all, because geologists had very little to work with : there was little or no fossil evidence, and the rocks had been frequently subjected to intense deformation and metamorphism. Modern geologists are learning a great deal more about this era: the reconstruction of ancient plate movements and radioactive dating techniques are enabling earth scientists to separate metamorphic events and identify different 'provinces' within the ancient rocks.

Pre-Cambrian rocks are found on all the continents. They occur in large areas that have a gentle topographic convexity known as shield areas, in the cores of folded mountain areas, and at the bottom of deeply eroded canyons such as the Grand Canyon. The shield areas of the world consist of wide areas of crystalline metamorphic rocks which comprise the ancient cores of all the continents. In Europe the Pre-Cambrian is represented by the Baltic Shield (covering regions of Finland and Scandinavia, sometimes known as Fennoscandia), and in North America by the enormous Canadian Shield.

The early part of the Pre-Cambrian was probably a period of extensive igneous activity, during which the earth's first primitive atmosphere was produced as gases were released from the hot liquid rocks. This atmosphere was probably rich in water vapour, ammonia, and carbon dioxide, and lacking in oxygen. The atmosphere first

The Canadian Shield, Northwest Territory of Canada.

Pre-Cambrian life – *Charonia masoni* from Hanging Stone Rocks, North Quarry, Woodhouse, Bedfordshire.

changed when the temperature dropped sufficiently for the water vapour to condense and the first rain fell. Eventually the earth cooled enough for water to remain on the surface in liquid form, and the accumulation of sediments began. The atmosphere changed slowly as ultra-violet light produced ozone in the upper atmosphere, and early bacterial organisms began to produce oxygen; later, primitive algae released more oxygen through photosynthesis, which broke down carbon dioxide, releasing oxygen. The oxygen content of the atmosphere was gradually increased and the carbon dioxide content decreased.

The Pre-Cambrian was a period of intense tectonic activity: mountain building and erosion took place on a large scale. At the

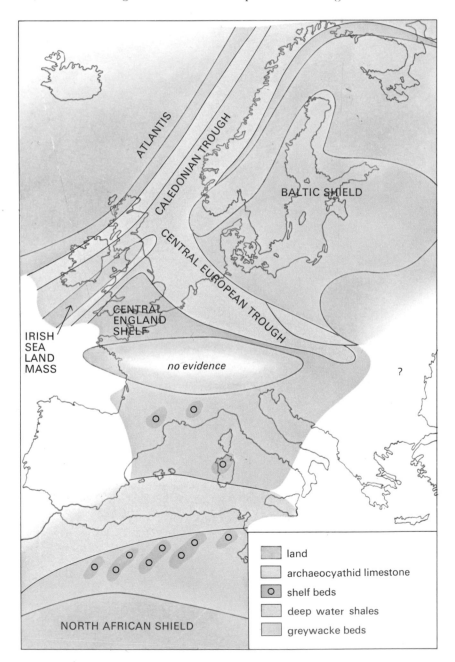

The palaeography of the Lower Cambrian.

ATLANTIS

CALEDONIAN TROUGH

CENTRAL EUROPEAN TROUGH

BALTIC SHIELD

CENTRAL ENGLAND SHELF

IRISH SEA LAND MASS

no evidence

?

NORTH AFRICAN SHIELD

land

archaeocyathid limestone

shelf beds

deep water shales

greywacke beds

centre of the Canadian Shield are folded rocks 3000 million years old, which are surrounded by the roots of successive mountain chains. There is also firm evidence of repeated glaciation in this area, as there is in north west Scotland.

Early geologists thought that the Pre-Cambrian rocks contained no fossils; specimens have been found, but they are rare, because very ancient organisms rarely had hard structures which would last as fossils, and because many remains will have been destroyed by metamorphic activity. The oldest known organism, *Eobacterium*, was found in the Figtree Formation of Pre-Cambrian rocks in southern Africa. In younger strata, a variety of multi-celled fossil organisms are found. The rocks of the Hediacara Hills in Australia, which are representative of the late Pre-Cambrian, have produced fossils of sponges, jellyfish, worms, and primitive Echinoderms and Arthropods.

The Cambrian

During the marine transgression that divides the Cambrian from the Pre-Cambrian, a deep trench, probably a destructive plate margin, developed offshore from the continental mass which was then where north east Europe is now. This trench covered what is now Norway, Scotland, and Ireland, with a branch thrusting into central Europe.

The area continued to sink throughout the Cambrian: sandstone and limestone beds were deposited in the shallow marine areas and shale in the trough area, while in the central part greywackes accumulated. Greywackes are sedimentary rocks formed from particles which are mainly rock fragments produced by the rapid erosion of continental areas; they are indicative of instability in the area. Most Cambrian rocks are formed from detritus from the interior of continents.

The Cambrian is rich in fossils. Great fossil reefs, produced by Archaeocyathids, organisms intermediate between sponges and corals, are found: in the Adelaide geosyncline in eastern Australia there are such formations hundreds of metres thick and over 500 kilometres long. The most abundant fossils from the period are the Trilobites. The shapes of these creatures changed with time, so that their fossils are good guides in rock dating. Graptolites were widely diffused by the end of the Cambrian; their fossils are found in the shale deposits laid down during the period.

The Ordovician

The break between the Cambrian and the Ordovician period was originally defined by an unconformity in the rocks of northern Wales, where sedimentary rocks lie on folded and eroded Cambrian rocks.

A section through North Wales.

Silurian

Ordovician

Cambrian

Pre-Cambrian basement

fault lines

NW

Anglesey

Snowdonia

Berwyn Hills

SE

Longmynd

Elsewhere there are no unconformities, indicating that the high sea level and mild climate of the Cambrian persisted well into the succeeding period. The great bulk of Ordovician rocks are sedimentary, a reflection of the warm, quiescent climate that made the land arid and desert-like ·and the seas calm and warm. Intense erosion filled the trough around Scotland and Norway with coarse greywackes, and submarine volcanic activity began.

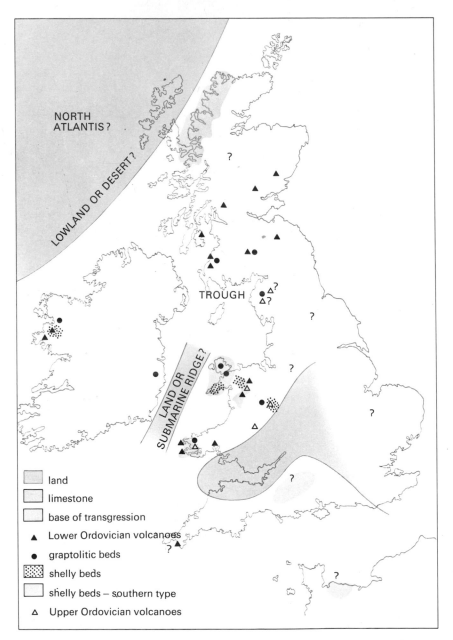

The palaeography of the Lower Ordovician.

NORTH ATLANTIS?

LOWLAND OR DESERT?

TROUGH

LAND OR SUBMARINE RIDGE?

land
limestone
base of transgression
▲ Lower Ordovician volcanoes
● graptolitic beds
▦ shelly beds
□ shelly beds – southern type
△ Upper Ordovician volcanoes

470 million years ago, in the early Ordovician period, the trough began to close, and the surrounding area crumpled to form mountains. The volcanic activity associated with this process metamorphosed many of the sedimentary layers. By the end of the

period, 440 million years ago, the Caledonian mountains had been formed along the north western fringe of the area.

Shale continued to be deposited in the area of the trough which is now Wales, and volcanic activity developed in the area now covered by southern Scotland and Ireland. The results of this are still preserved in the Lake District. The deposition of sedimentary rocks continued along the shelves of the continental masses. At the same time, central England was raised above sea level by marginal plate movements.

During the Ordovician Trilobites proliferated, reaching their peak in both numbers and variety. Graptolites and Brachiopods were widespread in the seas, and corals became prominent; the first reef building corals date from the Ordovician. This period saw the emergence of the first Vertebrates, primitive fish, whose fossils have been found in the Ordovician sandstones of Colorado.

The Silurian

Sedimentary deposition continued during the Silurian period, which lasted from 440 million years ago until 400 million years ago. The trough areas of southern Scotland, Ireland and Wales were filled with greywacke, while shale continued to be deposited on the margins. In the shallow marine areas, impure limestones and shales were deposited. The area of central England, which had been raised during the Ordovician, sank to just below sea level, and limestones were deposited on it, while the remaining islands became fringed with coral reefs. At the end of the period, the trough closed along its whole length as the continents of Europe and America moved together and joined. The collision, known as the Caledonian Event, produced a chain of mountains stretching from Norway through the Scottish Highlands

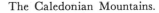
The Caledonian Mountains.

and northern Ireland to the Appalachians in America. The heat released by the collision formed granite masses (Shap Fell in the Lake District is a notable example), which were emplaced through the area at the close of the period. There was less activity in North America at this time, leaving behind very few unconformities between Silurian rocks and those of the succeeding period.

Life advanced during this period, which saw the first plants take hold on the bare rocks. In the seas, the Graptolites spread everywhere – the shale deposits laid down during the period are rich in their fossils. The Brachiopods continued to prosper, and new varieties of Trilobite appeared, armoured with carapaces and spikes. This development reflected the threat from the development of other Arthropods, which increased in numbers and size. The largest of these advanced invertebrates were the predatory Eurypterids, scorpion-like creatures which could grow to a length of seven feet. They were a threat to all other forms of life, including the primitive fish; these small jawless creatures developed heavy defensive armour. Late in the period, shark-like fish with jaws appeared.

The Devonian

The events of the Cambrian, Ordovician and Silurian periods (known as the lower Paleozoic era) left a trough running across what is now central Europe; the areas fringing the trough, including what are now Devon and Cornwall, were areas of marine sedimentation. North Devon was a shelf area where deposition also took place, while the rest of the British Isles and north western Europe formed a land area ringed by the Caledonian mountains. Rain and floods eroded the mountains and spread thick sequences of sand and mud over wide areas. Many basins between were filled with deposits of quartz grains coloured red by a coating of iron, which formed a conspicuous sequence of rocks known as Old Red Sandstone. This sequence is particularly widespread in Scotland, Ireland and western England, and is also found in eastern Europe and North America, where the Catskill beds of the northern Appalachians are analogous to the Old Red Sandstones of Great Britain. The distribution of Devonian sediments in Europe and North America confirms that the continents were once joined together.

The coastline migrated frequently over northern Devon, so that shallow marine and river deposits alternate; these deposits are known as marine Devonian. The Midland Valley in Scotland contained a rift valley which was associated with much volcanic activity; this is now thought to have been a transform fault along which the northernmost part of Britain moved about sixty-five miles. North west Europe and northern Scotland were part of a large depression filled with fresh and brackish water known as the Orcadian Basin, which was the source of a wide range of sedimentary deposits.

During the Devonian period, the plants consolidated their hold on the land. In the seas, the Eurypterids were still dominant; fossils found in the sedimentary deposits of Devon and Cornwall indicate that the Brachiopods and Trilobites remained widespread. The Old Red Sandstone deposits of the Orcadian Basin contain a rich variety of fossil fish. Many of these were armoured, with bodies covered

Above: fossiliferous limestone, typical of the middle Silurian.
Above left: Snowdon, the highest mountain of the Caledonian Chain in Wales.
Below left: a thrust associated with the Caledonian movements.
Below: metamorphosed Devonian marine slates, Old Delabole Slate Quarry, North Cornwall.

in bony plates, but some had cartilaginous skeletons and gill slits, and were the ancestors of modern sharks and rays. A great change occurred late in the period, when the first amphibians moved out from the sea to the land. The red sandstones of eastern Greenland contain numerous fossils of a salamander-like amphibian with four well-adapted legs.

The Carboniferous

The Carboniferous period, known in America as two periods, the Mississippian and the Pennsylvanian, lasted from 350 million years ago until 280 million years ago. Its start is marked by a marine transgression, when the sea level rose until much of the interior of North America and most of the British Isles were submerged. By the middle of the period, great thicknesses of limestone were being deposited: in the interior of the United States, there are vast sheets up to 2000 feet thick. This limestone contains a fossil fauna rich in corals and Brachiopods. In the British Isles, the rising waters left deposits of pebbles overlain with sandstones and then with limestone.

By the middle of the period, the trough covering Cornwall, Devon and central Europe was beginning to close as the African plate, carrying much of present day Europe, moved into the joint continent of Europe and North America. The collision produced a great mountain chain, known as the Hercynian chain, running from Poland to Alabama. This activity disturbed the pattern of sediment-

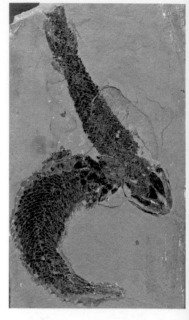

Fossil fish in the Caithness Flags of the Old Red Sandstone.

Carboniferous limestone landscape showing waterless uplands and deep gorges produced by collapsed caverns, Gordale Scar, near Malham, Yorkshire.

Left
Shale interbedded with coarse sandstone characteristic of the middle Carboniferous period, Mam Tor, Castleton, Derbyshire.

ation in the British Isles, where coarse sandstones began to alternate with the thinning limestones.

The second half of the period was characterised by the widespread development of swamps where luxurious vegetation flourished. Alongside the giant plants, the first true conifers appeared. The sea level continued to vary, and when it rose to cover the deltaic swamps, the remains of the vegetation sank to the bottom. When the sea subsided, the rotting vegetation was left covered with sediments which crushed it, with the help of the down-warping of parts of the land caused by the plate collision, to form coal. Great beds of coal were built up. A typical sequence was:

Younging ↓

Coal
Seat earth (fossil soil)
Shale
Sandstones

Dolerite sill intruded during the Hercynian mountain building period, Whin Sill, Northern Pennines, England.

Cornish granite produced by igneous activity associated with the Hercynian mountain building period, Hay Tor, Dartmoor, Devon.

The coal beds contain the remains of many plants, including giant ferns.

The rise of the Hercynian mountains affected the climate of the area, producing a rain shadow which eventually led to the whole area of Europe to the north west of them becoming a desert.

Although new forms of life emerged during the period, many of the older invertebrates continued to thrive: Carboniferous marine beds contain numerous fossil Goniatites, while the shale deposits are rich in the remains of thin shelled aquatic bivalve molluscs. On land, the amphibians increased in number and variety; they were joined by insects, some of enormous size. Some animals, notably the Trilobites and Eurypterids, were in decline, while others, like the primitive fishes, disappeared altogether.

The Permian

The Permian period, which lasted from 270 million years ago until 225 million years ago was characterised by desert conditions, which are marked in the strata by the appearance of red sedimentary deposits known as New Red Sandstones. The early part of the period saw the deposition of coarse sandstones, and volcanic activity. The harsh conditions meant that relatively few fossils were preserved. In the second half of the period, the sea level rose, and a shallow basin known as the Zechstein Sea covered much of the desert of

Closely bedded strata characteristic of the early Permian period, Trebarwith Strand, North Cornwall.

north western Europe; a similar basin, the Guadaloupe Basin, extended over what is now western Oklahoma, western Texas and part of New Mexico. The arid climate evaporated these salt lakes, leaving thick deposits of salts and minerals known as evaporites. The end of the period is marked by the deposition of red marls, mixtures of clay and limestone.

The Permian was a period of glaciation in the southern hemisphere: glacial deposits are found in southern Africa, Brazil, Australia and Antarctica. These areas were all joined as part of a supercontinent at this time, and were covered by a glacial ice cap centred in present day Transvaal in South Africa.

By the Permian period, both amphibians and reptiles were fully established on land, and both are well represented by fossils. In the sea, the Trilobites had died out, while the Brachiopods had assumed new forms: many developed spines which could be used to attach themselves to the bottom or to other Brachiopods. Some rocks in western Texas consist almost wholly of these types of Brachiopod shell cemented together by limestone. Marine life of the period is on the whole poorly represented by fossils; some sharks have been found, and many Ammonites, large shelled Cephalopods. The vegetation changed, with the gradual disappearance of the largest plants of the Carboniferous and the increasingly wide distribution of the conifers.

The Triassic

The rocks of the Triassic period, which lasted from 225 million years ago until 195 million years ago were originally defined on the basis of three series found in Germany:

	The Bunter	— continental river deposits
Younging	The Muschelkalk	— marine deposits
	The Keuper	— continental lake deposits

Rhaetic beds deposited at the end of the Triassic period, Aust Cliff, Gloucestershire.

56

The Muschelkalk is not found in the British sequence. The Bunter rocks consist of variegated sandstones, deposited in shallow depressions, with very little fossil flora or fauna. They are overlain by the Muschelkalk (in Germany), shelly marine limestones, which are followed by the varicoloured sandstones and marls, containing some evaporite outcrops, of the Keuper. The Keuper is itself overlain by the Rhaetic beds, consisting of black shales, sandstones and thin limestones, which mark a marine transgression. The beds contain a number of fossils, notably in the Rhaetic Bone Bed.

In general, the Triassic was a quiet period, though there was some localised mountain building and sporadic volcanic activity in various parts of the globe. Erosion of the mountainous areas continued; the climate remained very dry, as indicated by the red desert sandstone deposits found from northern America to eastern Asia.

Fossils found in the Triassic rocks of central and western Europe reveal that the reptiles continued to develop, with the ancestors of modern crocodiles, snakes, lizards, and turtles appearing. At the beginning of the period, large coral reefs were formed, striking examples of which remain in the Dolomite mountains. Large forests of conifers spread on the land. At the end of the period, the dinosaurs were appearing. The evidence of some very rare fossils suggests that the end of the Triassic also saw the appearance of the first true mammals.

The Jurassic

The Jurassic period started with a marine transgression 196 million years ago, and lasted until 135 million years ago. The sea rose

Jurassic limestone rich in ammonites.

to cover the whole of the British Isles except for the Scottish Highlands, the Pennine Ridge, central and northern Wales and the Thames valley. The depth of the sea water varied, and there were three submarine ridges, centred on the Mendips, the north Cotswolds, and the Humber, which rose and fell during the period and influenced the pattern of sedimentation. The basins between the ridges continued to deepen as the area as a whole was subsiding. The early part of the period was characterised by the deposition of shales and oolitic limestones – limestones formed of spherical rock particles which grow by accretion round a nucleus. These limestones were often rich in iron. Later sedimentation occurred in the deltaic northern basin, and at the close of the period the whole area was subjected to the deposition of clays. At this stage, the sea was retreating from the British Isles.

In the east of North America, there are no Jurassic sedimentary rocks, as the area was being elevated at the time. In the west, a large

Jurassic beds exposed in cliff, near Lulworth, Dorset.

Chalk, typical of the sediments deposited in the upper Cretaceous period.

sea, the Sundance Sea, extended from the Arctic as far south as New Mexico; this was a shallow lagoon, and its sandstone and shale sediments are a rich source of fossils.

The Jurassic was dominated by the Dinosaurs, which grew to gigantic sizes during their evolutionary development. The earliest known bird, *Archaeopteryx*, appears during the Jurassic. The seas contained a wide variety of invertebrates, among which the Ammonites and Belemnites were very numerous. The sediments of the period are rich in Ammonite fossils.

The Cretaceous

The Cretaceous period, which takes its name from the Latin word for chalk, lasted from 135 million years ago until 64 million years ago. It began with a marine transgression which almost completely submerged Europe. As the sea rose, clays and shales were deposited,

59

rich in fossils of Ammonites and bivalves. These deposits alternate with deposits of sandstone, suggesting that the area was a large delta, where sea and river waters enjoyed successive periods of dominance. Later layers are characteristic of truly marine conditions with sandstones rich in the mineral glauconite (which imparts a characteristic green colour), and clays. Both sandstones and clays contain many Ammonites and bivalves. In the second half of the period, the sea reached its greatest extent, leaving relatively little land above the surface. This land was low-lying, and the lack of erosion allowed the deposition of thick layers of very pure white limestone (chalk) from Ireland to southern Russia. This chalk, the most famous exposure of

Cretaceous chalk cliffs, Durdle Door, St Oswald's Bay, Dorset.

60

which forms the white cliffs of Dover, contains fossil Echinoids, Belemnites and bivalves, but few Ammonites, which were becoming extinct. The end of the Cretaceous saw the slow withdrawal of the sea, and the first stages in the separation of the North American plate from the European plate which opened the Atlantic ocean.

In the west of North America, sedimentation continued as the area of the Jurassic Sundance Sea was again inundated, this time to a greater depth. This seaway, the Rocky Mountain Seaway, was destroyed by the deformation and uplift that folded the sediments to form the beginning of the Rocky Mountains. These movements were accompanied by volcanic activity, and great masses of granite known as batholiths were extruded from the depths of the earth.

During this period, flowering plants appeared, and trees developed towards their modern forms. Insects of all kinds proliferated. The Ammonites completely disappeared at the end of the Cretaceous, after a period of slow decline. The Dinosaurs, too, were in decline, except in the seas, where giant reptiles were still dominant. By the end of the period, the rise to dominance of the warm blooded mammals was well under way.

The Tertiary

The Tertiary comprises the major part of the Cainozoic era, and includes the Eocene, Oligocene, Miocene, and Pliocene periods. It extends from 64 million years ago until 1 million years ago. In the British Isles, it is represented by the rocks of the Thames and Hampshire basins. The Eocene and Oligocene were periods of sedimentation in the marine, brackish, and fresh water of a deltaic environment. Typical deposits are clays and sands containing fossil bivalves and Gastropods. During the Miocene, the Alpine mountain chains were raised up as a result of the collision between Africa and Europe which began about 30 million years ago. The impact raised a large dome of chalk stretching from Hampshire into

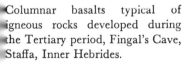

Columnar basalts typical of igneous rocks developed during the Tertiary period, Fingal's Cave, Staffa, Inner Hebrides.

France, the eroded remains of which form the downs of south east England. During the Pliocene period, southern England was again submerged; this event is marked by an erosion surface on the underlying rocks, but there is little evidence of sedimentary deposits from this period.

The surface of the earth that we know today gradually took shape during the Tertiary. The Atlantic steadily widened as the Americas moved slowly westward to their present positions. About 50 million years ago India began its long collision with Asia, which has still not quite ended, and the Himalayas were formed.

Tertiary deposits contain many fossils of land mammals, which had evolved rapidly to a position of dominance. Many of the forms subsequently became extinct, but those that survived led ultimately to the species of today.

The Quaternary

The Quaternary period covers the last million years of earth history; it contains two periods, the Pleistocene and the Holocene. The Pleistocene was marked by extensive and widespread glaciation known as the Ice Age. The climate changed, becoming much cooler, and glaciers which had formed in the mountains moved down to fill the valleys and spread over the plains. A huge ice cap spread until it extended south of the Great Lakes in North America, over Britain and central Europe, and into the Russian plains almost to the Volga. In Britain, the ice covered most of the country north of the Thames, while the area to the south became tundra-like and inhabited by mammoths and sabre-toothed tigers. The ice scoured the

Coombe deposits – slurry flows produced in areas of chalk during the Pleistocene Ice Age, Black Rock, Brighton, Sussex.

Boulder Clay produced by the Pleistocene Ice Age. Note the pebbles of igneous and sedimentary rocks enclosed in the fine clay matrix. Railway cutting at Glencraig Church, County Down.

rocks and carved out the valleys and lochs that make up the mountain and lake scenery of Scotland, the Lake District, and Wales. It is possible that the Ice Age is not yet over and that we are in an interglacial period; the ice may return in the next few hundred thousand years.

The Holocene period represents the last 20,000 years since the ice retreated, the period which saw the rise to dominance of modern man.

Rolling topography produced in lowlands by the Pleistocene Ice Age. Cavanacow, Pomeroy, County Tyrone.

Part 2

Minerals

A mineral is a naturally occurring inorganic chemical compound. The proportions of its components are fixed, and it has a set of chemical properties which, taken together, distinguish it from all other minerals. Each mineral has a fixed chemical formula and a definite internal structure that is expressed in its external crystalline form, although some minerals such as calcite exist in more than one form. Some rocks are composed entirely of a single mineral: quartzite, for example, is wholly made up of quartz (silicon dioxide) and therefore has the same chemical formula and properties as the mineral. Most rocks, however, are mixtures or aggregates of minerals and do not have the fixed structure and properties that any single mineral will have by virtue of being a particular chemical element or compound. In general, the term mineral is not used in its purest sense but is commonly extended to cover substances which are formed by organic processes, such as coal, oil, and bedded phosphates.

All minerals are composed of atoms or molecules arranged in regular patterns. An atom is the smallest fraction of any element that can exist by itself and still show the properties of that element. Although the diameter of a single atom is only about one hundred millionth of a centimetre, it is made up of yet smaller components known as sub-atomic particles or elementary particles. A large number of these have been discovered, but only three of them are important as permanent components of ordinary substances. They are protons, neutrons, and electrons.

The proton carries a positive electric charge, which is taken as the unit of charge; its mass is taken as the unit of mass. The neutron, as its name indicates, is electrically neutral, and has the same mass as the proton. Protons and neutrons together form the nucleus of atoms apart from those of the element hydrogen, which has a nucleus consisting of a single proton. The electron is a much smaller particle, with a mass approximately 1/1850th of that of a proton; for practical purposes, the whole mass of the atom is concentrated in the protons and neutrons that form the nucleus. The electron carries a negative electric charge equivalent in intensity to the positive charge of the proton.

The internal structure of an atom can be accurately represented only in terms of extremely abstract mathematical formulae; however, a convenient non-mathematical analogy is adequate to account for the properties of atoms that will concern us in this book. In this view, the atom resembles a miniature solar system with electrons revolving in orbits about a central nucleus of protons and neutrons. The reason that the electron orbits the nucleus rather than being drawn into it by mutual electrical attraction is that it behaves as a wave rather than as a particle. Thus the notion of a fixed orbit is a misleading one: the electrons are better described as occupying shells, or as being in the form of shells, a reasonable description of a complex mathematical function which expresses the probability of finding electrons in certain places around the nucleus.

The simplest atom of all is that of hydrogen, which consists of one proton and one electron. Its mass is thus approximately that of a proton. The total electric charge is zero, since the negative charge of the electron is balanced by the positive charge of the proton. All atoms are electrically balanced in this way: the total positive charge of the protons always equals the total negative charge of the electrons. Thus the number of protons always equals the number of electrons. The next heaviest element is helium, which consists of two protons, two neutrons, and two electrons. Each subsequent heavier element contains more protons, neutrons and electrons. As the number of electrons increases, they fill a series of shells, each of which has a maximum capacity. These shells are designated K, L, M, N, O, P, Q. The K shell has a capacity of two electrons, the L shell eight, the M shell eighteen, and the N shell thirty two; the O, P and Q shells are never filled in any known element, but their theoretical capacities are fifty, seventy two and ninety eight respectively. However many shells there are, the outer shell has a maximum capacity of eight electrons (with the exceptions of hydrogen, helium and lithium, where the outer shell is the K shell).

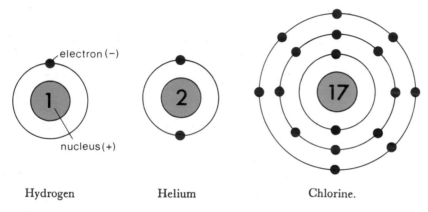

Hydrogen   Helium   Chlorine.

Each element can be assigned an atomic number, which is the number of protons that one of its atoms contains. The atomic number of an element is the number of positive charges on the nucleus of one atom of the element. Thus oxygen, which consists of eight protons, eight neutrons and eight electrons has an atomic number of eight; uranium, with 92 protons, 146 neutrons and 92 electrons has an atomic number of 92.

The original concept of atomic weight was to express the weight of an atom in terms of the weight of an atom of hydrogen. Since the weight of a hydrogen atom is not significantly different from that of the single proton forming its nucleus, this amounted to expressing the weight as the number of protons and neutrons in the nucleus. Thus oxygen, with eight protons and eight neutrons in its nucleus, has an atomic weight of 16; uranium, with 92 protons and 146 neutrons, has an atomic weight of 238. The molecular weight of a compound is the sum of the atomic weights of the elements forming it. Water consists of two hydrogen atoms joined to one oxygen atom, so its molecular weight is $2 \times 1 + 16 = 18$. Nowadays both atomic and molecular weights are referred to the atomic weight of carbon, C_{12}, and not hydrogen, as a standard.

When atomic weights are measured relative to carbon they turn out not to be whole numbers: iron, for example, has a measured atomic weight of 55.84. Even simple hydrogen departs from unity, with a measured atomic weight of 1.008. The reason for this apparent anomaly lies in the structure of the nucleus: the number of neutrons associated with the protons can vary, giving rise to variants of elements known as isotopes. Iron has 26 protons, and exists in forms with 28, 30, 31 and 32 neutrons; these isotopes have atomic weights of 54, 56, 57 and 58. The atomic weight of an element is written as a subscript to its chemical symbol, so that these isotopes are written as Fe_{54}, Fe_{56}, Fe_{57}, Fe_{58}. All these isotopes have 26 protons and thus have all the properties of iron. Most common elements exist in nature as a mixture of isotopes, which accounts for their fractional atomic weights. Isotopes are present in constant proportions in most samples of elements, so that the average atomic mass is constant. The gas chlorine, for example, consists of 75% of the isotope Cl_{35}, with 17 protons and 18 neutrons, and 25% of the isotope Cl_{37}, with 17 protons and 20 neutrons, giving an atomic weight of 35.5.

Early attempts to classify the elements were based on their atomic weights, because it appeared that elements of a similar chemical character possessed atomic weights related by an arithmetical progression. Mendeleeff arranged the elements in a Periodic Table, consisting of a series of vertical rows called groups containing elements with similar chemical properties. The horizontal rows are called periods.

THE MODERN PERIODIC TABLE

0	I	II	← Transition Elements →									III	IV	V	VI	VII
																H 1
He 2	Li 3	Be 4										B 5	C 6	N 7	O 8	F 9
Ne 10	Na 11	Mg 12										Al 13	Si 14	P 15	S 16	Cl 17
Ar 18	K 19	Ca 20	Sc 21	Ti 22	V 23	Cr 24	Mn 25	Fe 26	Co 27	Ni 28	Cu 29	Zn 30	Ga 31	Ge 32	As 33	Se 34	Br 35
Kr 36	Rb 37	Sr 38	Y 39	Zr 40	Nb 41	Mo 42	Tc 43	Ru 44	Rh 45	Pd 46	Ag 47	Cd 48	In 49	Sn 50	Sb 51	Te 52	I 53
Xe 54	Cs 55	Ba 56	▼ 57–71	Hf 72	Ta 73	W 74	Re 75	Os 76	Ir 77	Pt 78	Au 79	Hg 80	Tl 81	Pb 82	Bi 83	Po 84	At 85
Rn 86	Fr 87	Ra 88	▽ 89–103	104												

▼Lanthanides or Rare Earths	La 57	Ce 58	Pr 59	Nd 60	Pm 61	Sm 62	Eu 63	Gd 64	Tb 65	Dy 66	Ho 67	Er 68	Tm 69	Yb 70	Lu 71

▽Actinides	Ac 89	Th 90	Pa 91	U 92	Np 93	Pu 94	Am 95	Cm 96	Bk 97	Cf 98	Es 99	Fm 100	Md 101	No 102	Lw 103

Across the table, for example from sodium (Na) to chlorine (Cl), the properties change from metallic to non-metallic: sodium is a metal and chlorine is a gas. Down the table, elements become more metallic in their properties: oxygen (O) is a gas and tungsten (W) is a metal. Elements in the same group often crystallise in similar forms, and often replace one another in minerals.

Mendeleeff's basic principle of classification is still valid, but the discovery of isotopes led to the realisation that atomic number was more important than atomic weight, and the modern Periodic Table is compiled using it as a basis. The elements are arranged horizontally in order of increasing atomic number, and a new row or period is started every time an element is reached which has a full outer shell of electrons. The vertical groups or families of elements all have the same number of electrons in their outer shells, and it is this that gives them their similar properties. Because of certain anomalous elements called transition elements, which are classified according to the number of electrons in the penultimate shell, there are some long periods, which increase Mendeleeff's eight column table to the modern eighteen column table.

Atoms can gain or lose electrons and become ions. These are atoms which have lost their electrical neutrality and become charged: a loss of electrons results in a positively charged ion, since the positively charged protons exceed the negative electrons in number, and conversely a gain in electrons results in a negatively charged ion. The attraction between positive and negative ions is the source of chemical bonding, which takes place according to the Electronic Theory of Valency.

Group O of the Periodic Table contains five gases (to which helium should be added), neon, argon, krypton, xenon, and radon. These are exceedingly stable and do not normally combine with other atoms; they are known as the inert or noble gases (by analogy with the similarly inactive noble metals which include platinum and gold). Their atomic structure is characterised by eight electrons in their outermost shell, a stable pattern which is the key to most chemical bonding. The Electronic Theory of Valency is based on the principle that when elements react, that is when positive and negative ions combine, they usually attain the electronic structure of a noble gas, so that their nuclei become surrounded by a stable octet of electrons. For example, the sodium atom has only one electron in its outer shell: were it to lose this, it would show the stable pattern of the inert gas neon. Chlorine, on the other hand, has seven electrons in its outer shell: were it to gain one, it would attain the configuration of the inert gas argon.

When a sodium atom transfers an electron to a chlorine atom, the sodium atom becomes a positively charged sodium ion, and the chlorine atom becomes a negatively charged chlorine ion; the two ions are held together by electrostatic forces resulting from their complementary charges and form the compound known as sodium chloride (common salt which is the mineral halite or rock salt).
This kind of bond between ions of opposite electrical charge is known as an electrovalent or ionic bond. Electrovalent bonds are strong and results in crystals that are hard and have a high melting point. Nearly all minerals are bonded in this way.

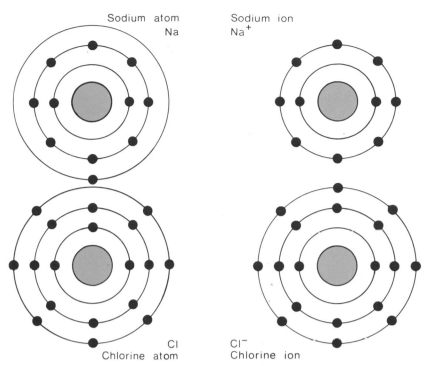

Sodium atom
Na

Sodium ion
Na$^+$

Cl
Chlorine atom

Cl$^-$
Chlorine ion

Diamond.
Graphite.

Atoms can also attain the electronic arrangement of a noble gas by sharing electrons, so that, in effect, two outer shells overlap, and form one shell which includes two nuclei. Each atom contributes one electron to the shared pair, forming what is known as a covalent or homopolar bond. No electrons are gained or lost, and no ions are formed. Thus hydrogen, with one electron, needs one more to attain the stable pattern of the inert gas helium, and chlorine, with seven electrons in its outer shell needs one more to attain the pattern of argon: the two gases can combine by forming a covalent bond by which two atoms are shared giving each the stable pattern of the nearest inert gas.

The crystal structures of compounds formed by covalent bonding depend largely on the shape of their component molecules, on the ease with which they can be packed in a three dimensional jig-saw. The forces which hold the molecules together are the weak van der Waal's forces: these are the weak forces of attraction between the molecules of all solids, and are the result of residual electrical effects. The only solids which are entirely dependent on these forces for their structure are the inert gases, for example argon in the solid state. Covalent compounds are usually weak, with low melting and boiling points: they are usually volatile liquids and gases at room temperature. An important exception among minerals is diamond, which consists of a crystal structure of five carbon atoms linked by covalent bonds. The other crystalline form of carbon, graphite, consists of layers of carbon atoms linked by covalent bonds, with the parallel layers being held together by van der Waal's forces. While the structure of diamond is very strong, that of graphite is weak, as it easily cleaves along the planes between the layers of atoms.

A variant of the covalent bond is the dative bond in which both shared electrons are donated by one atom. It occurs, for example, when a hydrogen ion combines with an ammonia molecule to give an ammonium ion. Once formed, the bond is indistinguishable from other covalent bonds.

A piece of metal is made up of a large number of crystals, each of which consists of an array of the nuclei and inner shells of the atoms permeated by a cloud of electrons from the outer shells of the atoms. The atoms of the metal all contribute to this cloud of electrons which holds the positive ions together. This metallic bond differs from an electrovalent bond in that it acts on like metal ions, not on ions of different elements. The structure of a metal is roughly analogous to a collection of ball bearings suspended in a lump of jelly: the ball bearings give the lump solidity and the jelly gives it cohesion. This structure is responsible for the commonly observed characteristics of metals: the electrons hold the positive ions tightly together, giving high densities, boiling points and melting points; the mobility of the electrons within the cloud gives metals their thermal and electrical conductivity, as well as ductility, tensile strength, and malleability. Metallic bonds occur in native metals and in some minerals that contain sulphides.

The hydrogen atom has a unique ability to form two bonds with one electron, as when it comes between two oxygen atoms in the structure of water and ice.

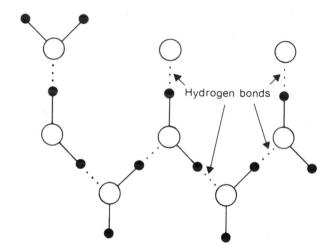

Hydrogen bonds

This linkage is very weak, but vital, since it accounts for the extra-ordinary properties of water. It is usually called a hydrogen bond, though this is a misnomer, as it is not a bond but an intermolecular force resulting from the high degree of polarisation of the water molecule. It is vital to life: it holds the non-identical twin molecules DNA and RNA together in a double spiral form; the breaking down of hydrogen bonds is partly responsible for the tenderising of meat when it is cooked. Hydrogen bonding is thought to occur in minerals which are produced by weathering.

In any mineral there are frequently two or more of the various types of bond linking the components. The atoms or molecules which compose a mineral are linked to form regular structures called crystal lattices. Each mineral has its own distinctive crystal lattice (though this may vary slightly depending on the circumstances of the mineral's crystallisation). The study of crystal lattices is known as crystallography, and provides one way of classifying minerals.

A crystal is a solid of regular shape enclosed naturally by flat faces in a regular and symmetrical manner; the shape of the crystal is an expression of the internal arrangement of the atoms. Every crystal is made up of certain atoms or groups of atoms arranged in a three dimensional pattern which is repeated throughout the crystal, producing a lattice structure. The lattice is built up of a number of unit cells, a unit cell being the smallest complete unit of the pattern. Thus the unit cell of the mineral halite is a cube of eight cubic sodium chloride molecules.

Crystals form when a mineral solidifies from a gaseous or liquid state – a process known as crystallisation. A mineral can crystallise in a number of characteristic shapes known as habits; these arise from variations in the lattice structure caused by the conditions in which the crystal grows. Variations of habit can have many causes, including the speed of crystal growth and the presence of impurities in the cooling liquid. Thus the mineral calcite (calcium carbonate) can occur as the elongated crystals of dogtooth calcite or the flattened crystals of nail-head calcite. In some cases crystals from a particular locality are characterised by their habit.

Dogtooth calcite from Cumberland.

When a mineral crystallises in an enclosed space, there may not be sufficient room for crystals to develop separately, and the result is a crystal mass in which some faces of each crystal are visible.

Crystal aggregate of olivine and feldspar.

Alternatively, the mineral may develop into a massive form which is made up of closely packed crystal grains but which shows no external signs of the internal crystal structure; this is known as a crystalline aggregate.

Alabaster in massive crystalline form.

A large number of crystal habits have been recognised – the most common are :

Acicular – needle-like crystals
Bladed – flat elongated crystals
Capillary – very thin crystals
Columnar – column-like crystals
Cubic – crystals with six equal rectangular faces
Dodecahedral – crystals with twelve unequal rectangular faces
Octahedral – crystals with eight square faces
Platy – thin, extensive plate-like crystals
Prismatic – crystals which resemble joined prisms
Pyramidal – crystals which resemble joined pyramids
Tabular – thick platy crystals

Crystallography

In the classification of minerals by their crystal lattices, the most perfect form of each crystal is used, the crystal which would develop in ideal conditions without external restraints or influences. A crystal grows by the addition of unit cells to the lattice structure in a regular way so that the crystal possesses a continuous symmetry. This crystallographic symmetry is not the same as geometrical symmetry : it depends on the internal atomic structure of the crystal, which is reflected in the angles between the faces of the crystal and not in the shape of the faces. A crystal can be defined by the form of symmetry it possesses. Within a particular form of symmetry, however, more than one crystal habit may be able to develop.

Opposite page.

Top: acicular crystals of actinolite from Zillertal, Austria.

Centre right: bladed crystals of selenite from Mexico.

Centre left: capillary crystals of plumosite (a variety of boulangerite) in quartz, from Wheal Boys, St Endellion, Cornwall.

Bottom left: columnar crystal of beryl from Mozambique.

Bottom right: cubic crystals of galena from Tri-State, Kansas.

74

76

There are three basic criteria or elements of symmetry in crystals, the plane of symmetry, the axis of symmetry, and the centre of symmetry.

The plane of symmetry is the easiest to visualise : an object has a plane of symmetry if it can be divided into two identical halves. In other words, such a plane divides the object in such a way that the two halves are mirror images of each other. A cube has a maximum possible number of such planes, nine.

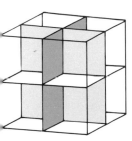 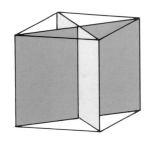 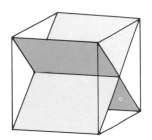 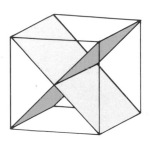

Planes of symmetry.

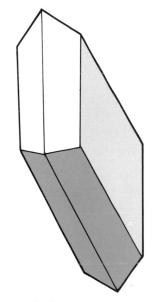

A crystal of gypsum.

The axis of symmetry can be visualised as an imaginary line about which an object can be rotated so as to present the same appearance more than once in a complete rotation. For example, a line drawn vertically through the centre of the top of a square table would be an axis of symmetry, a fourfold one because the table presents the same appearance four times when rotated through 360 degrees. In the case of a crystal an axis of symmetry occurs when the crystal can be rotated so that the same configuration of faces is visible on more than one occasion as it passes through 360 degrees. There are a number of different types of axis depending on the number of times the configuration of faces is repeated.

A centre of symmetry is present in a crystal if an imaginary line can be passed through the centre of the crystal from any point on its surface (a face, a point, or an edge) to a similar point on the opposite side.

The criteria of symmetry can be illustrated by reference to the common mineral gypsum. In its usual crystal form, as illustrated below, it has one plane which divides the crystal into two identical halves – the only plane of symmetry for this crystal. At right angles to this plane is an axis of symmetry : rotation about this axis causes the crystal to take up the same position twice in a complete rotation, so that it is a diad axis. For every face, edge or point of the crystal there is a similar face, edge or point in a corresponding position in the other half – therefore the crystal has a centre of symmetry.

Mathematical analysis has shown that there are only thirty-two possible combinations of axes, planes and centres of symmetry in crystals. These are classified into six crystal systems by reference to their crystallographic axes – of which there are three or four passing through a common point, the centre of the crystal.

77

System	Crystallographic axes

Isometric (Cubic)   Three mutually perpendicular axes of equal length.

Halite   Spessartite   Chromite   Sal Ammoniac

Tetragonal   Three mutually perpendicular axes: the two in the horizontal plane are of equal length, the vertical axis is either longer or shorter than the other two.

Cassiterite   Torbernite   Calomel   Chalcopyrite

Hexagonal/Trigonal   Three axes of equal length in the horizontal plane which intersect at angles of 60 degrees, and a fourth vertical axis either shorter or longer than the other three perpendicular to the plane which includes them.

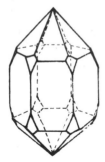    

Quartz   Vanadinite   Siderite   Ilmenite

Orthorhombic   Three mutually perpendicular axes all of different lengths.

  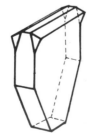 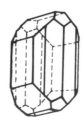 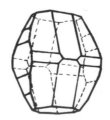

Strontianite   Lepidocrosite   Forsterite   Humite

Monoclinic — Three unequal axes, two at right angles and the third making an oblique angle with the plane of the other two.

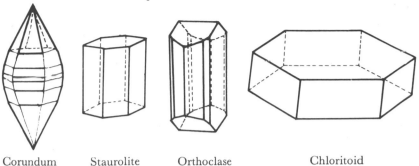

Corundum   Staurolite   Orthoclase   Chloritoid

Triclinic — Three unequal axes all intersecting at oblique angles to each other.

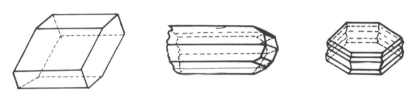

Kyanite   Polyhalite   Albite

The Hexagonal and Trigonal systems are described using the same axes, because the crystals of the two systems are very similar. Some crystallographers treat the Trigonal as a separate system with its own axes.

The crystal systems are best illustrated by reference to specific examples; the minerals chosen form well defined crystals so that it is relatively easy to determine which system they belong to.

ISOMETRIC (CUBIC)   *Galena*   lead sulphide (PbS), forms cubic crystals easily recognised by their lead-grey colour and metallic lustre.

Galena from North Yorkshire.

Halite   sodium chloride (NaCl) forms cubic crystals which are colourless when pure, but which are often tinted yellow or red. They have a glassy appearance.

Fluorite   calcium fluoride (CaF$_2$) usually forms cubic crystals, though octahedral and dodecahedral forms are also found. Pure fluorite is transparent and colourless, but it is very rare in this state. The crystals have a glassy appearance, and may be green, yellow or purple, or, more rarely, blue, pink or brown.

Above: halite from Imperial County, California.
Left: fluorite from Hights Mine Weardale, County Durham.

TETRAGONAL   *Cassiterite*   tin dioxide (SnO$_2$) forms thick prismatic crystals with a brilliant metallic lustre. Various colours are found, the most common being black or brown.

Cassiterite from Trevaunance Mine, St Agnes Cornwall.

HEXAGONAL
or
TRIGONAL

Apatite is a phosphate of calcium with either fluorine ($Ca_5F(PO_4)_3$) or chlorine ($Ca_5Cl(PO_4)_3$) present. It forms hexagonal prismatic crystals topped by hexagonal pyramids. They are usually pale sea-green or bluish green with a glassy appearance.

Calcite calcium carbonate ($CaCO_3$) forms needle-like prismatic crystals with a variety of colours and lustres.

Quartz silicon dioxide (SiO_2) forms hexagonal prismatic crystals terminated by positive and negative rhombohedra. Complex modifications occur, as well as highly deformed crystals. Almost any colour and lustre is possible.

Below: apatite – francolite, a variety of fluor-apatite from Fowey Consols, Cornwall.
Bottom: calcite from Oskaloosa, Iowa.
Right: quartz from Rhodesia.

ORTHORHOMBIC   *Topaz*   aluminium fluosilicate in a hydrous form $(Al_2SiO_4(F,OH)_2)$ forms prismatic crystals which are often white or yellow with a dull glassy appearance.

MONOCLINIC   *Gypsum*   hydrated calcium sulphate $(CaSO_4.2H_2O)$ forms tabular prismatic crystals which are colourless or white, sometimes grey, yellowish, or red, with a pearly appearance.

TRICLINIC   *Microcline*   potassium aluminium silicate $(KAlSi_3O_8)$ forms tabular crystals which can be green, white, pale yellow or red, with a dull glassy appearance.

Above: gypsum from Edlington Brickworks, Doncaster, Yorkshire.

Above left: topaz from Russiá.

Left: Microcline from Colorado.

82

In practice, few minerals form crystals of sufficient quality for their crystal system to be easily recognised – for teaching purposes wooden or plastic block models of crystals are used to show students what the perfectly formed crystals would look like. Crystallographic analysis based on crystal systems is generally beyond the scope of the amateur mineralogist and collector – it requires facilities that are available only to a professional in a highly equipped modern laboratory. Crystals are examined by X-ray diffraction, and the three-dimensional structures are represented on a plane surface by a mathematical technique known as stereographic projection.

THE CHEMICAL CLASSIFICATION OF MINERALS

Because minerals are compounds of the atoms of various elements, it is possible to classify them on the basis of their chemical constituents. Nearly every element known to man is represented in some mineral, but most are relatively uncommon: eight elements account for 97% of the weight of the earth's crust and 98% of its atoms. These eight are:

Element		% by weight	% by atoms
Oxygen	O	46.60	62.55
Silicon	Si	27.72	21.22
Aluminium	Al	8.13	6.47
Iron	Fe	5.00	1.92
Magnesium	Mg	2.09	1.84
Calcium	Ca	3.63	1.94
Sodium	Na	2.83	2.64
Potassium	K	2.59	1.42

The two most common elements, oxygen and silicon, account for 74% of the crust by weight and 84% of the crustal atoms. They combine to form silicon dioxide (SiO_2), known as silica, an important mineral which occurs abundantly in a number of different forms, the most common being quartz. The wide range of silicon compounds (silicates) are the most important rock-forming minerals.

The fundamental unit in the structure of silicate minerals is a tetrahedral arrangement of Silicon and Oxygen ions, in which the Silicon is situated at the centre and Oxygen at the four corners

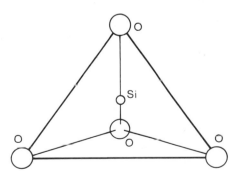

This structure is expressed chemically as $(SiO_4)^{-4}$, the −4 indicating that the unit has a net negative charge of four units. The modified covalent type bonds between the silicon atoms are very strong, but

the structure is not stable by itself because the electric charges on the component ions do not balance one another. Stable structures are formed when SiO_4 tetrahedra are linked in various ways by the sharing of two or more of their oxygen atoms between adjacent units, forming complex lattice structures in which ions of other elements may be accommodated. The range and variety of these structures is so great that minerals are divided into two basic chemical classes, silicates and non-silicates.

The non-silicate group of minerals covers all minerals that are not based on the $(SiO_4)^{-4}$ tetrahedron. These are classified in groups based on chemical composition and structure. The most obvious division is between native elements like gold and silver which occur in nature uncombined with other elements, and minerals which are compounds. These are further divided into groups on the basis of the elements they contain: thus minerals formed of elements combined with oxygen are classified as oxides, and include quartz and cassiterite; those formed of elements combined with sulphur, for example galena are classified as sulphides. Classification in this way yields eight major groups, some of which have minor subdivisions:

Native elements
Oxides
Hydroxides
Sulphides, tellurides and arsenides
Sulphates
Carbonates, nitrates and borates
Phosphates, chromates, arsenates, vanadates, etc.
Halides (commonly chlorides and fluorides)

The oxides and hydroxides are sometimes grouped together; the molybdates and tungstates are sometimes treated as separate groups rather than being included with phosphates, chromates, etc.

Among the minerals in each group are:

Native elements: Carbon (in the form of diamond or graphite), gold, silver, copper, platinum, arsenic, antimony.

Native gold from Transylvania, Rumania.

Native silver from Zacatecas, Mexico.

Native copper from Santa Rita, New Mexico.

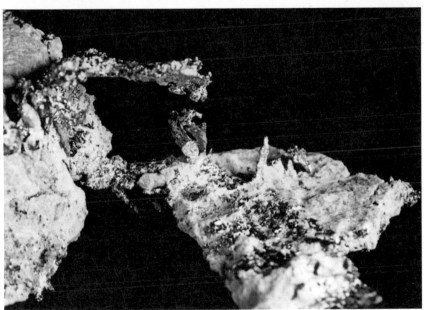

Oxides: Quartz (silicon dioxide, SiO_2), rutile (titanium dioxide, TiO_2), spinel (magnesium aluminium oxide, $MgAl_2O_4$), hematite (iron oxide, Fe_2O_3), cassiterite (tin oxide, SnO_2), corundum (aluminium oxide, Al_2O_3).

Hydroxides: Brucite (magnesium hydroxide, $Mg(OH)_2$), gibbsite (aluminium hydroxide, $Al(OH)_3$).

Sulphides: Pyrite (iron sulphide, FeS_2), cinnabar (mercury sulphide, HgS), blende (zinc sulphide, ZnS), galena (lead sulphide, PbS), orpiment (arsenic sulphide, As_2S_3), pentlandite (nickel iron sulphide, $(Fe,Ni)_9S_8$).

Red rutile from Glen Lochay, Scotland.

Spinel in calcite from Franklin, New Jersey.

Botryoidal hematite from Mozambique.

Cassiterite.

Corundum.

Pyrite from Italy.

Cinnabar from Humbolt County, Nevada.

Blende from Roughton Gill, Cumberland.

Sulphates:	barytes (barium sulphate, $BaSO_4$), anglesite (lead sulphate, $PbSO_4$), gypsum (hydrated calcium sulphate, $CaSO_4.2H_2O$).
Carbonates:	Calcite (calcium carbonate, $CaCO_3$), magnesite (magnesium carbonite, $MgCO_3$), malachite (copper carbonate, $Cu_2CO_3(OH)_2$).
Phosphates:	Apatite (calcium fluo-phosphate, $Ca_5F(PO_4)_3$ or calcium chloro-phosphate, $Ca_5Cl(PO_4)_3$), turquoise (basic hydrous phosphate of aluminium and copper, possibly $CuAl_6(PO_4)_4.(OH)_8.4H_2O$), autunite (hydrated phosphate of calcium and uranium, $Ca((UO_2)_2(PO_4)_2.10-12H_2O)$.
Halides:	Halite (sodium chloride, $NaCl$), sal ammoniac (ammonium chloride, NH_4Cl), fluorite (calcium fluoride, CaF_2).

Top left: barytes from Washington County, Missouri.

Top right: anglesite from Yuma County, Arizona.

Centre left: calcite – phantom calcite from Chihuahua, Mexico.

Centre right: malachite from the Congo.

Right: turquoise from Arizona.

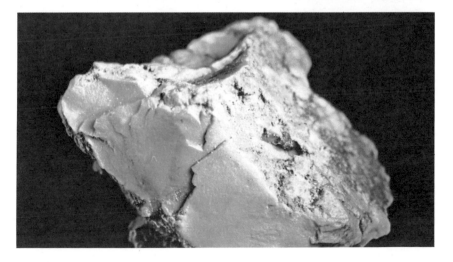

Fluorite from Cornwall.

The silicates are classified on the basis of their atomic structures, as revealed by X-ray analysis. The SiO_4 tetrahedra may combine by the mutual sharing of an oxygen atom, and current classification is based on the relatively few ways in which units may be linked together.

The nesosilicates or orthosilicates consist of separate SiO_4 tetrahedra stacked together in a regular manner throughout a crystal structure, with the tetrahedra joined only through other positive ions which lie between them. Minerals built up in this way include the olivines, the garnets, and the aluminium silicates.

The olivines are a series of nesosilicates with the general formula R_2SiO_4, where R may be magnesium (Mg) or iron (Fe) or both. At

Olivine.

Garnet crystals in schist, from Zillertal, Austria.

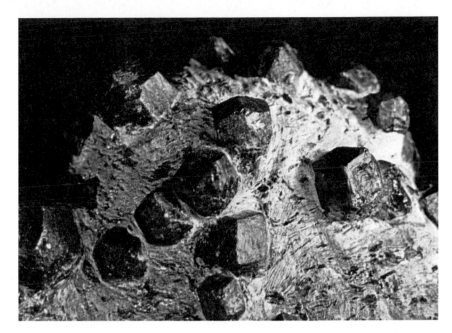

one end of the series is forsterite, magnesium silicate (Mg_2SiO_4); at the other end is fayalite, iron silicate (Fe_2SiO_4). In between the ratio of magnesium to iron can vary continuously. Olivine, magnesium iron silicate, $(Mg,Fe)_2SiO_4$, is the general name given to the intermediate minerals. Olivine in which magnesium predominates forms the upper layer of the earth's mantle.

The garnet family consists of a group of minerals with the general formula $M_3^{2+}R_2^{3+}(SiO_4)_3$, where M is a metallic ion carrying two positive charges which may be calcium, magnesium, iron or manganese, and R is a metallic ion carrying three positive charges, which may be iron, aluminium, chromium, or titanium. There are two species, pyralspite and ugrandite, each with three subspecies,

Almandine garnet from Zillertal, Austria.

Massive grossularite garnet from South West Africa.

forming a complex, continuously variable series:

	Pyrope	$Mg_3Al_2(SiO_4)_3$
Pyralspite	Almandite	$Fe_3Al_2(SiO_4)_3$
	Spessartite	$Mn_3Al_2(SiO_4)_3$
	Uvarovite	$Ca_3Cr_2(SiO_4)_3$
Ugrandite	Grossularite	$Ca_3Al_2(SiO_4)_3$
	Andradite	$Ca_3Fe_2(SiO_4)_3$

Natural garnets contain either the three minerals of the pyralspite species or the three minerals of the ugrandite species in varying proportions.

The aluminium silicates all have the formula Al_2SiO_5, but exist in different forms, known as polymorphs, depending on the temperature and pressure at which they were formed. Thus andalusite is formed under fairly high temperatures and low stress, sillimanite at a higher temperature and under more stress, and kyanite under high stress.

Andalusite from Dover Mine, Mineral County, Nevada.

Sillimanite from Chester, Connecticut.

Kyanite from Russia.

The nesosilicates are chemically diverse, but they share certain similar physical properties: they generally form crystals with equal dimensions; they are generally hard; they have high specific gravities and indices of refraction.

In the sorosilicates, or pyrosilicates, two SiO_4 tetrahedra share one oxygen atom, and are in turn linked through other positive ions to form an expanded network. The combination of the two tetrahedra forms a unit with the formula Si_2O_7. Relatively few natural silicates have this structure; one that does is melilite, $CaMgSi_2O_7$, which is found in the great lava fields in central and eastern Africa.

The cyclosilicates, or metasilicates, have ring structures, in which each SiO_4 tetrahedron shares two of its oxygens with neighbouring tetrahedra. Three member and six member rings are found. A six member ring is shown here.

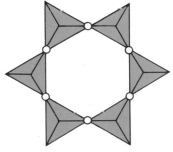

93

The mineral benitoite, $BaTi(Si_3O_9)$, is built up of three member rings; beryl, $Be_3Al_2(Si_6O_{18})$, is made up of six member rings.

The inosilicates exist in two forms, single and double chains. In the former each tetrahedron is joined to its neighbours through two oxygen atoms to form a single open chain. In the second type two single chains are joined through oxygen atoms so that the tetrahedra share alternately two and three oxygens.

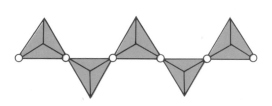

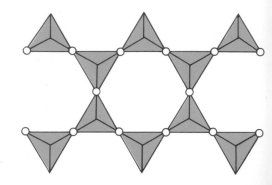

The pyroxenes, important rock-forming minerals, have a single chain structure, with a general formula $R_2Si_2O_6$, where R may be magnesium (Mg), iron (Fe), or calcium (Ca), or more rarely zinc (Zn), or manganese (Mn); in other types, R is a combination of sodium (Na), or lithium (Li) and iron or aluminium (Al). Aluminium, which has an atomic diameter very similar to that of silicon, and an identical charge, is able to replace silicon in the tetrahedra: this is known as lattice substitution. There are many varieties of pyroxene, with atoms of one metal replacing those of another within the limits of the formula; only aluminium can replace silicon. Important pyroxenes are enstatite ($MgSiO_3$), diopside ($CaMgSi_2O_6$), spodumene ($LiAlSi_2O_6$), augite ($Ca,Mg,Fe,Al)_2(Al,Si)_2O_6$ and aegirine $NaFe(Si_2O_6)$.

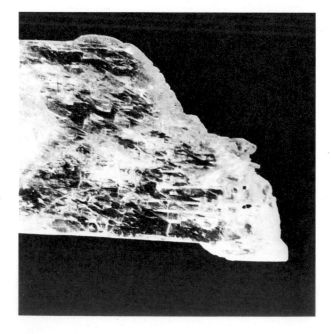

Double chain structures are found in the amphiboles, a large group of rock-forming minerals with the general formula $R_{7-8}(Si_4O_{11})_2(OH)_2$, where R may be magnesium (Mg), iron (Fe), calcium (Ca), sodium (Na) or aluminium (Al), or any combination of them. A typical example is tremolite, $Ca_2Mg_5(Si_4O_{11})_2(OH)_2$. Hornblende has aluminium replacing some of the silicons in the chains. Other amphiboles include actinolite, riebeckite and glaucophane.

Hornblende from Worcestershire.

Left: enstatite.

The phyllosilicates have a sheet structure which is formed when the SiO_4 tetrahedra are linked by three of their corners.

Far left: spodumene from Brazil.
Left: aegirine — aegirine-augite from Highland Grove, Ontario.

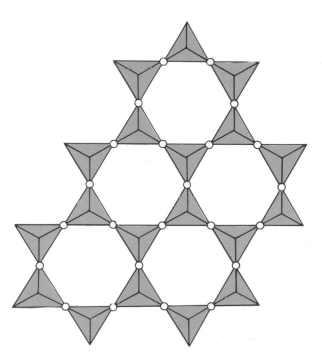

This structure can extend indefinitely in a two-dimensional network or 'sheet'; it is found, for example, in the mineral pyrophillite, $Al_2Si_4O_{10}(OH)_2$. The sheets lie one on top of another, and the weak bonds between them allow the sheets to slide over each other. The characteristically flaky minerals in this class include two important groups, the micas and the clays. The micas, whose chemistry is very complex, have about one in four of the silicon atoms replaced by aluminium; thus the mica muscovite has the formula $KAl_2(AlSi_3)O_{10}(OH)_2$. Muscovite forms a series in which the relative composition varies, as does another important mica, biotite, $K(Mg,Fe)_3(AlSi_3)O_{10}(OH,F)_2$. The clay minerals are basically hydrous aluminium silicates, which occur as minute flaky crystals having the phyllosilicate sheet structure. Examples are kaolinite, $Al_4Si_4O_{10}(OH)_8$, and pyrophillite, $Al_2Si_4O_{10}(OH)_2$.

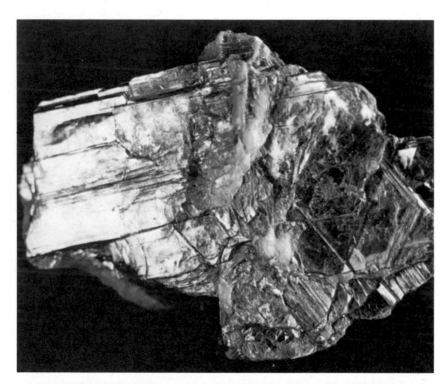

Muscovite from Norway.

Biotite – phlogopite from Goulᵈ Lake Mine, Kingston, Ontario.

The tectosilicates have a structure consisting of a three-dimensional framework which is formed when each SiO_4 tetrahedron is linked by all four corners, so that every oxygen ion is shared between two tetrahedra.

Minerals which have this structure include quartz, tridymite, and cristobalite, which are all forms of silica, SiO_2, but differ in the arrangement of the linked tetrahedra. The tectosilicates include the feldspars, in which aluminium replaces some of the silicon at the centres of the tetrahedra. When one aluminium ion substitutes for one of the four Silicon ions in the basic structural unit $(SiO_2)_4$, the unit $(AlSi_3O_8)$ is formed, which requires a positive ion with a single charge to complete the molecule. If potassium (K) is introduced, orthoclase, $KAlSi_3O_8$, is formed. If sodium (Na) is introduced, albite, $NaAlSi_3O_8$,

Albite from Portland, Connecticut.

Celsian from Benallt Mine, Rhiw Aberdaron, Caernarvonshire.

results. If two aluminiums replace two silicons in the $(SiO_2)_4$ unit, a positive ion with a double charge is needed to restore electrical neutrality. This can be calcium (Ca), in which case anorthite, $CaAl_2Si_2O_8$, is formed; if barium (Ba) is introduced, celsian, $BaAl_2Si_2O_8$, is formed. Albite and anorthite are the end members of a continuous series called the plagioclase feldspars; the intermediate members are said to be isomorphs of the two end members – which means that although their chemical composition varies, all these minerals have the same crystal form and crystal structure. Another way of describing the varying composition of these feldspars is as a solid solution of one mineral in another, the term referring to the fact that this solid resembles a liquid solution in that it remains homogeneous when its components are varied over a certain range. The range of plagioclase feldspars between pure albite and pure anorthite is divided into sections as follows:

	% Albite	% Anorthite
Albite	100	0
Oligoclase	90	10
Andesine	70	30
Labradorite	50	50
Bytownite	30	70
Anorthite	10	90
	0	100

Thus oligoclase can be described as a solid solution of anorthite in albite, and bytownite as a solid solution of albite in anorthite.

Oligoclase from Sweden.

MINERAL ENVIRONMENTS

A method of mineral classification which does not depend on laboratory techniques but on observation of the geological environments in which minerals have been formed. Most minerals are the result of processes that have taken place in the earth's crust or upper mantle; they are either components of rocks or associated with them.

The most common minerals are the hundred or so species which form the major constituents of rocks, the rock-forming minerals. The most plentiful of these are silica (the oxide of silicon), the silicates of aluminium, iron, magnesium, calcium, sodium, and potassium (the six most abundant elements after oxygen and silicon), and the oxides and carbonates of these elements. For example, the common rock granite is composed mainly of quartz (SiO_2), feldspar (for example orthoclase, $KAlSi_3O_8$), and mica (for example biotite, $K(Mg,Fe)_3(AlSi_3)O_{10}(OH,F)_2$).

There are well over 2000 other mineral species which are not rock forming. In terms of abundance, they are minor minerals, though many are of great economic importance. They are known as accessory minerals because they are not essential to the formation of a particular rock type but merely occur in small quantities in the rock when it has formed under certain chemical and physical conditions. Granite is often found with zircon (zirconium silicate, $ZrSiO_4$) and iron oxide (Fe_2O_3). In some bodies of rock, accessory minerals are present in large segregations known as mineral deposits; when these contain valuable elements that repay extraction, they are known as ore deposits. This has led to accessory minerals being misleadingly called ore minerals – not all of these minor minerals are ores in the recognised economic sense of the word. For a deposit to be mined economically, it must contain about two hundred times the average amount of the metallic mineral normally found in rocks. The chief nickel ore mineral, for example, is pentlandite (($Fe,Ni)S$), which is found in association with the mineral pyrrhotite in Sudbury, Ontario, Canada. Vast quantities of pyrrhotite are mined for the relatively small amount of pentlandite it contains.

Grains of zircon.

Pentlandite from Russia.
Right: pyrrhotite in quartz, from
Monte Somma, Italy.

The nature and location of rock-forming minerals is dependent on
the type of rock they form. Rocks are divided into three main
classes, the igneous rocks, the sedimentary rocks, and the metamorphic
rocks. It is estimated that 95% of the earth's crust is composed of
igneous rock, rocks which were originally molten. Beneath the earth's
surface, molten rock material exists as a magma, a silicate-rich
chemical solution which can contain crystalline and gaseous constituents. Many magmas originate in the low velocity zone of the
upper mantle, from where they pass upwards through fractures and
fissures in the crust, propelled either by the weight of rocks above or
by earth movements. On their way to the surface, magmas melt and
dissolve some of the rocks they pass through, complicating their
original chemical composition. At the same time, the magmas lose heat
to the surrounding rocks, and as they cool, they become thicker,
less fluid, and thus less mobile. These changes can cause magmas to
solidify before they reach the surface, forming large bodies of intrusive
igneous rocks known as plutonic rocks. Magmas which reach the
surface of the earth and erupt through fissures and cracks in the form
of volcanoes are called lavas; they flow out on to the surface and cool
to form sheets of igneous rocks called extrusive or volcanic rocks.
When magmas solidify very near the surface, filling fissures in the
surrounding rocks or forming thin sheets between layers, they form
what are sometimes known as hypabyssal rocks. Among the common
igneous rocks, granite and gabbro are plutonic, basalt and rhyolite are
extrusive, and dolerite and felsite are hypabyssal.

All sedimentary rocks are ultimately derived from pre-existing igneous
rocks exposed on the earth's surface. They may take the form of fragments resulting from the disintegration of earlier rocks, in which case
they are known as clastic rocks. These are usually produced by mechanical weathering or erosion, processes which can affect the composition of
the minerals they contain. The fragments can be consolidated into a
single mass either by welding, due to the weight of overlying rock

beds, or by cementation, when the spaces between the fragments become filled by the deposition of a binding material such as calcium carbonate or silica. Quartz grains, for example, are cemented firmly together by precipitated mineral matter to form sandstones.

Whereas quartz survives the weathering process intact, many minerals are chemically changed by it. Some are dissolved and carried in solution to the sea. If a part of the sea becomes cut off from the main body so that the rate of evaporation of the water exceeds the inflow of water, the water is eliminated and deposits of the dissolved salts are left behind. Minerals formed by this kind of evaporation at the surface are known as evaporites. Certain chemical conditions within a body of water may cause precipitation of dissolved minerals; ironstones and some limestones are formed in this way. Cherts are formed by the precipitation of silica within partial solutions of pre-existing rocks. The process by which this takes place has been a much debated geochemical problem, but some cherts are known to be the result of biological processes. These cherts are formed from the silica skeletons of organisms such as radiolarians and diatoms. Other rocks with an organic origin include coal, phosphates, and some limestones. All rocks formed by chemical or organic action consist of new minerals, which are distinguished from the inherited minerals formed into new rocks by mechanical processes.

Rocks undergo significant changes not only by weathering at the earth's surface, but also far below it. At considerable depths in the crust, where temperatures and pressures are higher than those prevailing at the surface, minerals become unstable and the atoms of which they are composed rearrange themselves. New minerals may form and old ones disappear, or structures may be changed by recrystallisation. Rocks which are formed as a result of these alterations are known as metamorphic rocks. The primary factor controlling metamorphism is depth, for both pressure and temperature rise with increasing depth, but it can also be brought about by earth movements which result from plate tectonics, or by the proximity of molten igneous rocks. During the process of metamorphism, nothing is added and nothing is subtracted. Any type of igneous or sedimentary rock can be metamorphosed, and the process can be repeated through a series of changes.

When a magma emerges from the depths into the upper portion of the earth's crust, it changes the rocks it comes into contact with. These changes, known as contact metamorphism, are caused by the rise in temperature associated with the presence of the magma. The metamorphic rocks are formed as a metamorphic aureole, a zone of rocks surrounding the igneous body at the contact surface. Regional metamorphism is a slower process which affects large areas of the earth's crust. It occurs as a result of rises in temperature and pressure caused by deep-seated earth processes. Dislocation or dynamic metamorphism results from movement higher in the crust, such as the large scale thrusts and faults associated with periods of mountain building. When there are no hot rocks involved in the process, no new minerals are formed: existing ones are broken down and distorted into new forms.

In all forms of metamorphism, the new minerals develop from rock

102

that is molten or partially molten. Rocks formed from a partially molten state often contain the remains of the structure and texture of the original rock and its minerals (relicts) along with the new minerals.

Rock-forming minerals	Accessory minerals	Extractable elements
Actinolite	Apatite	Phosphates
Andesite	Blende	Zinc
Augite	Beryl	Beryllium
Bauxite	Cassiterite	Tin
Biotite	Cerussite	Lead
Bytownite	Chlorite	
Calcite	Epidote	
Diopside	Fluorite	
Dolomite	Galena	Lead
Halite	Gypsum	
Hornblende	Hematite	Iron
Labradorite	Jadeite	
Leucite	Lepidolite	Lithium
Magnesite	Malachite	Copper
Microcline	Pentlandite	Nickel
Muscovite	Phillipsite	
Nepheline	Phlogopite	
Oligoclase	Pyrite	Sulphur, iron
Olivine	Riebeckite	
Orthoclase	Rutile	Titanium
Pyrope	Sphene	
Quartz	Spinel	
Serpentine	Zircon	Zirconium

Rock type	Rock-forming minerals	Accessory minerals
Igneous	The major silicates: feldspars, micas, pyroxenes, olivines, quartz.	Mainly silicates or oxides: rutile, sphene, spinel, epidote, chlorite.
Sedimentary 1. clastic	Residual mineral grains: quartz, calcite, dolomite, iron minerals (as cement).	Heavy minerals which survive erosion: pyrite, rutile, zircon.
2. chemical	Limestones, ironstones, evaporites: calcite, chalybite, halite.	Normally heavy minerals if any.
3. organic	Calcite; phosphates.	Normally heavy minerals if any.

Metamorphic		
1. contact	Cordierite, anorthite, diopside, andalusite.	
2. regional	Chlorite, epidote, micas, garnets, aluminium silicates.	Very wide range depending on the initial chemical composition and mineral content.
3. dynamic	Very variable.	

MINERAL RECOGNITION

The amateur geologist can identify and classify minerals by using simple physical and chemical tests, some of which can be carried out in the field when the specimen is being collected. The physical properties of minerals are usually studied and evaluated as the first step in the process of identifying minerals.

The most obvious physical property of a mineral is its colour. Unfortunately, the colours of minerals vary greatly, so that in many cases this property is of little or no diagnostic value. Quartz, for example, is usually colourless or white, but it is also found in pinkish yellow, pink, red, violet, purple, grey, brown, green and even black forms.

Left: colourless quartz from Rhodesia.

Below: rose quartz from South Africa.

Right: smoky quartz.

Many minerals exhibit a wide range of colours. Minerals can appear to be different colours depending on whether they are wet or dry, or whether they are examined under artificial or natural light.

The streak of a mineral is the colour of its powder, which is usually revealed by rubbing it on a plate of unglazed porcelain known as a streak plate. Hard minerals may have to be scratched with a knife or file. The colour of the streak may or may not be the same as the colour of the mineral in a mass: usually it is a lighter shade of the body colour, though there are many exceptions, such as black hematite which has a red streak, and pyrite which has a brassy yellow body colour and a greenish-black streak.

The lustre of a mineral is the appearance of its surface when light shines on it rather than through it. The reflective properties of an unweathered surface of a mineral depend on a number of factors, including transparency, reflectivity, and the structure of the surface layers. There are two general types of lustre, metallic and non-metallic. Metallic lustre is the ordinary lustre of metals. The several types of non-metallic lustre are defined by descriptive terms that are largely self-explanatory:

Adamantine – brilliant, like cut diamond
Vitreous   – like glass or quartz
Resinous
Waxy
Greasy
Silky
Satiny
Pearly
Pitchy
Dull
Earthy

Although the surface appearance of a particular mineral may vary, lustre is regarded as a diagnostic feature.

Opposite page.
Top left: quartz and agate with vitreous lustre, from Brazil.
Bottom left: adamite with resinous lustre, from Durango, Mexico.
Top right: chalcedony with greasy lustre, from Prieska, South Africa.
Bottom right: molybdenite with greasy lustre, from Wisconsin.

Specular hematite with adamantine lustre, from Cumberland.

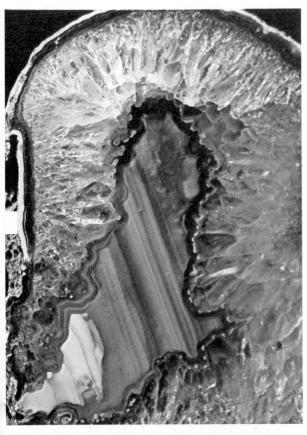

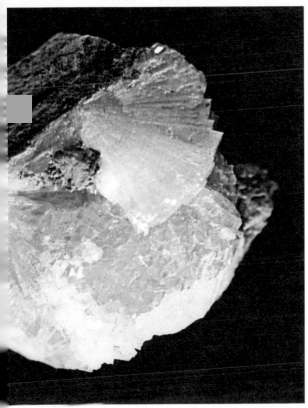
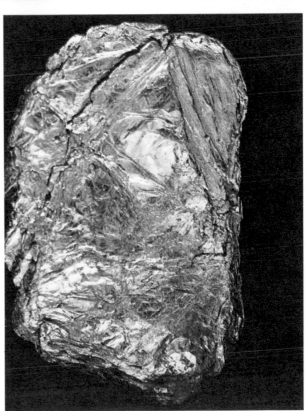

Above left: talc with dull lustre.
Right: bauxite with earthy lustre, from Arkansas.

Opposite page.
Top left: Tiger's Eye with silky lustre, from South Africa.
Top right: satin spar with satiny lustre, from Nottinghamshire.
Bottom left: tremolite with pearly lustre, from New York State.
Bottom right: pitchstone with pitchy lustre, from Scotland.

The determination of hardness is one of the most important tests in the identification of minerals. There are many ways of measuring hardness, based on the resistance of minerals to scratching. A comparative scale of hardness was drawn up by the Austrian mineralogist Moh:

1. Talc
2. Gypsum
3. Calcite
4. Fluorite
5. Apatite
6. Orthoclase
7. Quartz
8. Topaz
9. Corundum
10. Diamond

Hardness 1 indicates the most easily scratched and hardness 10 the maximum resistance to scratching. Thus diamond will scratch all other natural minerals, while corundum will scratch all minerals with a hardness of less than 9. A knife can be used for rough hardness tests in the field: the average hardness of knife blades is slightly more than 5, so all minerals can be divided into two groups, those that can be scratched with a knife and those that cannot.

The relative density of a mineral is expressed in terms of its specific gravity, which is the ratio of its weight in air to the weight of an equal volume of water and is thus a measure of the mineral's density compared with the density of water. It is measured in the laboratory by

Flint showing conchoidal fracture, from Gravesend, Kent.

weighing the specimen in air and in water, using a Walker's steelyard or a Jolly's spring balance. In the field, a rough guide can be obtained by feeling how 'heavy' a mineral seems in comparison with other minerals of known specific gravity. The specific gravities of minerals vary over a wide range, from mirabalite (a hydrated sodium sulphate, $Na_2SO_4.10H_2O$) at 1.5 to platinum at 19. The average range is between 2.5 and 7.

The tendency of many minerals to split along certain regular planes is known as cleavage. The planes are closely related to the atomic structure of the mineral, and occur parallel to actual or possible crystal faces. The number of cleavage planes and their direction are constant in all specimens of a given mineral, although the quality may vary. The number of possible cleavages ranges from none to six (minerals having five cleavage directions are not known). Cleavage is described by specifying the crystal face parallel to which it takes place and its degree of perfection, which may be :

Poor, imperfect — indistinct and irregular
Good, distinct — clear but may be irregular
Perfect — clear and regular

The quality of cleavage varies from mineral to mineral. Muscovite, for example, cleaves easily and perfectly; many other minerals are very difficult to cleave.

All surfaces of breakage in minerals other than planes of cleavage are covered by the term fracture. There are five types of fracture :

Conchoidal — The mineral breaks with a curved concave or convex fracture, often with small undulations resembling the lines of growth on a shell.
Even — The fracture surface is flat or nearly flat.
Uneven — The fracture surface is rough and irregular, consisting of minute elevations and depressions.
Hackly — The surface is irregular and studded with sharp angular projections.
Earthy — Soft irregular surface, as in the fracture of chalk.

Certain minerals such as the micas and talc do not fracture : they are elastic and cleave perfectly along parallel planes.

Jasper showing even fracture, from South Africa.

Fayalite showing uneven fracture, from Rockport, Massachusetts.

Sodalite showing hackly fracture.

Magnetite showing earthy fracture. Ma-on-shan Mine, Kowloon, Hongkong.

Complete chemical analyses of minerals are complicated and time-consuming, but a few simple tests requiring a minimum of apparatus can be used to detect the presence of many elements and to determine some key chemical properties. Simple analysis requires the following

A bunsen burner or spirit burner.

A charcoal block.

A platinum wire – a short length of platinum wire bent into a loop and fused into a glass rod.

A closed tube – a glass test tube about two inches long with an internal diameter of $\frac{5}{16}$ of an inch closed at one end and open at the other.

An open tube – a glass tube about 4–5 inches long, with an internal diameter of $\frac{5}{16}$ of an inch open at both ends and with a slight bend a third of the way along it.

A blowpipe – a piece of metal tube bent at right angles, with a mouthpiece at one end and a finely perforated nozzle at the other. This is used to direct the flame from the bunsen burner on to the mineral sample by continuous blowing. To keep up a steady bast, the cheeks should be kept inflated and air drawn in through the nose. The air inlet of a bunsen burner can be adjusted to give a blue oxidising flame, a yellow reducing flame or an intermediate flame containing areas of both colours. When the air inlet is fully open, the flame has an inner blue cone, and its hottest part, the point of fusion, is just outside this cone. The nozzle of the blowpipe is inserted into an oxidising flame; the fine jet of flame produced can then be directed as required. The point at which oxidation of substances placed in the jet of flame takes place most readily is located just outside the visible area of the flame. With a yellow reducing flame, the gas is not completely burned and will combine with oxygen from substances introduced into the flame : this removal of oxygen is termed reduction. The blowpipe nozzle is placed outside a reducing flame and used to direct it on to the specimen which must be completely surrounded by flame. However, if the object is placed too far into the flame, a deposit of soot may form on it.

Fluxes – these are substances which are added to specimens in order to make them fuse more rapidly. The ones commonly used are borax (hydrous sodium borate, $Na_2B_4O_7.10H_2O$), microcosmic salt (hydrated sodium ammonium hydrogen phosphate, $NaNH_4HPO_4.4H_2O$), and sodium carbonate ($Na_2CO_3.10H_2O$).

Acids – dilute (10%) and concentrated solutions of hydrochloric, nitric and sulphuric acids give certain characteristic reactions.

Six basic tests can be performed on a mineral sample using these items. In tests for reaction to acids, a small sample is usually treated with hydrochloric, sulphuric, and nitric acid in that order, using a different sample for each acid. Dilute acid is used first, then concentrated if no action occurs. If there is still no reaction, the specimen may be heated carefully in concentrated acid. Common reactions, which indicate the presence of particular groups, are as follows :

Effervescence in hydrochloric acid, with carbon dioxide released	Carbonate
Effervescence in hydrochloric acid, with hydrogen sulphide released (smell of bad eggs)	Sulphide
Gelatinisation with hydrochloric acid	Silicate
Brown fumes produced when sulphuric acid added	Nitrate
Greenish fumes (chlorine) produced when manganese dioxide is added to sulphuric acid and the specimen	Chloride

In flame tests, some of the powdered mineral specimen is introduced into the blowpipe flame on the platinum wire. A brief flash of colour may be imparted to the flame; the colour is often intensified by moistening the mineral with nitric acid. Characteristic colours produced are :

Calcium	Brick red
Strontium	Violet red
Lithium	Crimson
Sodium	Yellow/orange
Copper	Emerald green
Potassium	Violet

In closed tube tests, a small quantity of the mineral is powdered, placed in the tube, and heated in the flame of the burner or lamp. Air is immediately driven out of the tube, so that the specimen is heated largely out of contact with the oxygen of the air. Water driven out of the mineral collects as drops towards the cooler mouth of the tube; any volatile constituents will collect in the same way, forming a sublimate near the mouth of the tube. The sublimates of certain elements can be distinguished : sulphur forms an orange sublimate; antimony forms a white sublimate; lead forms a white sublimate which fuses into yellow drops; and mercury forms a sublimate of silver globules.

In open tube tests, the powdered mineral is placed towards one end of the tube and heated in the burner flame. A current of air flows through the tube, allowing constituents of the mineral to combine with oxygen. Sublimates may again be formed on the cooler parts of the tube : white, forming near the specimen, indicates antimony; black, with a reddish tinge, indicates mercury; sulphur dioxide fumes indicate the presence of sulphur. Some of the oxides formed have characteristic colours : the brown mineral limonite is converted into a black oxide of iron and expelled water collects on the cooler parts of the tube.

A flux is a substance which when added to a mineral causes it to fuse more rapidly than would happen if the mineral were heated by itself. The platinum wire is heated to redness and then dipped in the flux, which adheres as a small droplet to the loop. The droplet is then heated again until it fuses into a small bead. The procedure is repeated until a spherical bead about $\frac{1}{8}$in. in diameter is built up in the loop. This hot borax bead is applied to the powdered mineral so that a small quantity sticks to it; the bead is then re-fused in the oxidising flame of the burner. The colour of the bead, when hot and cold, is noted, and the process is repeated using the reducing flame. Certain ions impart characteristic colours to the bead, which indicate to a certain extent the nature of the mineral under examination.

Using Borax as flux:

Colour in oxidising flame	Colour in reducing flame	Element
Greenish-blue	Opaque red	Copper
Yellow	Bottle green	Iron
Deep blue	Deep blue	Cobalt
Reddish-violet	Colourless	Manganese
Reddish-brown	Opaque grey	Nickel
Yellow	Pale green	Uranium
Pale yellow	Brown	Molybdenum

Using microcosmic salt as flux:

Colour in oxidising flame	Colour in reducing flame	Element
Greenish-blue	Opaque red	Copper
Yellowish to brownish-red	Red	Iron
Blue	Blue	Cobalt
Violet	Colourless	Manganese
Yellow	Yellowish-green	Uranium
Yellow	Reddish-yellow	Nickel
(Insoluble skeleton in clear bead)		(Silica)

Charcoal is infusible, a bad conductor of heat, and a reducing agent: the carbon of which charcoal consists readily combines, when heated, with oxygen from the specimen. The specimen is powdered, and placed in a shallow depression near one end of a charcoal block. The oxidising flame of the blowpipe is directed on to the specimen and any reactions are noted. The process is then repeated using the reducing flame. Certain elements when present in a mineral will oxidise and volatilise, with the oxide being deposited as a sublimate on the cooler portion of the charcoal near or at a distance from the specimen. If the specimen crackles and spits when heated, a fresh sample should be prepared and mixed into a thick paste with water before repeating the test. The nature, colour, and smell of the encrustation left on the charcoal are all indications of the nature of the elements present. Thus arsenic compounds give a white encrustation far from the sample, while antimony gives a white encrustation near the sample. Magnesium, aluminium, and tin form white sublimates; zinc forms a yellow sublimate which becomes white on cooling; lead forms a dark yellow sublimate, while sulphur gives off sulphur dioxide fumes which have a characteristic sharp, pungent smell. The white encrustations can be distinguished from each other if cobalt nitrate is added to them and then strong heat applied. They change colour as follows: green – zinc; bluish-green – tin; brownish-green – antimony; pink – magnesium; blue – aluminium. Some compounds, when heated in the reducing flame with sodium carbonate as a flux, are reduced to metals which appear as small globules. Metals obtained in this way include copper, silver, gold, lead, and bismuth.

In order to identify an unknown mineral, the tests outlined above should be performed in a logical order. The specimen should first be examined physically (see tables at the end of this book), with its colour, streak, lustre, hardness, cleavage, fracture and approximate specific gravity being noted. If the specimen has a clear crystal form it may be possible to identify it crystallographically. If no clear result emerges, or if confirmation is needed, the various chemical tests should be tried.

Part 3

Rocks

IGNEOUS ROCKS

A rock is a collection of minerals. There are hard rocks and soft rocks which may contain the same minerals but in different forms. Collections of minerals which have crystallised from molten matter create igneous rocks. Mineral grains cemented together after being eroded from pre-existing rocks form sedimentary rocks. When either igneous or sedimentary rocks have been subjected to changes of temperature and pressure they are converted into metamorphic rocks. Igneous rocks are formed when magma from within the earth's crust or mantle rises to the surface through cracks or fissures in the overlying rocks. A magma is any hot mobile material which is capable of penetrating the rocks of the crust: the normal form is a complex and highly variable high temperature solution of silicates containing large or small proportions of water (in the form of vapour) and other gases. Magma is not merely liquid rock: the dissolved gases in it affect its behaviour when it rises to the surface. At depth, these gases are held in solution by the pressure, but when this is reduced, as when a fissure appears in the surrounding rock layers, the gases form bubbles within the magma (in the same way that bubbles form in a fizzy drink when it is opened and the pressure released). The gases released push the magma to the surface, sometimes with explosive violence, as in the extreme case of the eruption of the volcanic island of Krakatoa in the Indonesian archipelago in 1883.

Magma is formed only under exceptional conditions. Earthquake records and seismic studies indicate that the earth's crust and upper mantle are generally composed of solid material. Beneath the crust, temperature increases with depth, so that at a depth of 35 kilometres, near the base of the continental crust, the temperature is 500–600 °C. At the surface, this would be sufficient to melt most rocks; but pressure also increases with depth, and an increase of pressure raises

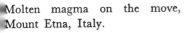

Molten magma on the move, Mount Etna, Italy.

the melting point of materials, so that rock remains solid at this depth. Thus for magma to form, there must be either a local increase of temperature or a local decrease of pressure. There are two areas within the crust where these factors seem to apply.

Analyses of seismic data reveal a layer in the upper mantle where P and S waves decrease in velocity. This Low Velocity Zone is regarded as consisting of melted or partially-melted rocks. The reasons for its existence are still the subject of investigation, though it is thought that heat produced by concentrations of radioactive material within the mantle could account for it. Once in a molten state, the magma works its way towards the surface, either by melting away the overlying rocks or by forcing them aside. The original pure melt is contaminated in the process, as it absorbs chemical content from the rocks through which it passes.

The other area in which magmas are produced is where continental and oceanic plates collide. As the oceanic plate slides beneath the continental plate, the friction creates enough heat for partial melting to occur. The magma thus produced rises through tensional cracks on the landward side of the continental plate, forming an arc of volcanic islands.

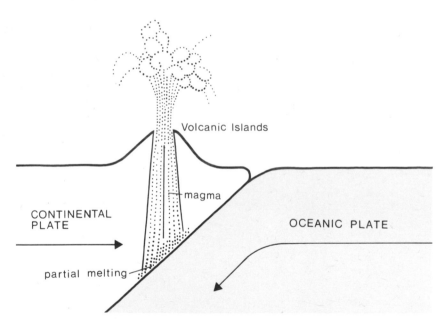

Magmas produced by this plate tectonic activity will also be modified chemically on their way to the surface.

The varieties of magma that are found at the surface can be accounted for by the circumstances of their production, so that the differences between them are attributed to the differences in the rock layers through which they have passed on their way to the surface. According to one theory, there is one primary or primitive magma from which all other magmas, and consequently all igneous rocks, are derived. This magma is supposed to have the chemical composition of a basalt; when it cools from the molten state, minerals crystallise from it in a set sequence:

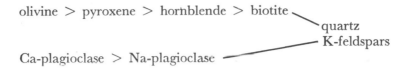

olivine > pyroxene > hornblende > biotite
quartz
K-feldspars

Ca-plagioclase > Na-plagioclase

(> = Decreasing temperature)

The minerals in the upper row make up what is known as a discontinuous reaction series. This means that as the magma cools, each mineral in turn separates out from the magma, a reaction that takes place within a definite temperature range. The minerals in the lower row, the plagioclase feldspars, form a continuous reaction series, in which, as we have already seen, there is a continuous gradation of composition between the end members of the series, anorthite (Ca-plagioclase, $CaAl_2Si_2O_8$), and albite (Na-plagioclase, $NaAlSi_3O_8$), starting with anorthite which crystallises first. The crystallisation of the discontinuous and continuous series proceeds simultaneously in the magma, so that Ca-plagioclase appears at the same time as olivine or pyroxene, and Na-plagioclase at the same time as hornblende or biotite. As each mineral crystallises, the remaining melt becomes increasingly rich in silica. In a magma that was moving, the first minerals to crystallise would be left behind, so that the last rocks to crystallise would be highly silicic. Thus the sequence of rocks formed would be: basalt − olivine − gabbro − diorite − quartz monzonite − granite. This provides a reasonable mechanism by which the wide variety of igneous rocks might be produced from a single primary magma. The rocks resulting from the crystallisation of the last part of the magma would have compositions quite different from the rocks made up of the first crystals to separate out. However, though this process certainly occurs on a local scale, there is increasing evidence that it does not operate universally.

Though the single magma theory is inadequate, it is no longer thought necessary to postulate a whole series of basic magmas, one for each type of igneous rock. Current opinion favours the idea of two magmas, with all rocks being derived from them or from mixtures of them. The basic magma has a composition similar to basalts, and is essentially the magma of the one magma theory; its probable origin is in the Low Velocity Zone. The other magma is silicic, and is thought to occur where plates bend down into the mantle, as at a continental-oceanic plate margin. This silicic magma is the source of granitic rocks, which are only found in continental areas.

Magmas which reach the earth's surface and flow out over it are known as lavas; they cool to form extrusive rocks which have either a fine crystalline grain or a glassy texture. Magma which is trapped at some depth within the crust and crystallises slowly forms intrusive rocks, which have a coarse crystalline texture. Intrusive rocks which form large bodies fairly deep within the crust are known as plutonic rocks; those which form smaller intrusions fairly near the surface are known as hypabyssal rocks.

The largest form of plutonic intrusion is the batholith, a mass of igneous rock which has been pushed up from below through the overlying rock strata.

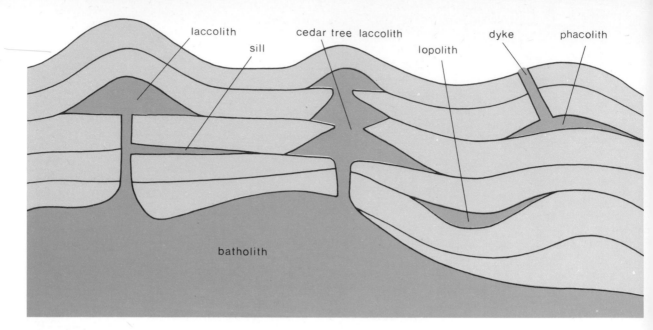

The rock layers are displaced and broken, so that batholiths are examples of discordant intrusions. Batholiths appear at the surface after erosion has removed the overlying rock layers; they form the central granitic masses of many of the great mountain ranges. Their great size means that they have no observable bottom, though they are believed to reach a maximum depth of about six miles. A batholith is usually defined by its size, which is an exposed surface area of 40 square miles or more; an exposed intrusive body with an area less than this is known as a stock.

A lopolith is a saucer-shaped igneous intrusion which is formed when magma flows into rock strata and causes them to sag under its weight. The shape of the roof does not matter, but the floor must sag. A feeder pipe, through which the magma flowed, is often discernible. Because the rock layers are displaced but not broken, a lopolith is an example of a concordant intrusion.

When a more viscous magma forces its way into rock layers, it tends to arch the overlying rocks upwards rather than spreading sideways: the result is a dome or arch-shaped intrusion known as a laccolith. The rock layers are not broken: a laccolith is another concordant intrusion. If the pressure of the magma is sufficient, the roof may be lifted until it fractures, releasing magma into the rock layers above, where another laccolith may form. This process may be repeated to form a multiple or cedar tree laccolith. Because the rock layers are broken, this is a discordant intrusion.

When magma is intruded into rock strata which subsequently undergo folding, another sort of concordant intrusion, a phacolith, may be formed.

Any rather small, more or less vertical mass of intruded igneous rock is known as a plug or bysmalith. A volcanic plug or neck is formed in the nearly circular vertical feed channel through which magma rises to the surface in a volcano. The solidified lava is often exposed by erosion, forming a very conspicuous feature in the landscape.

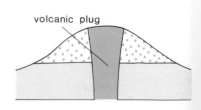

Daouda – an eroded volcanic plug in the Ahaggar Mountains of the Sahara.

Dolerite dyke.

In hypabyssal intrusions, the magma cools more rapidly than in plutonic intrusions, so that the grain size of the constituent minerals is smaller. Felsite and dolerite are rocks typical of hypabyssal intrusions. Sills are formed when magma intrudes into pre-existing strata without breaking them. They are thus concordant and are frequently sheet-like and roughly horizontal. Sills which occupy a small area may be confined to one plane and thus remain concordant, but large sills commonly break at intervals and continue in a different plane. Dykes are vertical tabular or wall-like bodies of igneous rock which have been intruded into pre-existing fractures in the rock strata. When they are exposed at the surface, they commonly form ridges that can sometimes be traced for miles. Dykes are discordant, and vary in thickness from a few inches to hundreds of feet. They generally occur as large numbers of parallel or radiating intrusions known as a dyke-swarm.

Extrusive rocks such as rhyolite and basalt are formed by rapid cooling, and thus do not develop large crystals; they are characteristically fine grained or glassy. The most common type of extrusive

123

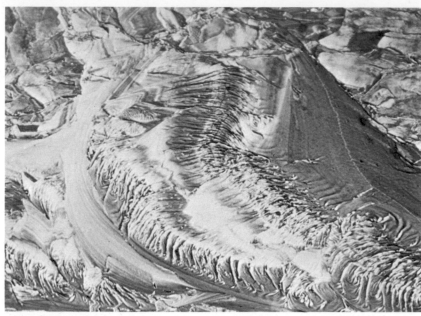

Hawaiian shield volcano, Kilauea.

Stromboli – a typical cone volcano which lies off the coast of Sicily.

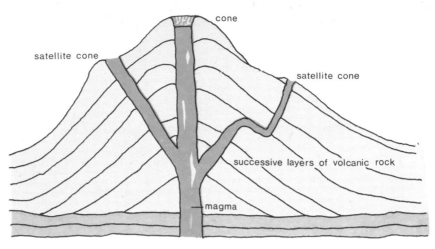

cone

satellite cone

satellite cone

successive layers of volcanic rock

magma

igneous rock is the lava flow, which flows out from a volcanic vent to form an extensive sheet if the magma is fluid or a thick lens or dome if it is viscous. Free flowing lavas form shield volcanoes, like those of the Hawaiian Islands. The gases escape easily from these highly fluid lavas, so that the eruptions are non-explosive and fairly continuous, and the resultant volcanic dome is widespread with gentle slopes. Mauna Loa in Hawaii is the largest active volcano in the world; it rises 13,680 feet above sea level, and about 30,000 feet above its base on the ocean floor, with a maximum slope angle of only about twelve degrees. It has been built by thousands of individual lava flows.

Volcanoes created by extrusion of viscous, gas-filled silicic magmas are cone volcanoes: they are steep sided cones from which lava and debris are ejected in violent eruptions. The viscous magma solidifies rapidly, building up large cones around the vent. The magma also blocks the vent, causing the trapped gases to build up pressure until the cone breaks and the lava erupts. This eruption does not always take place through the central vent: in some cases the cone gives way at a lower level, forming a smaller satellite cone on the side of the main structure. Mount Etna has over two hundred of these satellite cones. When the pressure is not relieved in this way, it may build up until it is released in an explosive eruption. Clouds of magma droplets and solid fragments broken from earlier lavas and from the walls of the volcano are blown into the air and shower down at various distances from the volcano according to their sizes. This material forms pyroclastic igneous rocks. Volcanoes fed by viscous magmas tend to erupt periodically. Between eruptions, they become choked by congealed magma, and there may be a long period of quiescence when the volcano appears extinct, but during which it is building up to another eruption. The longer the quiet period, the more violent the eruption is likely to be: Vesuvius appears to have been quiet for centuries before the eruption which destroyed Pompeii in A.D. 79.

Fissure eruptions occur when lava wells up through a long crack in the earth's surface rather than through a roughly circular opening. They produce, through repeated eruptions, great sheets of lava which may accumulate to thicknesses of several thousand feet and which may spread over hundreds of square miles. Such an outpouring of lava occurred on the Deccan Plateau of western India, which is a huge area of basaltic lava. Fissure eruptions are taking place today in Iceland, which lies along the mid-Atlantic ridge. In this case, the lava that rises into the fissure is associated with the growth and movement of oceanic plates.

The Classification of Igneous Rocks

Igneous rocks are classified on the basis of their chemical composition, using the percentage of silica (SiO_2) as the distinguishing feature. This leads to a four-fold chemical classification:

Over 66% SiO_2	—	ACID igneous rocks
52–66% SiO_2	—	INTERMEDIATE igneous rocks
45–52% SiO_2	—	BASIC igneous rocks
Under 45% SiO_2	—	ULTRABASIC igneous rocks

The first three of these groups contain rocks which are rich in silica and are known as saturated igneous rocks. A fifth division of igneous rocks occurs when silica rich minerals are replaced by minerals which are poor in silica (such as the feldspathoids, which contain more alumina than silica); these rocks are known as the undersaturated igneous rocks.

Classification by overall chemical composition has limitations: it is bound to classify together rocks which differ widely in mineral content and appearance. Thus a granite and an obsidian may have identical chemical compositions, yet they are totally dissimilar in appearance. The igneous rocks are more practically divided into groups called clans which have a similar mineral content and a common chemistry.

The GRANITES correspond to the acid group of igneous rocks. They are rich in free quartz (SiO_2) and contain feldspars, such as orthoclase and oligoclase, together with micas.

Rocks which contain little or no free quartz but are rich in orthoclase, oligoclase and plagioclase feldspars, and which contain some amphiboles, correspond to the intermediate group of igneous rocks. There are two clans: the SYENITE clan, comprising rocks in which orthoclase and oligoclase make up more than 50% of the feldspar content; and the DIORITE clan in which plagioclase makes up more than 50% of the feldspar content.

The GABBRO clan corresponds to the basic group of igneous rocks. It consists of rocks which contain very little or no free quartz and alkali feldspars (orthoclase and oligoclase) but are rich in plagioclase feldspar, amphiboles and olivine.

The ULTRAMAFIC clan corresponds to the ultrabasic group of igneous rocks. It consists of rocks which contain no quartz or feldspar but which are rich in pyroxenes, amphiboles and olivine.

The undersaturated igneous rocks again form a class of their own. Each clan can be subdivided into plutonic, hypabyssal and extrusive igneous rocks to give a total classification of igneous rocks:

		PLUTONIC	HYPABYSSAL	EXTRUSIVE	UNDERSATURATED
ACID SiO₂ over 66%	GRANITE CLAN	Granite	Micrograuite	Rhyolite	
INTERMEDIATE SiO₂ 52–66%	SYENITE CLAN	Syenite	Microsyenite	Trachyte	Nepheline-syenite
	DIORITE CLAN	Diorite	Microdiorite	Andesite	
BASIC SiO₂ 45–52%	GABBRO CLAN	Gabbro	Dolerite	Basalt	Nepheline-gabbro
ULTRABASIC SiO₂ less than 45%	ULTRAMAFIC CLAN	Many variations			

The predominant minerals of an igneous rock frequently determine its general appearance, and its colour can often give some idea of its composition. The minerals which form igneous rocks can be divided into two groups, the felsic minerals, which are light coloured, and the mafic minerals, which are dark coloured. Quartz, feldspar, and the feldspathoids are felsic, while olivine, pyroxene, the amphiboles and the micas are mafic. Thus rocks made predominantly from quartz, which is usually colourless and transparent, and feldspars, which are pale coloured, are usually pale in colour. Four subdivisions of the igneous rocks have been suggested based on the percentage of dark mafic minerals in the rock as determined from a thin section.

Leucocratic rocks – light coloured – less than 30% mafic minerals.
Mesocratic rocks – medium coloured – 30–60% mafic minerals.
Melanocratic rocks – dark coloured – 60–90% mafic minerals.
Hypermelanic rocks – very dark coloured – 90–100% mafic minerals.

The colour of a rock provides only a very rough means of classification, and it has its dangers if used in the field. For example, very fine grained or glassy rocks tend to look dark whatever their composition; and weathering changes the colour of exposed rocks, so that it is necessary to examine freshly broken surfaces.

The texture or structure of a rock is a more useful guide to its nature; indeed it reveals more about the origin of most rocks than does mineral composition. For example, sandstone and granite may have virtually the same mineral composition, but totally different textures: the mineral grains of the sandstone are rounded from wear and held together by a natural cement, indicating a sedimentary origin, while the grains of granite are intergrown crystals which could only have formed at high temperature and pressure.

The texture of a rock depends on the relative sizes of the component mineral grains and the relation of these grains to each other. In igneous rocks it stems from the way that the rock cooled and solidified

127

from the magma. The rate at which a rock cooled influences the most obvious textural feature of a rock, its grain size. Coarse-grained rocks are the result of slow cooling, which allows time for the atoms to arrange themselves and so to produce large crystals (between 5mm and 300mm across); more rapid cooling produces medium-grained rocks with smaller crystals from 1mm to 5mm across; fine-grained rocks, with crystals less than 1mm across are produced by still more rapid cooling. Very rapid cooling, such as takes place when magma suddenly erupts into the atmosphere, gives no time for crystallisation to take place and glasses are formed. Rocks which are entirely glass are said to be holohyaline or vitreous; rocks which are part glassy and part crystalline are said to be hyalocrystalline; wholly crystalline rocks are said to be holocrystalline.

The conditions for the growth of fully crystalline coarse-grained rock, namely slow cooling under sufficient pressure to hold in the volatile components, are found in magmatic chambers well down in the earth's crust; such rocks are thus characteristic of deep-seated plutonic intrusions. Medium-grained minerals are found in minor intrusions like sills and dykes. Extrusive volcanic rocks are often fine-grained or glassy because eruption at the earth's surface brings about rapid cooling. However, despite their common origin in eruptions, different volcanic rocks have different textures, for a number of reasons: the crystals may start to grow at different times and may grow at different rates; cooling may occur in several stages; crystals grown during one stage may be partially or wholly dissolved during another; eruption may end the process at any stage.

Complex cooling produces the distinctive porphyritic texture. This is found in fine-grained or glassy rocks in which a few scattered crystals have grown to a larger size than the rest. The individual large grains are known as phenocrysts, and the enclosing rock as the groundmass. This texture suggests that the rock cooled in two stages: the large crystals, the phenocrysts, were formed under conditions of slow cooling, probably before eruption; the fine-grained groundmass was formed in conditions of rapid cooling, probably after eruption.

Porphyritic texture in granite from Silvermine Bay, Lantau, Hongkong.

The Granite Clan

Granite is a light coloured rock composed essentially of quartz and feldspar, with small amounts of other minerals, chiefly mica (usually biotite and/or muscovite) and amphiboles (usually hornblende). In addition, tiny scattered grains of accessory minerals, such as magnetite, ilmenite, apatite, zircon, sphene, topaz, fluorite, andalusite, cordierite, and garnet may be present. In some granites, the feldspar is almost exclusively of the alkali type (orthoclase, microcline), but a typical granite contains about 30% each of alkali feldspar, plagioclase feldspar and quartz. All granites contain over 66% silica, including over 30% free quartz.

Granites are sub-divided into three rock types on the basis of their relative feldspar content. Alkali granites have a feldspar content which includes more than 66% of alkali feldspars (feldspars in which alkali metal ions, such as those of sodium or potassium, are held in spaces in the silicate framework structure). Adamellite is a variety of granite containing alkali feldspars and plagioclase in roughly equal amounts; neither the alkali feldspars nor the plagioclase makes up more than two-thirds of the feldspar present. Granodiorite is not strictly a granite, though it is commonly referred to as one; it contains quartz and plagioclase feldspars, which are predominant — not more than one-third of the total feldspar content is made up of alkali feldspar.

The volcanic or extrusive equivalent of an alkali granite is a rhyolite, which contains the same minerals in the same proportions

Below: porphyritic adamellite – Shap granite from Westmorland.
Bottom: granodiorite from Leicestershire.
Right: banded rhyolite from Hurricane, Utah.

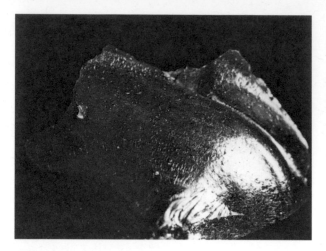 

but which has a texture so fine that the individual grains cannot be recognised with the naked eye. If the rock is composed entirely of glass, it is called obsidian. The extrusive equivalent of adamellite is rhyodacite (or toscanite); the extrusive equivalent of granodiorite is dacite. Both these rocks are difficult to distinguish from rhyolites. There are also hypabyssal equivalents of the three granite rock types, as shown in the table:

Left: obsidian from California.
Right: microgranite from Cornwall.

Alkali feldspar as % of total feldspar	Plutonic	Hypabyssal	Extrusive
greater than 66%	Alkali granite	Microgranite	Rhyolite
66 – 33%	Adamellite	Microadamellite	Rhyodacite
less than 33%	Granodiorite	Microgranodiorite	Dacite

Mineral content includes over 30% free quartz.

The plutonic forms are generally course-grained holocrystalline leucocratic rocks; they are often porphyritic, with phenocrysts of feldspar. The hypabyssal forms are medium grained holocrystalline leucocratic rocks which are sometimes porphyritic. The extrusive forms are fine grained hyalocrystalline or vitreous leucocratic rocks; they are occasionally porphyritic, in which case the phenocrysts are small feldspar crystals fixed in a vitreous groundmass. The totally vitreous form, obsidian, is a distinctive black glass.

Granites are the principal rocks of the upper part of the earth's crust; they are the igneous rocks that occur most extensively at the earth's surface. The magma which forms them is thought to be produced by heating and partial melting of rocks deep in the crust. It is squeezed to the surface when plate movements fold rock layers to produce mountain chains. Thus granites form the cores of the earth's great mountain chains, and can be seen in the peaks of the Alps, the Rockies, and the Himalayas. Granites resist erosion, and in many areas granite masses stand above the general level of the land, forming large rounded domes like the 'Sugar Loaf' at Rio de Janeiro.

Huge, deep-seated batholiths of enormous volume are fairly common – a notable example is the Sierra Nevada in California. Numerous smaller batholiths are found, like those in Brittany and Cornwall.

The magmatic theory is not the only one put forward to explain the origin of granitic rocks. Many geologists are convinced that granites should not be considered as igneous rocks at all, but rather as products of extreme metamorphism of material that was originally volcanic or sedimentary rock. The process is known as granitisation. All the chemical constituents of granite are found in some sedimentary rocks, and it was originally thought that if these were heated sufficiently they could be transformed into granite without going through a molten stage. However laboratory experiments suggest that granitisation requires appreciable melting of the original rock before granite is produced, so that the distinction between granite formed by granitisation and granite formed by igneous activity becomes so fuzzy as to be virtually meaningless. As might be expected, there is no general agreement over the proportion of granites formed by each process. The term granitisation is now used to describe the formation of granitic rocks by partial melting where little overall movement of the melted material takes place.

There is some mystery about the origin of pegmatites, which are coarse-grained rocks containing large crystals intergrown in an irregular fabric. Most geologists regard them as the end product of the lengthy sequence of events that occurs during the cooling and differentiation of magma. As minerals crystallise from a cooling granitic magma, water and the volatile constituents which contain the rarer elements of the magma become concentrated in the remaining liquid portion. These include light elements like boron, lithium, and beryllium whose atoms are too small to be incorporated into the crystal structures of the common rock-making minerals, and heavy elements like tungsten, tin, niobium, and tantalum whose atoms are too large. This last portion of the magma is a highly mobile fluid;

Pegmatite from Cornwall.

it is expelled into the surrounding rocks where the pegmatites crystallise, usually in the form of irregular segregations, veins, or small dykes or sills. They are generally small bodies of rock, rarely more than a mile in maximum dimension.

Pegmatites are of great interest to the mineral collector as they are the source of many rare minerals, such as tourmaline, beryl, and topaz, and of gem-quality specimens of more common minerals. Because they crystallise from a watery, mobile solution, the crystals found in pegmatites are large. The largest crystals ever recorded were found in them. Among them are the famous giant spodumene 'logs' at the Etta mine in the Black Hills of South Dakota. Microcline (potash feldspar) is the most abundant pegmatic mineral: it forms large crystals, usually milky-white, but coloured red by the presence of iron in some locations. Amazonite, a rarer form, is bright green; it is found in the Urals in Russia and at Pikes Peak, Colorado.

The Syenite Clan

The syenites are a group of intermediate igneous rocks similar in composition to the granites but with less quartz. They are made up of alkali feldspars (over 50% of the total feldspar content) and plagioclase feldspar (under 50% of total feldspar content), along with some dark minerals, usually hornblende and biotite mica. Syenites crystallise from magmas containing enough silica to form silicates but with none left over to form quartz; this may be present as an accessory mineral, but it never forms more than 10% of the rock. Other accessory minerals which may occur in small amounts include apatite, sphene, zircon, and magnetite. Pegmatites associated with syenite often contain rare minerals.

Syenite itself is plutonic, and normally occurs as a medium to coarse-grained holocrystalline leucocratic rock. It sometimes forms separate bodies, but is more usually found in the form of marginal features around granites. The hypabyssal form is microsyenite, a

Syenite from Drachenfels, Germany.

medium-grained holocrystalline leucocratic rock which is occasionally porphyritic. It often forms dykes and sills. The volcanic equivalent of syenite is trachyte, a light coloured fine-grained hyalocrystalline leucocratic rock. It is said to be an alkaline rock because its feldspars contain sodium or potassium rather than calcium (as in plagioclase). It can contain limited amounts of both quartz and plagioclase. It is frequently porphyritic, and examples with very large phenocrysts occur.

The syenites are all associated with granites. Syenite itself often forms laccoliths. Trachytes occur extensively in fairly stable continental areas as small lava flows or as small dykes; larger deposits are associated with rift movements – they are widespread in and around the Rift Valley of East Africa.

Trachyte from Somerset.

The Diorite Clan

Diorites, like syenites, are intermediate igneous rocks. They consist essentially of plagioclase feldspar, together with one or more of the minerals biotite, hornblende, augite and hypersthene. Quartz may be present in small amounts, up to 10%; alkali feldspar may make up to one-third of the total feldspar. Common accessory minerals include sphene, magnetite, ilmenite, and apatite, in the form of small grains.

Diorite, the plutonic form, is a dark coloured, coarse-grained holocrystalline mesocratic rock; it is usually equigranular, though porphyritic types, with feldspar phenocrysts, are found. It occurs either in large batholith complexes in association with granites, or as small intrusive bodies associated with gabbros. The hypabyssal equivalent is microdiorite, which differs from diorite only in its texture, which is finer. It is a medium-grained holocrystalline mesocratic rock, which is often porphyritic with feldspar phenocrysts. The fine-grained volcanic equivalent of diorite is andesite, a hyalocrystalline leucocratic rock; it is often porphyritic, containing phenocrysts of plagioclase feldspar, augite or hornblende set in a

Diorite from Cumberland.

groundmass too fine-grained to reveal its crystalline texture to the naked eye. Andesite is named after its major occurrence, in the Andes in South America, where it is a dominant rock. It also commonly forms the volcanic islands on the landward side of continental-oceanic plate boundaries. Like all the diorites, it is derived either from a mixture of basic and silicic magmas, or from a basic magma contaminated by its passage through the surrounding rocks. The ring of andesitic islands surrounding the Pacific is known as the Andesite line: it marks the dividing line between oceanic plates, where basalts are produced, and continental plates, where trachytes and rhyolites are produced.

Andesite from Somerset.

The Gabbro Clan

The gabbros are a group of basic igneous rocks with a silica content between 45% and 55% and little or no free quartz. They consist of plagioclase feldspars (commonly in the form of labradorite), a pyroxene (augite and/or hypersthene), and very commonly, substantial amounts of olivine. Accessory minerals include quartz, hornblende, biotite, magnetite and ilmenite. In some bodies of gabbro there may be segregations of magnetite and ilmenite large enough to form giant iron ore deposits, as at Kiruna in Sweden.

Gabbro, the plutonic form, is much less common than its extrusive counterpart, basalt. It is a coarse-grained holocrystalline melancratic rock and is usually equigranular, though porphyritic forms do occur. It generally forms small scale intrusions, but very thick intrusive sheets such as the Bushveld complex in South Africa and the Duluth

Gabbro from Cornwall.

Dolerite from County Durham.

135

Gabbro in the United States are also found. The hypabyssal equivalent is dolerite, a dark, heavy medium-grained holocrystalline melanocratic rock. Porphyritic forms are uncommon, but ophitic forms, in which large grains of pyroxene enclose a number of small tabular plagioclase crystals, occur frequently. Dolerites are found as dykes and sills, often of large dimensions, usually in association with flows of basalt, their volcanic equivalent. Basalt is normally a dark, dense, fine-grained holocrystalline or hyalocrystalline melanocratic rock, occasionally containing a little glass, and often porphyritic with phenocrysts of feldspar, olivine or augite. It occurs extensively throughout the world as lava flows – there is more basalt at the earth's surface than all the other extrusive rocks combined. In many parts of the world, the flows extend to form great plateaux thousands of feet thick, such as those of the Deccan in India and of the Columbia River in the United States. Basalts are virtually the only rocks found in the floors of ocean basins, where they are extruded from mid-oceanic ridges. Basalt shows a particular type of columnar jointing, with large hexagonal prisms forming at right angles to flows, dykes or sills; a notable example is the Giant's Causeway in Antrim, Northern Ireland.

Quartz-rich gabbros occur, with free quartz up to a maximum of 10% of the total mineral content; the plutonic form is known as quartz gabbro, the hypabyssal form as quartz dolerite, and the extrusive form as tholeite.

Amygdaloidal Basalt from Northern Ireland.

136

Columnar jointing in basalt, as found at the Giant's Causeway, County Antrim, Northern Ireland.

The Ultramafic Clan

Ultramafic rocks consist essentially of ferromagnesian minerals, rock-forming silicates which contain iron and magnesium to the virtual exclusion of quartz, feldspar and feldspathoids. In other words, they

137

Dunite from The Lizard, Cornwall.

are composed of dark-coloured mafic minerals rather than light coloured felsic minerals. Ultramafic rocks may be combinations of olivine, pyroxene, amphiboles or micas. Many are monomineralic, that is they consist of only one mineral: hornblendite is a rock consisting solely of the mineral hornblende.

Ultramafic rocks are all plutonic, though they sometimes occur on the surface where they have been extruded with the basaltic magmas. The peridotites consist largely of olivine, with some pyroxene; one type is monomineralic, consisting of olivine alone. Chromite is a constant accessory mineral. Dunite is an almost pure olivine rock; pyroxenites consist largely of pyroxene. Magnetite, chromite, spinel, sphene, and garnet are found as accessory minerals. Certain ultramafic rocks contain special minerals: platinum is found in some dunites, and a mica peridotite, kimberlite, contains diamonds.

Ultramafic rocks are generally coarse-grained holocrystalline melanocratic rocks; porphyritic types are rare. Wholly ultramafic masses are rare, because of the way these rocks are formed. When a basic magma cools, the silicate minerals olivine and pyroxene are among the first to crystallise; their high specific gravities cause them to sink to the bottom of the magma. Thus layers of dunite and peridotite are often found at the base of thick gabbro sheets, as in the Sudbury Nickel Complex in Canada and the Bushveldt Complex in South Africa. Ultamafic deposits are exploited for their accessory ore minerals such as chromite, which is the only source of the metal chromium.

The Undersaturated Igneous Rocks
These are rocks containing feldspathoid minerals rather than quartz and feldspar. Feldspathoid minerals are formed from magmas

which are poor in silica : most of the available silica is taken up in the formation of ferromagnesian minerals (pyroxenes, amphiboles, micas, etc.); the amount of silica remaining is insufficient for quartz or feldspars to form, so feldspathoids, which have much less silica in their lattices, are formed. Since they are undersaturated with silica, feldspathoids can never occur in association with free quartz : if any free silica had been present in the magma it would have combined with the components of the feldspathoid to form feldspar. All feldspathoid minerals contain sodium and/or potassium – that is they are rich in alkalis. The most common feldspathoids are nepheline

Nepheline from Bancroft, Ontario.

(NaAlSiO$_4$) and leucite (KAlSi$_2$O$_6$). Rocks which are formed from silica-deficient magmas include feldspathoid syenite, feldspathoid diorite, and feldspathoid gabbro, and their hypabyssal and extrusive equivalents. The number of rock types containing feldspathoids is large, but the most common are nepheline syenite and leucite syenite, in which these minerals take the place of some of the feldspar of ordinary syenite. The largest single mass of such rocks is in the Kola peninsula in north west Russia. In general, the textures and modes of occurrence of the undersaturated rocks are similar to those of the normal varieties.

The Pyroclastic Igneous Rocks

These are a group of extrusive igneous rocks, with a similar chemical and mineralogical composition to lava flows, which are ejected during violent volcanic explosions. They consist of solidified magma, mineral crystals, and volcanic glass shattered into fragments by the action of the hot volcanic gases; the fragments are often cemented together by a vitreous mineral substance with a composition similar to the parent magma. There are three types of pyroclast. Those formed from live lava vary from quite fine spray to volcanic bombs, clots of lava which congeal, at least externally, before they reach the ground. A second type includes pyroclasts formed from dead lavas and those torn from the walls of the volcanic conduit or from obstructions in the vent. The third type is formed from pre-existing crust rocks brought up from beneath the volcanic cone. Except in very violent eruptions, the larger fragments usually fall back near the crater and roll down the inner or outer slopes forming agglomerates or deposits of the coarser volcanic breccia. Deposits which are fairly fine (with a grain size of less than 2mm) are known as tuffs; very fine deposits are called ash. The coarsest deposits are normally found near the volcano, and the finest furthest away.

Pyroclastic rocks often resemble cinders or ashes; large deposits have a layered and bedded appearance similar to that of sedimentary rocks.

Volcanic agglomerate from Somerset.

Tuff from Yuma, Arizona.

SEDIMENTARY ROCKS

Sedimentary rocks are formed at or near the earth's surface by the accumulation of material as a result of natural geological processes taking place there. These processes may be mechanical, involving the physical breakdown of pre-existing rocks by weathering or erosion, the transport of the debris and its subsequent deposition and re-assembly as new sediments; they may be chemical, involving the chemical disintegration of rocks by the action of substances dissolved in rain water, the removal of material in solution and its subsequent precipitation and deposition; or they may be organic, requiring the action of living creatures, as when plant roots split rocks, or when reefs are built by corals.

Rock Weathering

Weathering is the breakdown of rocks *in situ*: no transportation is involved. It is the result of the response of rocks to their physical and chemical environment on the earth's surface. Weathering may be mechanical or chemical; in most climatic conditions, the processes of mechanical and chemical weathering are complementary – disintegration increases the surface area of material exposed to the atmosphere and thus provides greater opportunity for chemical

Frost shattered mountains: Y Glyder Fach in Wales, with Snowdon in the distance.

weathering, while chemical reactions frequently produce bulky new minerals which help to disrupt the rock mechanically. In some climates, one or other process may be dominant so that the characters of the rocks produced are finally dependent on climatic conditions.

Mechanical weathering results in physical shattering of rocks. Where the minerals of a rock and its texture have developed at high temperature or under great pressure, internal stresses may develop at normal temperature and pressure, causing the rock to expand and finally to fracture. This process is known as unloading.

The dominant force that produces rock disintegration is the action of frost. When water freezes to form ice its volume increases by 9%, so that water freezing in the cracks and pores of a rock will exert great pressure, as much as a ton to the square inch, on the confining surfaces. Grains are forced apart and fragments split off. In many regions, daily fluctuations of temperature across the freezing point of water are common, and this cyclical repetition of freezing and thawing exerts enormous disruptive pressure on rocks. Outcrops of rock in high latitudes and in mountainous regions are very susceptible to weathering by this process, which is responsible for the jagged outlines of high mountains.

Rocks exposed to continuous intense sunlight have their outer surfaces heated to very high temperatures, which causes the outer layer to expand. Rapid cooling after sunset or by rain causes thermal

Frost shattered boulder: Dhaulagiri, Nepal.

stresses that are considered to be sufficient to cause cracks to develop between the grains of the rock so that it eventually crumbles. This process has not, however, been demonstrated experimentally: rocks subjected to hundreds of cycles of heating and cooling in the laboratory have failed to confirm the process. Examination of rock fragments supposedly formed by rupturing due to thermal stress reveal that chemical weathering may have first weakened the rock to a point where heating and cooling could fracture it. The temperature changes do not in any case penetrate very far beneath the surface of the rock, so that any disruption takes place at or very close to the surface.

Soft rocks, such as clays, may be affected by rainfall; rain running down a slope washes the finest parts to the foot of the slope where they accumulate as rainwash, leaving gulleys in the rock. Plants and animals may play a small part in mechanical weathering: tree and plant roots may widen crevices in rocks and soils, and burrowing animals and earthworms may loosen and mix soils.

Chemical weathering is the process by which the mineral constituents of rocks are altered chemically under conditions normally found at the earth's surface. As it falls, rain dissolves atmospheric gases, notably oxygen and carbon dioxide. On reaching the ground. it takes up material produced by the decay of plant and animal matter and so forms weak organic acids. These substances in solution can react with rock minerals to bring about chemical changes as rain water percolates through the surface layers of disintegrated

The typical stark topography of an area affected by rainwash near Norbeck Pass in the Badlands of South Dakota.

rocks. Igneous and metamorphic rocks contain minerals that are, in general, stable at the temperature of crystallisation, a temperature much higher than is normal on the earth's surface. Thus they are in false equilibrium and unstable when they outcrop at the surface. Quartz is one of the few common minerals that resist chemical weathering; it is broken down mechanically. The feldspars are converted into carbonates which dissolve, leaving alumina and silica which combine with water to form hydrated aluminium silicates – the clay minerals, which are chemically stable under the conditions of weathering. The ferromagnesian minerals are the least resistant to chemical change; biotite, for example, is altered to chlorite and limonite (hydrous iron oxide), which often form brown stains on weathered rocks.

The minerals which make up sandstones and shales are stable under normal atmospheric conditions, but the cement that holds the grains together usually is not and is thus subject to chemical weathering. The removal of the cement in solution leaves the rock porous and ready to crumble – a phenomenon known as beehive weathering.

Limestone, which consists predominantly of the mineral calcite (calcium carbonate, $CaCO_3$), reacts with rain water containing carbon dioxide from the air to form the soluble calcium bicarbonate $(Ca(HCO_3)_2)$. The bicarbonate is dissolved and removed, leaving the rock surface etched and fretted.

The products of chemical weathering are removed from the original site in solution in water. Material resulting from mechanical weathering is moved under the influence of gravity in mass movements. Slow mass movements occur as various forms of creep, a process by which weathered material moves slowly downhill. Rapid mass movements may take the form of flows, such as mud flows, in which the moving mass is continuously deformed, or slides, which move as a whole on a definite surface. The most common types are rock falls, landslides and landslips.

Erosion, Transport and Deposition

Flowing water is the primary means of removal, transport and deposition of material that goes to form sediments. The other agents of erosion and deposition are wind and ice. The main forms of flowing water are rivers, the sea and groundwater – water which moves through the surface layers of the earth.

A river can erode and transport material, depositing it at a point where gradient becomes more shallow. Erosion normally takes place in the upper reaches of a river, where the gradient is steepest and the velocity of flow highest. Fast moving river water may sluice away loose material like water from a hose; to make any impression on harder rock it needs suspended particles of sand or gravel which wear away the river bed by a filing action known as corrasion. Potholes are produced in a river's bed by pebbles being trapped in a hollow and then swirled round by the current. Erosion is increased by the higher volume of water and its more rapid rate of flow during flood conditions.

The material transported downstream by a river is called its load.

A river in action, soft and hard rock layers are eroded, producing this waterfall: Hell Gill Falls, Ravenstonedale, Yorkshire.

It consists of two parts, one carried in solution, and the other as solid particles. The soluble products of chemical weathering that are carried in solution include colloidal silica, the carbonates, sulphates and chlorides of calcium, magnesium, sodium and potassium, and the hydroxides of aluminium and iron. These are all carried by the river either to the sea or to an inland lake. Solid particles are transported in three ways. The smallest are carried in suspension; the size of particles carried in this way depends on the speed and degree of turbulence of the water. Slightly larger particles may be lifted temporarily

146

Clay deposition in the estuary of a river – the Couesnon seen from Mont St Michel, France.

into suspension and carried along in a series of short parabolic leaps; this process is known as saltation. The largest fragments which a current is capable of carrying are bounced or rolled along the stream bed in a process known as traction. Such material is abraded in the process and becomes reduced in size and partly rounded. Material picked up by flowing water will be carried until the velocity of the current falls below the original velocity at which it was picked up. Extremely fine particles, like those of clays, need the water to be still before they are deposited.

A river deposits its load when its velocity is lowered: this can be caused by a reduction in gradient or by an obstruction. A common point of deposition occurs where a stream flowing swiftly down a steep mountain slope reaches the flatter ground of a valley or plain. The transported material is deposited in a wide fan-shaped body known as an alluvial fan. Such deposition is often only temporary, and, in the end, most of the load is carried on to a lake or to the sea. In both cases, the velocity of the water is checked, and much of the load is deposited in a delta, a triangular area with its apex pointing upstream. Deltas are built outwards from the river mouth into the sea or lake by successive depositions in that direction. Fine-grained materials like clays which are transported as colloidal solutions (solutions in which extremely fine particles are kept suspended against gravity by electrical forces) are deposited easily in the sea because salt water causes flocculation, the formation of colloids into larger particles.

The sea erodes coastlines mechanically, by the force of moving water and the battering of rock fragments carried with it. The force of waves alone may be sufficient to break off rock fragments, which in turn become agents of further erosion as they saw into the coastal rocks. Wave erosion near the base of a cliff leads to undercutting followed by the collapse of the upper parts. In this way, the whole

Wave action on a cliff.

cliff recedes. The shaping of a coast by marine erosion depends largely on the properties and structure of the rocks that make up the coast. Soft rocks are more easily eroded than hard rocks; thus two 'classic' types of coastline can develop, depending on the orientation of alternate bands of hard and soft rock in relation to the coastline. Where hard and soft rocks occur in alternate bands parallel to the coastline, a concordant coastline is produced. If the sea breaks through the hard layer to the soft rocks behind, excavation takes place forming coves which extend as far as the next layer of hard rock.

Where hard and soft layers alternate at right angles to the coastline, a discordant coastline results. Erosion of the soft rocks by wave action

Right
This coastline is discordant on the right and concordant on the left. Ballard Down, Dorset.

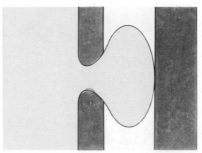

The shaping of a concordant coastline.

148

The shaping of a discordant coastline.

149

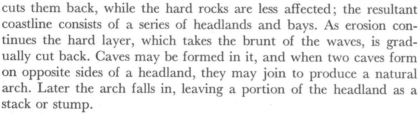

cuts them back, while the hard rocks are less affected; the resultant coastline consists of a series of headlands and bays. As erosion continues the hard layer, which takes the brunt of the waves, is gradually cut back. Caves may be formed in it, and when two caves form on opposite sides of a headland, they may join to produce a natural arch. Later the arch falls in, leaving a portion of the headland as a stack or stump.

Left: A coastline of headlands and bays, Lundy Bay, Cornwall. *Above and below right:* natural arches. *Above:* Lundy Bay, North Cornwall. *Below right:* Tenby, Pembrokeshire. *Below left:* a cave formed by wave action, Trebarwith Strand, Cornwall.

150

A stack – the Old Man of Hoy, Orkney.

Some rocks, notably limestones, are eroded chemically as well as mechanically by sea water.

Material eroded by wave action, together with that carried to the sea by rivers, may be moved about and deposited by waves and currents. Waves which strike the coastline obliquely transport material parallel to the coast by the process of long-shore drift. Attempts are frequently made to prevent this happening on beaches by building low walls or groynes perpendicular to the shore line; the moving material then piles up against the sides of the groynes facing the direction from which it is being transported.

Beaches are built by the action of incoming breakers near the shore-line; in the process, the particles are sorted according to size and density. The breakers can carry both large and small fragments towards the shore, but the less powerful backwash of each wave can only carry out the finer particles, so that the coarsest material is deposited at the top of the beach and increasingly finer material is left further down towards the sea.

Where long-shore drift takes place along an indented coastline, or where the coast changes direction, spits may be formed. The material being carried by long-shore drift is carried on more or less in a straight line and is deposited across the bay mouth, building up a ridge above the surface of the water. The spit extends by successive additions until waves or currents from another direction limit its

The size of the beach material can vary enormously. *Above:* Daymer Bay, Cornwall. *Below:* Tregastel, Brittany, France.

growth. Spurn Head spit, across the River Humber, for example, is formed by material eroded from the soft cliffs of Holderness and carried by long-shore drift to be deposited when it meets the current of the Humber. A bar is formed in a similar way to a spit, except that instead of one end terminating in open sea, it extends from one headland to another. Groundwater is rainwater that percolates into the earth's surface. Its movement and storage is controlled by the porosity and permeability of the surface rocks. Porosity is the proportion of a rock's volume that is empty space (for example, the minute spaces between mineral grains). Permeability is the capacity of a rock to transmit fluids. Clay has a high porosity, but its pores are very small and unconnected, so that its permeability is small. Limestone also has a high porosity and a high permeability. Groundwater also dissolves limestone, forming caves and underground channels; a typical limestone area has little or no surface drainage. Occasionally the roofs of limestone caverns collapse to form spectacular gorges. Notable examples of complex systems of limestone holes and caves are found in Kentucky and New Mexico, where the famous Carlsbad Cavern is nearly 4000 feet long, with walls 600 feet apart and a roof 300 feet high.

In addition to the water that flows as a stream through the network of underground passages in limestone masses, there is usually also a slow seepage of water from the innumerable joints and cracks in the roofs of the caves. As a drop of water containing dissolved limestone

hangs from the roof of a cave, it begins to evaporate and some of the calcium carbonate is deposited. Successive drops build up long icicle-like pendants known as stalactites. The drops that fall to the floor build up pillars known as stalagmites. Stalactites and stalagmites thus grow towards each other, and can unite to form pillars.

Wind can be an agent of erosion, transportation or deposition; it is most effective in arid or semi-arid areas, where loose material is

Spurn Head at the mouth of the River Humber, Yorkshire.

A gorge created by water erosion around a glacier, aided by small-scale cavern collapse, Gordale Scar, Yorkshire.

Stalactites and stalagmites at Easegill Caverns, Westmorland.

liable to be blown away because it is not held together by moisture or held down by the roots of vegetation. In humid areas, it is normally only significant on beaches or where man has laid large areas of soil bare by ploughing. Such agricultural land is vulnerable to denudation by wind action during an extended period of drought: the 'dust bowls' of Kansas and Oklahoma during the 1930s and 1950s were the result of wind action after crops failed to grow because of lack of rainfall.

In desert regions, the wind picks up hard grains of quartz sand and drives them aganist rock masses, causing wear and abrasion. This natural sand-blast is concentrated near ground level, between one and three metres above the ground, since sand grains are too heavy to rise

Zeugens.

156

far. It acts in a similar way to the artificial sand-blast that is used to etch glass and clean and polish building stones, eroding and polishing the surfaces in its path. Its action on exposed rocks is highly selective: it picks out all the weaknesses in the rock surface, attacking the soft layers, fractures and joints. Undercutting is a notable feature of wind erosion, particularly in areas where bands of hard and soft rock strata alternate. Where the layers are horizontal, the hard rocks may be left standing up above the level of the desert floor as mushroom-like zeugens.

Zeugens are often elongated in the direction of the prevailing wind. Where the strata are tilted, the softer layers are cut away leaving long passages between overhanging ridges known as yardangs.

Wind transports dust and sand in different ways. Dust particles (less than 0.06mm in diameter) can be carried in suspension, much as sediment is carried by a river. Such material can be lifted high into the air and carried far from its source even by winds of average velocity. Thus dust from the Sahara desert often falls on ships far out in the Atlantic, or on southern Europe. When the dust settles out of air suspension it builds a blanket deposit of minute uniform particles known as loess. The loess beds of western China, formed from dust carried by wind from the Gobi desert, cover an area the size of France to a thickness of several hundred feet.

Sand grains blown by wind form large sheets, which eventually pile up under continued wind action to form sand drifts and sand dunes. Sand grains driven by wind move in a series of short leaps in the process called saltation; which has already been mentioned in connection with river transportation. When the wind blows steadily from one direction, crescent-shaped dunes known as barchans are produced; the horns of the crescents point away from the direction of the wind.

If one end of a barchan becomes held in place by a damp patch or by vegetation, it may elongate to form a seif or longitudinal dune.

Barchan dunes in the Sahara.

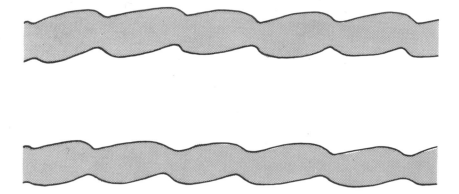

Transverse dunes extend at right angles to the wind direction. Complex dunes of irregular shape are also found.

Though desert landscapes are dominated by the structure of dunes suggesting that wind is the dominant geological agent, the action of water is equally significant, even though it flows freely only after torrential storms, which are very rare. Such desert storms cut deep channels known as wadis.

Complex chains of dunes in Saudi Arabia.

A wadi in Australia.

The present day geological work of ice is restricted to high altitudes or latitudes; even so, as much as 10% of the earth's land surface is covered by ice in the form of glaciers and ice sheets. The effects of the last great ice age are still very conspicuous: during this period a third of the land area was covered by ice.

The processes associated with action due to ice-masses are known as glaciation. Glaciers are formed where the climate is conducive to the accumulation of snow; such conditions occur in the high latitudes of both hemispheres and at high altitudes in any area. In such areas snow collects in large snowfields, and if the summer temperature is not too high, its thickness gradually increases over a period of years, until it eventually turns to ice under the pressure of its own weight.

This ice forms at the base of the snow layer, and as more snow piles up, the weight forces it outward and it begins to flow very slowly under the influence of gravity. In mountain regions, ice moves down valleys in tongue-like extrusions known as glaciers, which continue to advance as long as the supply of ice exceeds the loss due to melting. Glaciers usually move slowly, less than a foot a day, but some are known to flow more than fifty feet a day.

The base of a glacier is filled with a layer of frozen-in boulders and rock fragments which abrade the surface over which it moves. This smoothes the surface over which the glacier passes, and often leaves scratches and striations, and even large grooves. As a glacier moves downward, it tends to pluck material from the back of the slope on which it rests.

The present day work of ice is best seen at high altitudes, as here at Blick von Valuga-Gipfel, Austria.

A valley glacier, Chamonix, Switzerland.

160

The result is a great armchair-shaped hollow known as a cirque (or corrie). The steep back walls are often thousands of feet high. These hollows are often overdeepened (gouged out by glacial action), with a slight ridge at the front edge (which may also be formed from glacial debris), so that when the glacier eventually melts a small corrie lake or tarn is formed. These often stand at the head of a present-day river valley. If cirques develop on either side of a slope, a steep-sided, sharp-edged ridge known as an arête is left between them. A cluster of more than two cirques leaves a sharp central peak called a horn; the most spectacular example is the Matterhorn in Switzerland.

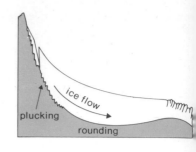

Cirque glaciers move under the influence of gravity until they reach a river valley, where several may coalesce to form a valley glacier. These glaciers act as agents of erosion, transport and deposition; they greatly modify the valleys through which they move. The glacier carries stones and rock debris which act as abrasives, and wear away the valley floor and sides, changing the V-shaped section of a river valley into a broad U-shape. Small crags are smoothed and rounded to form humps known as *roches moutonées*, because of their supposed resemblance to flocks of sheep. Any spurs projecting from the sides of the original valley are worn away, leaving truncated spurs. The weight of the ice scours away the bottom of the valley, over-deepening it, leaving a gouged out rock basin which may fill with

Kali Gandaki Valley, Nepal. Dissected sediments adjacent to the Himalayas.

The Matterhorn, Switzerland.

A U-shaped valley, showing a lake in the over-deepened trough, hanging valleys and alluvial forms. Wast Water, Cumberland.

water when the ice melts forming a ribbon lake or, if invaded by the sea, as in Norway, a fjord. The floors of such overdeepened valleys may descend well below sea level – Loch Morar in Scotland is over 1000 feet deep, though its surface is less than 50 feet above sea level. This overdeepening is greater in main valleys than in tributary valleys, so that the tributary valleys are left as hanging valleys, truncated at the walls of the main valley.

When the ice melts, these hanging valleys may be reoccupied by streams which flow into the main valley by cascading down the steep walls as waterfalls; Bridalveil Fall enters Yosemite Valley in Yosemite National Park, California, in this way. Where the gradient is less steep, masses of sediment may be deposited where the stream or river reaches the main valley floor to form an alluvial fan.

A U-shaped valley, showing a braided river channel flowing along the ice-gouged trough. Glen Feshie, south of Aviemore, Inverness-shire.

164

When valley glaciers reach the lowlands at the foot of mountains – the area known as the piedmont – they may coalesce to form a great sheet of ice, a piedmont glacier. A present day example is the Bering Piedmont Glacier in Alaska. As these glaciers spread slowly over the land, they tend to act as giant scrapers, smoothing and rounding the landscape, removing soil and superficial deposits and carrying these along with them. When the ice melts, large amounts of transported material are deposited as moraines. The material pushed forward by the front edge of the glacier is often left as a crescent-shaped barrier across a valley known as a terminal moraine. Sometimes several are found one behind the other, marking the positions where the glacier remained stationary for lengthy periods during its retreat. Transported material sometimes survives as ridges or shelves along the valley sides, but these lateral moraines are usually eroded away by stream action after the ice melts. The typical deposit left by a piedmont glacier or an ice sheet is ground moraine, which is formed by slow collapse of the ice during melting. It is generally sorted by the melt water; the finer material is washed out beyond the terminal moraine to form an outwash plain, while the heavier material remains as loose debris. The material laid down in an outwash plain (or fan) is coarsest near the terminal moraine, and grades outwards into boulder clay, a mixture of sand and boulders mixed with fine material which is usually loose and unconsolidated. The larger boulders found in boulder clay are known as erratics; these may have been transported a considerable distance, and identification of their source can establish the direction of travel of the glacier or ice mass. Thus, erratics found on the east coast of Britain can be matched only to rocks in the Oslo region of Norway, indicating that during the Great Ice Age, ice spread across the North Sea from Scandinavia to Britain.

The ground moraine left by ice sheets forms an irregular blanket, varying from a few to several feet thick. It usually has a gently rolling surface, but may be moulded into a series of small rounded hummocks known as drumlins. These are generally less than a hundred feet high, up to half a mile long, and steep at one end and tapered at the other. They occur in parallel clusters, with their steep ends facing the direction from which the ice came. Eskers are another characteristic feature of lowland glaciation: they are sinuous ridges of sand, gravel and boulders which run roughly at right angles to the terminal moraine with which they are associated. They have steep sides and narrow, flattish tops (not unlike railway embankments); they may be up to a hundred feet high and may extend for up to a hundred miles. They are almost certainly deposited by torrents of water derived from melted ice and flowing in confined channels beneath the glacier.

Diagenesis

The process by which loose, unconsolidated sediments are changed into hard sedimentary rocks is known as diagenesis. It takes place at low temperatures and pressures near the earth's surface, without any movement of the crust being involved. The most common processes are compaction and cementation; as sediments are buried by further sediments deposited on top of them, they are compacted.

As the grains move together under pressure, water is squeezed out from between them. Unstable constituents may be broken down, and the more soluble constituents dissolved. They may be carried in solution through the spaces (pores) between the grains and redeposited by crystallisation in open pore spaces, forming a cement which holds the grains together in a homogeneous mass. The cement may alternatively be brought in by groundwater percolating through the pores of the rock. Common cements are calcite, silica, and iron hydrates. This final stage of diagenesis in which loose sediment is cemented together into a massive rock is lithification. If compaction becomes extreme, the sediment may recrystallise. Normally this requires extreme pressure, such as results from earth movements, and is considered a metamorphic process. However, in limestone, recrystallisation frequently occurs during diagenesis. Limestone is made up of calcite grains which are the debris from small shelled organisms. These may be dissolved and recrystallised as a new structure of calcite which does not preserve the original organic structures. This process takes place near the earth's surface at normal temperatures and pressures.

The Classification of Sedimentary Rocks

Sedimentary rocks are commonly classified into two broad groups on the basis of the processes which led to their deposition. Rocks which have been built up by deposition of fragments split from pre-existing rocks by the processes of weathering and erosion are called clastic rocks. Rocks which are formed by chemical or organic processes are known as non-clastic rocks.

Clastic rocks are subdivided on the basis of the size of their component grains into three groups: the rudaceous clastic rocks, with grains ranging in size from 2mm upwards; arenaceous clastic rocks, with grains ranging to size from $\frac{1}{16}$mm to 2mm; and argillaceous clastic rocks, with grains less than $\frac{1}{16}$mm in diameter.

Non-clastic rocks are generally classified on the basis of their chemical composition. Thus carbonate rocks have a high carbonate content; siliceous rocks have a high silica content; ferruginous rocks have a high iron content; carbonaceous rocks have a high carbon content; phosphatic rocks have a high phosphate content; evaporites are rocks formed by the evaporation of fluids.

The mineral content of a clastic rock depends directly on the kind of rock which was eroded, transported and deposited to produce it. Quartz and heavy minerals, if present in the original rock, will remain chemically unchanged in the sediment; feldspars and micas will often be broken down to form clay minerals over a period of time. The presence of unaltered feldspar in a sediment is an indication that the area of deposition was not far from the source area, the area where the erosion took place.

Rudaceous clastic rocks consist of more or less rounded pebbles held together by a cement, which frequently consists of a sandstone or a limestone. Conspicuously large fragments enclosed in such rocks are known as phenoclasts. When the constituent fragments are sharply angular, the rock is termed a breccia; when they are rounded, the rock is termed a conglomerate. If there are relatively few grains in the supporting matrix of cement, so that the grains appear to 'float'

Conglomerate from Hertfordshire.

in it, the rock is termed a paraconglomerate (or parabreccia). If the grains are in contact, so that the cement merely fills the spaces between them, the rock is termed an orthoconglomerate (or orthobreccia).

If the rock is made up of grains of one material or mineral, it is termed a monomict; in an oligomict, grains of one kind of mineral predominate; a rock with grains of various materials is polymict.

The source area of the component grains that make up a rudaceous rock is important. If the rock consists of fragments of old material worn from a mountain range and transported and deposited in a distant river basin, it is called extraformational. Such rocks often show a considerable difference in age between the phenoclasts and the matrix of cement that encloses them. If the source of sediment is in the same area as the place of deposition, as when grains from a cliff are eroded and fall directly to their place of deposition as sediments, the resulting rock is called intraformational. Normally intraformational conglomerates are formed when the conditions of sedimentation change, as when the streams flowing across large river deltas change course laterally so that they erode recently deposited sediments and transport them for subsequent redeposition. In rocks formed in this way, there is little difference between the phenoclasts and the matrix holding them together.

Among arenaceous rocks, the range of possible textures (which depend on the environment in which the sediment was deposited) is expressed in terms of the relation between the size of the phenoclasts and the size of the grains of the matrix in such rocks. Sand is defined as having grains between 2mm and $\frac{1}{16}$mm in diameter; it has little or no cement, but it is changed by diagenesis to sandstone. Silty sand consists of sand particles in a fairly fine matrix, with the size of its grains ranging between $\frac{1}{16}$mm and $\frac{1}{256}$mm. Clayey sand has a very fine matrix with a grain size of less than $\frac{1}{256}$mm.

Quartzite sandstone from Northern Ireland.

Arenaceous rocks with sharp-edged angular phenoclasts are known as grits; those with rounded phenoclasts are termed sandstones. Pure quartz sands consist of well-rounded grains which result from prolonged erosion along the edges of shallow seas. When they are lithified by cementation with silica they form quartzitic sandstones – the total rock consisting of almost pure quartz. Sandstones which contain small amounts of feldspar in addition to the quartz are known as feldspathic sandstones; similarly the red, yellow or green sandstones which are cemented by iron hydrates are known as ferruginous sandstones. Sandstones containing mica (usually muscovite) are known as micaceous sandstones; the mica flakes tend to accumulate in layers, along which the rock splits easily, so that it is also known as a flagstone.

Arkoses are sandstones which contain feldspar grains (up to one third of the whole) and some other minerals, usually micas, in addition to the quartz. The grains are usually rather coarse and partially rounded; the cement is usually an iron compound, though it can be calcite. Arkoses are often found in current-bedded structures. They are produced by the rapid erosion and deposition of igneous masses which allows little time for the feldspars to decompose chemically.

Greywackes are dark coloured sandstones made up of a mixture of partially angular grains of many rocks and minerals jumbled together and cemented by a finer grained matrix. The grain size ranges from fine to coarse, so that graded bedding is a common feature of greywacke deposits. The absence of sorting and rounding suggest that erosion and deposition were rapid; it is currently thought that most greywackes were laid down by fast-moving, submarine turbidity currents flowing down slopes from shallow to relatively deep water.

Greywacke from South Wales.

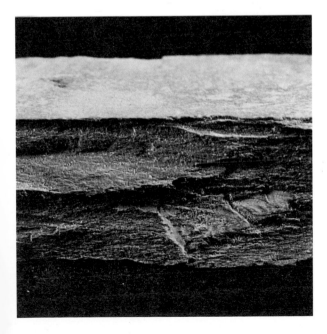

Below: Siltstone from Kaghan Valley, Pakistan.

Right: Mudstone from Gloucestershire.

Argillaceous rocks have constituent grains of less than 1/16mm in diameter. Those with grains ranging between 1/16mm and 1/256mm in size are known as siltstones; the grains are usually fine quartz particles mixed with clay minerals. Rocks with grains less than 1/256mm in diameter are known as mudstones or clays. Mudstones are formed from mud which has had the water squeezed out of it by the pressure from overlying layers of material. They are very cohesive and

Shale from Dorset.

Clay from Devon.

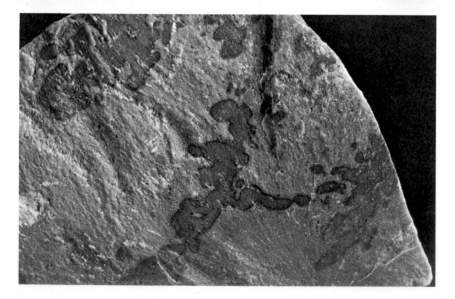

Marl from Gloucestershire.

tend to break irregularly. Mudstones with clay particles orientated parallel to the bedding planes tend to fracture easily along these planes; these are known as shales. Clays consist of a high proportion of fine flaky particles which are readily enveloped by thin films of water, making them moist and plastic. Marls are a mixture of clay and particles of calcium carbonate.

The non-clastic rocks are formed by chemical and biological action; they may be deposited directly on to the earth's surface, or produced by the diagenesis of sediments. They are classified according to their chemical content.

The carbonate rocks are generally known as limestones. The dominant mineral is normally calcium carbonate, which exists in two crystal forms, calcite and aragonite. Dolomite (calcium magnesium carbonate, $CaMg(CO_3)_2$), magnesite (magnesium carbonate, $MgCO_3$) and siderite (iron carbonate, $FeCO_3$) are also fairly common. All carbonate rocks may contain some sandy or clayey material.

The majority of limestone rocks are organic in origin; the exception

A typical limestone, from the Khyber Pass, North West Pakistan.

A crinoidal limestone from Somerset.

171

is aragonite, which is precipitated directly from sea water, particularly in the warm, highly alkaline conditions which characterise the warm currents of seas and oceans: it is precipitated as needle-like crystals in the waters around the Bahamas. Some limestones, notably those formed by secretion from living organisms such as corals, are part chemical and part organic in origin.

Organic limestones are derived from plant or animal fragments cemented or compacted into rock layers. Debris from one particular type of organism frequently predominates in limestone beds, and various types can thus be distinguished; these include shelly limestone, formed from the fossil shells of molluscs, crinoidal limestone, formed from the calcareous parts of the crinoid echinoderms, and foraminiferal limestone, formed from the remains of unicellular protozoa. Algal limestone is of plant origin, coming from the remains of algae which contain calcium carbonate. Chalk is a soft white limestone which is very fine grained; it is made up of foraminiferans, some fine shell material, radiolarians, and calcareous parts of unicellular algae, all cemented in a calcite matrix.

Limestones can be classified according to the type of matrix and the type of particles it cements. The three main constituents of any limestone are allochems, micrite and sparite (sparry calcite). Allochems are the granular parts of the limestone aggregate. They are of various types. Intraclasts are limestone fragments which are eroded from the floor of the sedimentary basin at the same time as sediment is being deposited. They range from sand-size grains to pebbles and boulders, which are usually aggregates of smaller intraclasts. Oolites are spherical or near spherical rock particles, usually about 1mm or less in diameter, which have grown by accretion around a nucleus. The nucleus is usually a tiny shell fragment or a sand grain; as it is

Chalk from Amesbury, Wiltshire.

A pisolitic limestone (pisolites are large oolites) from County Durham.

washed around in waves and currents this small particle serves as a centre around which deposition of successive coatings of calcium carbonate takes place. When examined under the microscope, oolites are found to consist of a number of concentric layers surrounding a nucleus. Limestone grains may be fossils, that is whole shells, or fragments of them. Pellets are ovoid particles of calcium carbonate which range in size from 0.25mm to 5mm in length; they have no internal structure at all, unlike oolites. They are thought to have been formed from faecal pellets which were excreted by molluscs, echinoderms, or other small invertebrate animals.

Micrite (or microcrystalline calcite ooze) forms one type of limestone matrix. It is a very fine-grained sediment, formed by chemical precipitation. Sparite cement is crystalline and more coarse-grained; it fills in the cavities or pores within pre-existing limestone. It is common in limestone formed from oolites or from well-rounded shell debris.

A combination of terms allows limestones to be characterised accurately. Thus oosparite is an aggregate of oolites cemented in a matrix of sparite; biosparite is an aggregate of fossil fragments in a matrix of sparite; oomicrite is composed of oolites in a matrix of micrite.

Limestone is formed in shallow marine environments, the same areas in which clastic rocks are deposited, so it is common to find mixtures of clastic and carbonate sediments. Calcareous sandstones are sandstones which contain quartz grains held together by a calcite cement; sandy limestones are similar, except that the quartz grains are larger.

Dolomite rock is a variety of limestone in which more than 15% of the calcium carbonate is replaced by magnesium carbonate.

Dolomite from Leicestershire.

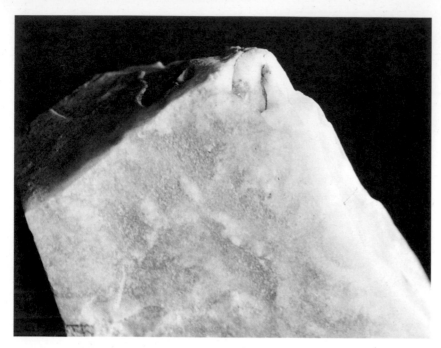

It is formed by a reaction in seawater in which magnesium ions are exchanged for some of the calcium in calcium carbonate ($CaCO_3$) to give calcium magnesium carbonate ($CaMg(CO_3)_2$). The process appears to require hot, very salty water, and thus accompanies evaporation. Dolomite rocks preserve the structure of the original rock to varying degrees; in some cases the reduction of volume that accompanies the change causes dolomites to become cavernous, with large pore spaces, which makes them potential reservoir rocks for oil.

There are various sedimentary rocks composed of silica, apart from the quartz sands. These siliceous rocks are frequently produced by diagenesis and often form localised deposits within other rocks. For example, cherts are found in the Carboniferous limestone deposits of the British Isles; they are aggregates of very fine silica crystals which occur as bands or layers of nodules in sedimentary rocks. Some are formed by the silification of limestone, a process in which the calcium carbonate is replaced by silica; others are of organic origin, being deposits of fossil radiolarians or diatoms, organisms which absorb silica. Flint is another siliceous rock, but the exact details of its formation are uncertain. It occurs in chalk deposits as nodules, which appear to have crystallised around a nucleus. The flint nodules characteristically occur in bands which may be visible in the exposed chalk of cliffs.

Sedimentary rocks which contain a significant amount of an iron mineral such as hematite, limonite, siderite, glauconite or pyrite, are known as ferruginous rocks. They are generally formed in the same way as clastic rocks or in the same way as limestones. Thus glauconitic sandstones (greensands) are sandstones in which some of the grains consist of the green, iron-bearing mineral glauconite. Clay ironstone, another clastic rock, is a mixture of siderite (iron carbonate, $FeCO_3$) and argillaceous sediment. Ferruginous oolitic limestone is a carbonate rock formed by the replacement of the calcium carbonate of limestone

Clay ironstone nodule.

Ferruginous sandstone from Wiltshire.

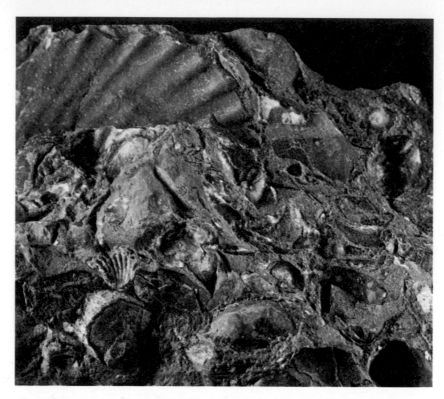

Ferruginous limestone – ironstone from Whitby, Yorkshire.

oolites by siderite, or by the deposition of an iron silicate (chamosite) in concentric layers around nuclei to form ironstone ooliths.

When plants and animals die, their tissues are usually broken down by bacteria and other organisms. However, rapid accumulation of organic debris may restrict the supply of oxygen, and make complete breakdown impossible. Under such circumstances the partially decayed organic debris is buried and converted by diagenesis into carbonaceous rocks – rocks whose main component is carbon, often combined with hydrogen in the form of hydrocarbons. Coals are carbonaceous rocks formed from the accumulation of vegetable debris in swamps or low coastal plains. A layer of loose vegetable matter is converted, first by chemical and bacterial action at the surface, and then by compression due to burial under subsequently deposited material, into a compact coal seam. The process has a series of stages, and may be arrested at any one of them; a series of coal types exists depending on the degree of compaction the vegetable matter has undergone. Peat is a loose material, a relatively little modified accumulation of plants which retains most of their structures. Lignite or brown coal represents a further stage in the transformation: it is more compact than peat, and a darker brown colour, but its vegetable origin is clearly visible in the plant structures it contains. Bituminous coal, the normal domestic coal, is dull black, brittle and hard, and shows only occasional traces of plant matter. Anthracite is shiny black, and structureless; it shows little or no trace of any organic structures.

Where the accumulation of vegetable matter takes place in a marine environment, the process of compaction and diagenesis probably results in the formation of oil, oil shales and natural gas. The exact

Right: Peat from Somerset.
Far right: Anthracite from South Wales.

Bone Bed from Gloucestershire.

nature of the process by which vegetable matter is converted to hydrocarbons is not fully understood at present.

The mineralogy of phosphatic rocks (rocks containing phosphorous) is complex. All marine sediments contain a proportion of phosphate, and under certain conditions this can rise to a considerable amount. Phosphates dissolved in water which flows through limestone can alter the rock to form phosphatic limestone. The phosphatic rocks known as primary phosphates include those formed from bone beds, deposits built up from those remains of vertebrates which contain abundant phosphates, usually bones, teeth, or scales. Examples of this kind of bed are found in Florida, and in the Rhaetic Bone Bed of south-western England. The occurrence of a bone bed often marks a sudden change in the past environment – the Rhaetic Bone Bed marks the beginning of the marine transgression which laid down the marine sediments of the Jurassic period.

Guano is composed of highly phosphatic excreta deposited in large accumulations on oceanic islands by birds or in caves by bats. It is slowly changed by diagenesis after deposition, and the result is a concentration of the insoluable calcium triphosphate. The soluble phosphates which are washed out during the process are carried downwards and may occasionally phosphatise any underlying limestone.

When a shallow lake has no outlet to the sea, or when an arm of the sea becomes cut off from the main body of water, both the sediments and the dissolved chemicals are trapped in one environment. As evaporation takes place at the surface of the water the chemical

177

solution becomes increasingly concentrated until the various salts crystallise out, forming deposits of evaporites. The process requires high temperatures and low rainfall; the ideal environment for the formation of thick deposits would seem to be an almost totally landlocked sea basin with tidal access to the ocean over a shallow sand bar.

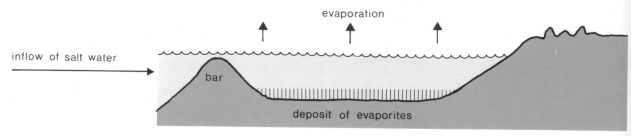

In this situation there would be an inflow of water at high tide to compensate for the water lost by evaporation, and the process of crystallisation would be nearly continuous. Most evaporites derive from salt water, which is rich in soluable salts. Crystallisation begins when the water has been concentrated to about half its original volume, with the least soluble salts separating out first. Thus gypsum, calcium sulphate, would crystallise before halite, sodium chloride; a concentration of up to sixty times normal would be required to precipitate thenardite, sodium sulphate, and potash, potassium sulphate. These last two are predictably uncommon in evaporite deposits. Thick deposits of halite are common : there are large ones in Texas, Louisiana, Cheshire, and in Germany at Anhalt.

Under certain conditions evaporites may develop from bodies of non-saline lake water; an example is the Great Basin region of Nevada and California where there are dried up lakes containing sodium borate and carbonate minerals among the evaporites.

METAMORPHIC ROCKS

A metamorphic rock is one which has been changed in mineral content, in texture, or both, as a result of a drastic change in environment. The chief agents of metamorphism are high temperature and great pressure. Under extreme conditions, with a drastic rise of both temperature and pressure, the metamorphosed rock may be virtually identical to an igneous rock. The borderline between the two types is ill-defined. Metamorphic alteration may be minor, or low-grade, with the original bedding or rock structure remaining visible, or major – high-grade – with the whole rock being recrystallised (though without ever having totally melted). Metamorphic rocks may themselves be metamorphosed again; this process is known as polymetamorphism.

Metamorphism occurs at considerable depths beneath the earth's surface, so it is impossible to observe the process directly. However, laboratory experiments provide some insight into the kinds of reaction that take place, and enable us to define limits within which the metamorphic process takes place. The temperature is perhaps the most important factor : below 200°C, the reactions are so slow that they have little effect (they shade into extreme diagenesis), and above 800–1000°C, the whole rock melts. So most metamorphism takes place between 200°C and 1000°C. Pressure during metamorphism is chiefly due to weight of overlying material, which increases with depth. The majority of metamorphic rocks have not been more than 20km below the surface. At this level, the pressure is 6000 atmospheres – that is 6000 times the atmospheric pressure at sea level. Some metamorphic rocks probably originate below this depth, but it is a rough limit for most metamorphic changes. The lower limit of pressure is the ordinary pressure of the atmosphere, if we include the types of change found near hot springs as examples of metamorphism.

Pressure can be of two kinds – confining or hydrostatic pressure; directed pressure or stress. The latter is due to earth movements. At low temperatures it may break down rocks mechanically; at high temperatures it may speed up chemical reactions or crystal growth. A final condition that determines the rate and often the nature of metamorphic processes is the presence of fluids filling the pores of the rocks. Between these interstitial fluids and the minerals of the rock there is a constant interchange of material which speeds up the process of chemical change, an aspect of metamorphism known as metasomatism.

Metamorphism which takes place at high temperature and under low pressure is known as contact metamorphism. It is usually associated with igneous activity, namely the intrusion of magma into a body of rock. The invaded or host rock is affected both by the heat emanating from the magma and by its chemical constituents. The heat induces recrystallisation of the area of the host rock nearest to the magma, and fluids from the magma may penetrate the host rock and promote the formation of new minerals (the process is called pneumatolysis). Contact metamorphism is most intense in the zone of contact between the magma and the host rock; metamorphic effects decrease with distance from this zone, which is known as the metamorphic aureole of the igneous body. Aureoles vary, depending on the type of rock invaded and the size of the intrusion. Large intrusions may have metamorphic aureoles up to a mile thick, while a small dyke or sill may modify only an inch or so of the rock it invades. Contact metamorphism can also take place on the surface, when lava flows out over pre-existing rocks.

Regional metamorphism takes place at high temperature and high pressure. It is associated with deep burial of rocks and with earth movements. Much of the pressure involved is directed pressure. In the great folded mountain belts of the world, regionally metamorphosed rocks occupy large areas. Regional metamorphism involves all the metamorphic agents working together, and its products are varied and complex.

Under conditions of high pressure and low temperature, dynamic metamorphism may take place in rocks subjected to dislocation as a result of powerful earth movements. Stress is the principal factor; rocks are broken up, and frequently reduced to fine powder. The mechanical destruction of the grains making up a rock is known as cataclasis. It does not result in the formation of any new minerals.

The Classification of Metamorphic Rocks

The metamorphic rocks are classified according to the form of metamorphism they have undergone and the nature of the original rock.

ORIGINAL ROCK	CONTACT META-MORPHOSIS	REGIONAL META-MORPHOSIS	DYNAMIC META-MORPHOSIS
Argillaceous clastic	Spotted rocks	Slate Phyllite Schist Gneiss	Cataclastite Mylonite
Arenaceous clastic	Quartzite	Quartzite	Cataclastite Mylonite
Calcareous	Marble	Marble	—
Impure calcareous	Calc-silicate hornfels	Calc-silicate schist	—
Acid igneous rock	—	Quartz schist Granulite	Cataclastite Mylonite
Basic igneous rock	Epidiorite	Epidiorite Schist Amphibolite Eclogite	—

Certain new minerals are produced by two types of metamorphism:

CONTACT	REGIONAL	BOTH
Andalusite	Chloritoid	Amphiboles
Brucite	Garnet	Feldspars
Cordierite	Glaucophane	Micas
Grossularite	Kyanite	Pyroxenes
Idocrase	Staurolite	Sillimanite
Wollastonite		

Contact Metamorphic Rocks

Spotted Rocks are produced by low grade metamorphism of argillaceous rocks. They are found towards the outer edge of metamorphic aureoles. The texture is modified so that it acquires a slaty cleavage – that is, it is easily broken into thin sheets. Small dark spots which are small nodules of chiastolite, graphite, rutile or iron ores, develop in the rock.

Hornfels is a medium or fine-grained granular rock which is formed as a result of metamorphism of argillaceous clastic rocks. It is found in the innermost parts of metamorphic aureoles. The texture is different from that of the parent rock, being more

Top left: Chiastolite slate from Devon.
Top right: Hornfels from Devon.
Bottom left: Quartzite from Shropshire.
Bottom right: Marble from Carrara, Italy.

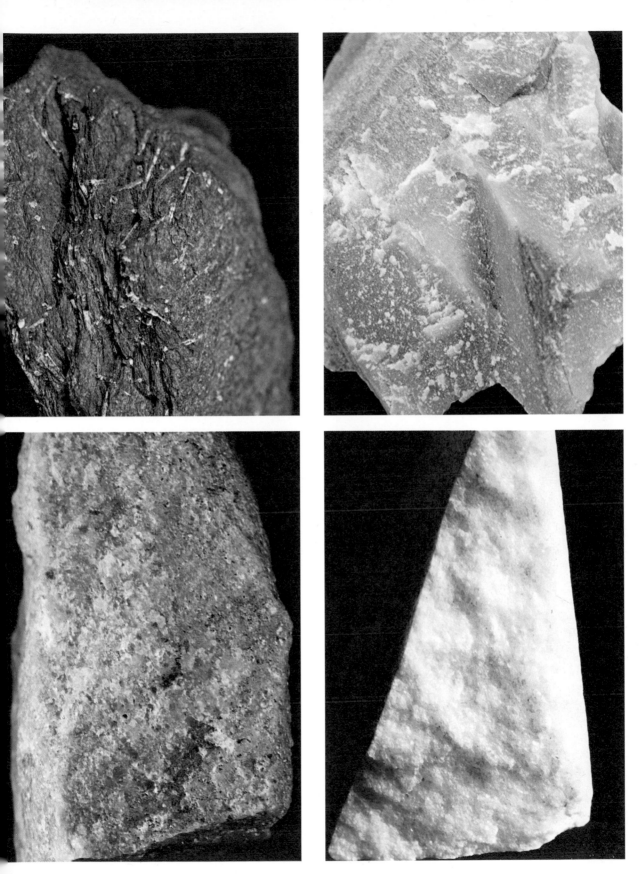

Above: Phyllite from Cornwall.
Right: Gneiss from Argyllshire.

granular (due to complete recrystallisation) and lacking any bedding or cleavage.

Metamorphism recrystallises the quartz grains of sandstone to form quartzite. An even-grained granular texture results, with variable grain size and no trace of the cementation found in the original rock. Impurities in the original rock may give rise to irregular grains of metamorphic minerals such as chlorite or biotite scattered through the rock. Feldspars, garnet, hornblende or epidote may also be present in this way.

Epidiorite is a granular rock produced by low-grade contact or regional metamorphism of basic igneous rocks.

Marble is the result of the metamorphism of limestone; it is recrystallised as rock with an even-grained texture, although the grain size may vary.

Regional Metamorphic Rocks

Slates are formed by low grade metamorphism of argillaceous clastic rocks. They undergo little recrystallisation, but develop a well marked cleavage in one direction. Minute flakes of mica and wisps of chlorite are usually present.

Higher grade metamorphism of argillaceous clastic rocks results in the formation of phyllite, a rock that is coarser grained and less perfect in cleavage than slate. It has a lustrous appearance due to the orientation of mica flakes along the line of cleavage. Mica and chlorite are usually present.

Schist is formed at higher temperatures, and is characterised by a parallel arrangement of the bulk of the constituent minerals. It is distinguished from phyllite by a coarser texture and a tendency towards a wavy cleavage, which leaves a clear alignment of mica flakes along the surface known as schistosity.

Gneiss is produced under conditions of fairly high temperature and pressure, and so is found in the hottest parts of areas of regional metamorphism. It is a coarse-grained banded rock, the bands representing the segregation of the component minerals into parallel streaks.

Opposite.
Top left: Clay slate from Cornwall.
Top right: Mica schist from Brittany, France.
Bottom left: Hornblende schist from Cornwall.
Bottom right: Mica garnet schist, from Cornwall.

183

The bands consist of alternate layers of schistose minerals (micas, amphiboles, and occasionally pyroxene) and granulose minerals (quartzo-feldspathic minerals). Many gneiss bodies are penetrated by granite veins or pegmatites.

Quartzite, identical to that produced by contact metamorphism, is also produced by regional metamorphism. Marble is also produced by regional metamorphism.

Calc-silicate schist is a rock very similar to the hornfels produced by contact metamorphism; it differs in having a schistosity along which flaky minerals such as micas are aligned. The bulk of the rock is in the form of various calcium and magnesium silicates. Quartz schist is a schist rich in quartz, with the quartz having been recrystallised into lenticular crystals which are aligned with the schistosity.

A higher grade of metamorphism of an acid igneous rock produces granulite, an even-grained granular rock with no schistosity. The component minerals are feldspars, pyroxenes, and garnets.

Amphibolite is produced by medium to high grade metamorphism of basic igneous rocks. It consists mainly of hornblende and plagioclase feldspar, which are often segregated into bands. There is some schistosity because of the alignment of the hornblende along one plane.

Eclogite is a very dense rock produced by the most extreme type of metamorphism. It is essentially a basic igneous rock which has been recrystallised under conditions of high temperature and pressure. The component minerals are normally garnet, pyroxene, and sometimes amphibole. The rock is granular and coarse grained.

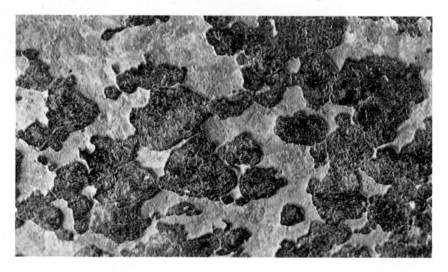

Eclogite from Rhodesia.

Dynamic Metamorphic Rocks

Cataclastite is rock that has been mechanically broken, and the constituents partly shattered, leaving angular pieces of uncrushed rock surrounded by finely crushed material.

If the shearing and dislocative forces that produce cataclastite are prolonged and intense, the individual crystals of the rock become fractured and the whole rock becomes more and more fine grained. This fine-grained rock is known as mylonite; it often has a banded or streaked appearance. It is found in areas of great tectonic dislocation.

ROCK RECOGNITION

In the field, the collector needs to be able to identify a rock both in its broad classification – 'Is this a sedimentary rock or an igneous rock ?' – and in more detail – 'Is this a limestone or a conglomerate?'. The first stage is to examine the rock in mass, to try to get some indication of the rock's type by studying the landscape in which it is found, and any distinctive features of the rock face as it appears at the exposure.

Raised areas often are often formed from rocks that are hard and resistant to erosion. Hills that rise suddenly from otherwise flat, low-lying land are often exposed bodies of igneous rock, such as batholiths, stocks, or volcanic plugs.

The characteristic scarp and vale topography of the Cotswold and Weald areas of England, indicate that bands of hard and soft rock alternate – in the Cotswolds, hard limestones alternate with soft clays. An escarpment is formed by combined vertical and lateral erosion by running water in areas where alternating layers of hard and soft rock have been upthrust so that they are gently inclined to the surface.

If the rock at the exposure consists of clearly discernible layers or beds lying one above the other, it is almost certainly sedimentary, though any one of the layers may be an extrusive igneous rock which has been overlain by sediments. Bedding may survive low grade metamorphism but all traces of it are destroyed by high grade metamorphism. The individual beds may vary in thickness from a few inches to many feet. The planes which separate the beds may show ripple marks, suncracks, rainpits, or fossil evidence – all indications of a sedimentary origin. If the rock shows no clear bedding, but occurs as irregular masses with extrusions which cut across bedded rocks, and if the rock texture is granular or porphyritic, it is probably igneous.

Joints are regular fractures running through rocks; there is no observable relative movement on either side of the fracture. They are found in both igneous and sedimentary rocks, and are caused by shearing or tension in the rock in response to earth movements. In igneous rocks joints are formed as the rock solidifies; in sedimentary rocks they are produced during the burial and the subsequent uplift of the rock layers.

Joints are weaknesses in rocks, and when exposed to weathering are readily widened by the action of rain, frost, wind, and plant roots. They tend to be the planes along which rocks split – the results can be seen in the tumbled blocks found at the base of most cliffs and steep slopes. Some rocks have a characteristic joint pattern: granite produces the castellated appearance of the cliffs at Lands End in Cornwall. Basalt and dolerite sometimes form distinctive hexagonal columns; examples are found at the Giants Causeway in Northern Ireland, and at the Devils Post Pile National Monument in Nevada.

After assessing the large scale features of the exposure, the collector should proceed to a more detailed small scale study. A hand specimen knocked off the rock enables its texture, mineral composition, structure and hardness to be examined. Fossil content and colour may also be important.

The first thing to note is the rock's texture, which is the result of the size and shape of the constituent mineral grains, their degree of crystallisation, and their relationship with one another. Igneous rocks generally crystallise as they cool from a hot magma. Extrusive varieties which have cooled rapidly, may be vitreous or cryptocrystalline – that is, their crystal structure is too fine to be seen by the naked eye. Small crystals (up to 2mm in diameter) are characteristic of hypabyssal rocks. Larger crystals are characteristic of plutonic igneous rocks. Igneous rocks with a complex cooling history have a porphyritic texture, in which large crystals are embedded in a finer grained groundmass; this texture is common in certain granites. Rocks which have undergone high grade metamorphosis usually have crystalline structures. Limestones, and some other sedimentary rocks which are composed of one mineral may become crystalline because of the pressure of overlying rock.

Most sedimentary rocks are non-crystalline. The mineral grains forming them are usually surrounded (or have the spaces between them filled) by a matrix of much finer material, frequently clay minerals. Some sedimentary rocks, like sandstones, consist of grains held together by a cement which is deposited in the pore spaces of the rock, usually by ground-water. Sandstones which have been laid down by wind action have grains with a smooth rounded outline. The pores in a rock may remain unfilled, leaving it porous as in the case of limestone.

Schistose texture is characteristic of some metamorphic rocks in which the crystals have regrown in the metamorphic environment. The alignment of crystals of flaky or platy minerals (such as micas) along the line in which pressure was applied at the time of metamorphosis leads to a distinctive cleavage which allows the rock to be split into slabs or sheets which have a rough or wavy surface.

After the texture of the hand specimen has been examined, an attempt should be made to identify the minerals which make up the rock. The constituent minerals determine the nature of a rock, and in combination with texture give a clear indication of the type of rock. Thus granites are crystalline rocks composed of quartz, orthoclase, plagioclase and micas, all minerals which are usually identifiable in hand specimens. Similarly, limestone is readily identified by its predominant mineral, calcite, and its fine texture. The identification of the mineral alone is not sufficient to define the rock: limestone and marble are both forms of calcite, but one is sedimentary and the other metamorphic, with the result that they have very different textures.

Metamorphic rocks display structures which can often be identified in hand specimens. Gneiss has a mineral composition resembling that of granite, but its constituents are arranged in a series of roughly parallel bands, each of which consists predominantly of one mineral (though rarely of one alone). The light coloured bands contain a predominance of quartzo-feldspathic minerals, while the dark bands contain a predominance of ferromagnesian minerals. The quartz or the feldspar may appear as knots (similar in appearance to those in wood), which are very large crystals that have survived metamorphism and cause the flaky or platy minerals surrounding them to be bent around them.

This feature, which is also found in schists (where the enclosed crystal is commonly a garnet), is called an augen structure.

Igneous rocks often have an amygdaloidal structure, which is visible in hand specimens. When magma is extruded on the earth's surface, it contains gases, which form bubbles when it solidifies. These form cavities in the rock which may be empty, or lined with crystals, or completely filled with minerals. The filled cavities often look like almonds, and are called amygdales (from the Greek word for almond). One of the minerals frequently found in them is agate, usually banded in layers with different tints. In the amygdales of some basalts are zeolites, minerals with a good deal of water loosely held in channels in their crystal frameworks.

Fossils are characteristic of sedimentary rocks. They are occasionally found in pyroclastic igneous rocks or in rocks that have been lightly metamorphosed, but in general fossils do not survive metamorphism. Any rock containing fossils should be assumed to be sedimentary unless there is a very good evidence (from texture, or from the rocks it is associated with) to the contrary.

Colour is less useful as a diagnostic feature in rocks than it is in minerals. Most types of sedimentary and metamorphic rocks exist in a range of colours, depending on the amount of impurity associated with the main constituents, and on the degree of weathering at the surface. Many rocks are tinted reddish-brown by oxides of iron. Igneous rocks, however, can be roughly defined in terms of colour, depending on whether they are leucocratic, mesocratic, melanocratic, or hypermelanic.

Some rock types can be identified by examining the other rocks that they are found associated with. Any body of intrusive igneous rock will be surrounded by a metamorphic aureole, a zone of metamorphosed rocks. The rocks nearest to the area of contact will be the most metamorphosed. Thus when, for example, a gabbro intrudes into a layer of slaty rocks, a highly metamorphosed rock, hornfels, produced by complete recrystallisation of the slate, is found in the innermost parts of the aureole, while the outer limits of the aureole will be found to contain spotted rocks, slates containing small nodules of andalusite and cordierite.

In another characteristic pattern, a contact metamorphic rock is overlain by an extrusive igneous rock (often with a ropy upper surface), which is in turn overlain by a sedimentary rock or by another extrusive igneous rock.

Regional metamorphic rocks usually cover large areas. Various grades are found, which reflect the temperature and pressure prevailing in the metamorphic environment at the time of metamorphosis.

Sedimentary rocks are very varied, and no general observations on their associations are possible. Some distinctive associations do occur. Conglomerates or breccias (rudaceous rocks) often represent a marine transgression, and the overlying deposits are often sandstones and limestones, rocks which are deposited in a marine environment. In conditions where the sea withdraws from an area, limestones are often found overlain by coarse sandstones and (particularly in carboniferous strata) by coal deposits. Deposits of sandstone and clay often alternate.

IGNEOUS ROCKS

General texture : normally crystalline.
Mineral content
The constituent minerals are abbreviated as follows :
Q=quartz   O =orthoclase   P =plagioclase   M= micas
A=amphibole   Py =pyroxenes   Ol=olivine   F= feldspathoids
The figures after the mineral indicate the percentage of the mineral in the total rock.
Minerals which are present in trace quantities are indicated by (t).

General rock type	Constituent minerals
Alkali granite	Q(30), O(60), P, M.
Adamellite	Q(30), O, P, M.
Granodiorite	Q(30), P(60), O, M.
Syenite	Q(10), O(50), P, A, M.
Diorite	P(50), Py, A, M, Q(t).
Gabbro	P, Py, A, Ol.
Ultramafic	Py, A, Ol, M.
Feldspathoid igneous rock	F, P, A, M, Py.

Texture

General rock type	Coarse-grained	Medium-grained	Fine-grained
Alkali granite	Alkali granite	Microganite	Rhyolite
Adamellite	Adamellite	Microadamellite	Rhyodacite
Granodiorite	Granodiorite	Microgranodiorite	Dacite
Syenite	Syenite	Microsyenite	Trachyte
Diorite	Diorite	Microdiorite	Andesite
Gabbro	Gabbro	Dolerite	Basalt

SEDIMENTARY ROCKS

General texture : normally non-crystalline (except limestones).
Composition
The constituent minerals are abbreviated as follows :
F= feldspar   Q=quartz grains   Cl=clay minerals C=calcite
I=iron minerals   R =rock fragments Ca =carbon
The figures indicate the percentage of the mineral, in the total rock; trace quantities are indicated by (t).

General rock type	Constituents
Sandstone	Q, Cl(t).
Siltstone	Q, Cl.
Rudaceous rocks	Q, R, F, Cl(t).
Greywacke	Q, R, F, Cl(t).
Impure sandstone	Q, R, Cl(t).
Arkose	Q, F(20), R, Cl(t).
Clay	Cl.

Limestone	C.
Sandy limestone	C, Q.
Marl	C, Cl.
Ferruginous limestone	C, I(10).
Ferruginous sandstone	Q, I(10)
Bituminous sandstone	Q, Ca.
Bituminous clay	Cl, Ca.
Peat or coal	Ca.

Texture

Texture is only important in the identification of clastic rocks:

Coarse-grained	Medium-grained	Fine-grained	Constituents
	Sandstone		Q, Cl(t).
Conglomerate/ breccia	Greywacke		Q, R, F, Cl(t).
		Siltstone	Q, Cl.
		Clay	Cl.
	Arkose		Q, F(20), R, Cl(t).

METAMORPHIC ROCKS

Texture/structure

Rock type	Texture/structure
Quartzite, Marble, Granulite, Eclogite, Epidiorite	Even grained
Hornfels, epidiorite	Fine grained
Slate, phyllite	Cleavage (by alignment of minerals in one plane)
Phyllite, schist	Schistosity (pearly appearance of cleavage surface)
Gneiss, amphibolite	Gneissose structure (banded appearance)
Schist	Augen structure

General texture: normally crystalline.

Mineral content

Q = quartz   F = feldspar   A = amphiboles   Py = pyroxenes
M = micas   C = calcite   Cl = clay minerals

Rock type	Constituent minerals
Hornfels	Cl.
Slate or Phyllite	Cl, M.
Quartzite	Q.
Marble	C.
Schist	Q, F, M.
Gneiss	Q, F, M, A, Py.
Amphibolite	A, F.
Epidiorite	A, F, Py.

Part 4

Collecting

The collector can save time and trouble by doing some research before setting out in search of specimens. Before visiting an exposure, you should find out as much about it as you can: you should try to discover what types of rock occur in the area, what the succession looks like, what minerals and fossils occur in the rocks.

Maps are essential in the field, for locating yourself both geographically and geologically. The best geographical map to use is one with a scale of six inches to one mile, like those produced by the Ordnance Survey in Great Britain and by the Department of the Interior in the United States. These show sufficient detail for the collector to locate his position to within a few yards – and it is always useful to know exactly where a particular specimen was found. Good geological maps are produced by the Institute of Geological Sciences (IGS) in Great Britain and again by the Department of the Interior in the United States. The IGS one inch to the mile series are generally available, but the more generally useful six inch maps arc not; however, they can be consulted at the IGS, and copies made. The Geological Society of America produces maps, guidebooks and reports on annual field trips organised by the Society. The collector needs to know how to read a map, and should carry a reliable compass to enable him to do so accurately.

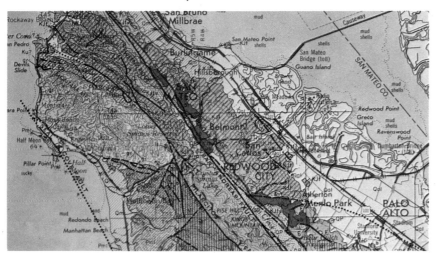

By using a geological map skilfully, you can locate exactly what type of rocks surround you and what geological processes have affected them. The illustration shows a section of a typical geological map. This particular example covers part of California, but in general appearance it is no different to a geological map produced in Britain or elsewhere. It is based on a geographical map and shows the names of physical features such as rivers, mountains or lakes, as well as settlements (towns and villages) and roads. It is therefore possible to locate yourself fairly easily with it. On this geographical map has been superimposed the nature of the rocks forming the land – those which occur immediately below the soil cover. The different rock types are coded with colours and letters (e.g. the pink area lettered 'gr' is composed of Mesozoic granite rocks); there is a key on the right-hand side of the map. This key is shown as a geological succession, with the oldest (in this case Pre-Cambrian) rocks shown at the bottom of

193

the key and the youngest at the top. The key is also divided into two columns according to whether the rocks are igneous or sedimentary in origin. Thick black lines on the map represent faults – particularly important here as the area contains the San Andreas Fault.

The detail shown covers the area north of Redwood City between San Francisco Bay and the Pacific Ocean. The most prominent rock in the area forms the bulk of Montara Mountain, the Mesozoic granite which is coloured pink. Its outcrop is almost totally fault bound. It is surrounded by Tertiary rocks. As it is Mesozoic in origin, it obviously cannot have been intruded originally into rocks which are younger in age. It must have been affected by some of the intense earth movements which have occurred in the area; the fact that it is surrounded by fault lines seems to bear this out. The most obvious example of the intense movements is the San Andreas Fault, which is seen as a thick black line crossing the map obliquely from top to bottom, coming close to Redwood City. The movements of this fault are indicated by the differing rock types which are in contact across it, as well as by the existence of ribbon lakes which follow the line of the fault just north of Redwood City. On either side of the fault are mainly Mesozoic sedimentary and igneous rocks (colour coded pale brown, green striped and purple), all of which have been intensively metamorphosed by the earth movements associated with the fault. Recent alluvial deposits (colour coded pale yellow) line the coast of San Francisco Bay and occurs in pockets on the Pacific coastline.

The collector's most essential piece of equipment is a geological hammer. There are two basic types, the crack hammer and the geologist's or chisel hammer. The crack hammer is a small sledge-hammer used for breaking rocks, for smashing open nodules or other large blocks of rock to ascertain if they contain anything of interest. The chisel hammer has a flat square head at one end and a chisel head at the other. The square end is often used in combination with a separate chisel. A 2lb chisel hammer is best, but an additional 1lb one may also be useful. Another type of hammer is similar to the chisel hammer except that it has a pointed head, known as a pick head, instead of the chisel head. It is not unlike an ice axe in appearance. It is useful for dealing with soft sedimentary rocks, when the pointed end can be used for probing or hacking. A convenient weight for this type of hammer is 1lb.

Chisels are necessary for removing specimens of hard rock. Ordinary cold chisels are ideal; smaller ones are used for the delicate job of removing crystals from rock masses, while the larger ones are hammered into fissures and cracks in rocks to split off samples for examination.

Other useful tools are a small trowel with a two or three inch blade, and a strong kitchen knife. The trowel is useful with soft sedimentary rocks such as clays, and the knife (a strong pen knife will do) is also useful for probing soft sediments. A pair of cheap goggles should be used to protect your eyes when you are hammering hard rock, which tends to splinter. A pair of strong gloves (gardening gloves are ideal) will protect your hands from cuts and grazes on the sharp edges of broken rocks.

A strong collecting bag is essential. A small canvas shoulder bag of the sort sold in government surplus stores is suitable for most purposes. A rucksack has several advantages: it leaves the hands free and allows fairly large quantities of specimens and equipment to be carried in relative comfort. Specimens should be wrapped in newspaper before being placed in the bag. They should be numbered, and the date and particulars of the location they came from recorded. More fragile specimens may break if harshly treated; they should be carefully wrapped in newspaper and as far as possible kept separate from heavy specimens. Smaller specimens are usually wrapped in newspaper and then placed in plastic bags, while the most fragile specimens are wrapped in newspaper or cotton wool and placed in a small box or tin (such as a pipe tobacco tin) to prevent them being damaged.

A small lens or pocket magnifying glass is essential for examining specimens in the field. The most suitable sort has a magnification of ten times and a half inch diameter lens which folds away inside a metal or plastic cover.

It is always worthwhile noting down exactly where you found a specimen and when you found it. A notebook and pencil should be carried for this purpose. The best procedure is to use an index number for each entry which corresponds to the number written on the paper in which the specimen is wrapped. Further notes should describe the nature of the exposure, the succession, if one is visible, and any other significant data. A camera is very useful for recording the exposure from which the specimen is taken. The frame number of the film should be noted with the other details about the specimen.

The search for mineral and rock specimens frequently involves visits to high, exposed places; in any case, the collector is liable to spend long periods out of doors in all kinds of weather. Clothing is important: an adequate waterproof outer garment such as an anorak is essential. Trousers should be heavy denims or corduroys. A sweater should be carried on any expedition that is liable to last more than a few hours. Footwear is perhaps the most important item, since the collector is liable to do a lot of walking over rough ground. Stout walking shoes or boots should be worn with fairly thick woollen socks. On expeditions into mountainous country, some extra items should be carried, including a waterproof torch, water and some food (apples, chocolates, nuts). If you are going well off the beaten track, you would be well advised to carry a polythene rescue blanket, which is a lightweight sheet of foil designed to keep out rain and snow, while keeping the person under it warm by reflecting his body heat.

There are a few other points which you should remember when collecting. If the site you wish to visit is common land, or is owned by the National Trust or some other public bodies there should be no problems, and you can go ahead and search for specimens. Some sites have rules which you should obey forbidding the 'hammering' of certain exposures. In all other cases, the permission of the owner of the land containing the exposure should be sought. In the case of a natural exposure, contact the owner and ask his permission to look at the site and take specimens. It is quite likely that he will be pleased and interested. Quarry or mine owners should also be written to in advance with an explanation of your interest and a suggested date for your visit. Usually there will be no objection, though you may be asked to sign an accident indemnity form. If you are lucky, you may be shown around by someone who has a personal knowledge of the area which may well augment your own.

An exposure of rock can be anything from a temporary hole in a road to a large coastal cliff; the essential feature is that the overlying vegetation and soil has been removed in some way so that the bedrock is exposed to examination. Temporary exposures result from road works, the digging of drains or foundations, or from landslips. They are all liable to be filled in or covered over within a fairly short period. If such an exposure looks geologically interesting, it is always worthwhile noting down the details of the succession exposed – the rock types revealed, the relationship between the rocks and any minerals or fossils they may contain – and then sending your notes to any geologist who is working in the area. The long trenches dug for drains, sewers, telephone cables or gas pipes are often very informative, since they are likely to cut across a whole series of rock formations.

Permanent exposures may also be man-made, for example road and railway cuttings; the latter are not public, so that the interested geologist should seek the permission of the railway authority controlling the area in which the exposure he wishes to examine is located. Man-made exposures which fall into disuse can rapidly become covered with debris and vegetation. Natural permanent exposures include all forms of natural rock face, such as cliffs, scars, river banks, ravines, and so on.

Old Delabole Slate Quarry, the deepest man-made exposure in Britain, excavated since the sixteenth century for its unique slate deposits which were laid down in the tropical seas of the Devonian period. The slate is used for roofing tiles, for example of the Houses of Parliament in London.

A temporary exposure produced by a roadside landslip at Nuthall, Nottinghamshire.

A natural inland exposure: bedded Triassic sediments – Keuper marl – at Colwick, Nottinghamshire.

A natural coastal exposure: the chalk cliffs of south eastern England – the Seven Sisters, near Seaford, Sussex.

Above: The Shap Blue Quarry, Westmorland.

Left: The cutting for the M6 motorway at Tebay, Westmorland, showing folded Paleozoic sediments.

Quarries are of particular interest to the geologist. Large amounts of material are removed for commercial exploitation, leaving wide areas of exposed rock which reveal much about the geology of the area. The Shap Granite Quarry in Westmorland, for example, exposes nearly the whole of a granite intrusion, in which the method and times of the intrusion of magma are clearly revealed, along with details of the associated mineralisation. The adjoining Shap Blue Quarry reveals how the intrusion of granite affected the surrounding rock by metamorphosing it and infiltrating it with mineral veins. The ironstone quarries of North Lincolnshire expose most of the lower Jurassic succession in the area. By simply walking down one of the access roads leading to the quarries, you can identify every bed in the succession. The Lane's Trap Quarry at Amherst, Massachussetts, is a famous source of igneous rocks.

Some road and railway cuttings, notably those made for large modern motorways and highways, reveal almost as much as large quarries. For example, the cutting on the northbound carriageway of the M6 motorway between Kendal and Penrith in England shows in perfect detail the folding of the lower Paleozoic sediments caused by the Caledonian uplift.

When the rock cutting takes place underground, as in mines, it is not possible for the amateur geologist to see the exposure. However, the spoil heaps associated with mines are good sources of minerals and fossils; they also provide information about the rocks beneath the surface. For example, it is possible to collect good specimens of the various tin materials from the spoil heaps of tin mines in Cornwall, while good specimens of lead minerals can be found in the spoil heaps of mines around Keswick, in Cumberland and in the Joplin district of Missouri.

Natural exposures vary considerably, depending on their location. Mountainous areas obviously tend to contain much larger areas of exposed rocks than lowland areas. Most such exposures are inland

A granite tor: Rough Tor, Bodmin Moor, Cornwall.

199

Left: A Carboniferous limestone scar, Gordale, Yorkshire.

Right: Cliffs expose varied rocks, and the surface is kept clean by wave action. *Above:* horizontal beds in Orkney. *Below:* Trebarwith Strand, Cornwall – typical cliff of sediments folded and faulted during the intrusion of granites when Cornwall was the heart of a mountain chain.

Below: An igneous rock surface may be so hard that brute force will fail to dislodge a specimen from it: granite at Tregastel, Brittany, France.

and are deeply weathered, so that fresh rock surfaces can be exposed only by hammering. Coastal exposures are the most fruitful: cliffs reveal large sections of the geological succession. Cliffs are subjected to continual erosion, so that the faces are normally fresh, particularly after winter storms.

The method of collection employed at an exposure depends on the kind of specimen being collected. Rocks, minerals and fossils require different techniques, as do varying textures of rock. The technique of collection is also dependent on the nature of the exposure, a fresh rock surface requiring a different method from a weathered surface or a spoil heap.

Igneous and metamorphic rocks are crystalline (or highly baked, in the case of rocks that have undergone contact metamorphosis) and hard: brute force will not dislodge a specimen, and even the use of a sledge-hammer on the rock face will only powder the surface and jar the collector's arm. A scientific approach is more effective. Look for any sign of weakness in the rock, such as a crack or projection, and attack it using a fairly heavy hammer (2lb) and a cold chisel. If there is a projection, the chisel should be applied to its base and given a few sharp blows with the hammer; the projection should crack along its base and break away, giving you your specimen. A crack can often be opened by a few blows from a chisel, so that fragments of rock break off. Some apparent weak spots may not res-

pond to this treatment. The only solution is to keep looking until you find one that does.

The hard sedimentary rocks include most lower Paleozoic sediments (which have been subjected to a great deal of tectonic activity), limestones and many sandstones. There are many fine exposures of Paleozoic rocks in the Gros Ventre area of Wyoming. The best example of a hard sedimentary rock is the Carboniferous limestone. As with igneous and metamorphic rocks, the collector has to search for weaknesses which he can exploit in order to get his specimen. In the case of sedimentary rocks, the bedding planes often form lines of relative weakness, particularly if the rock is fairly thinly bedded. By placing the chisel at right angles to the bedding plane, a slab of the rock can often be detached.

The soft sedimentary rocks, which include clays, shales, and some sandstones, often have the consistency of mud, particularly in some Mesozoic and Cainozoic deposits. When dry, they are easily broken by hand. Specimens can usually be removed with a small trowel or with a light, pointed hammer.

Minerals are collected in a slightly different way. In the case of a mineral specimen found embedded in a hard igneous or metamorphic rock which you want to remove, the technique is not to try removing the specimen from the rock, but to remove the whole piece of rock surrounding it, and to extract the mineral later at home or in a workshop. By attempting to simply extract the mineral from the rock

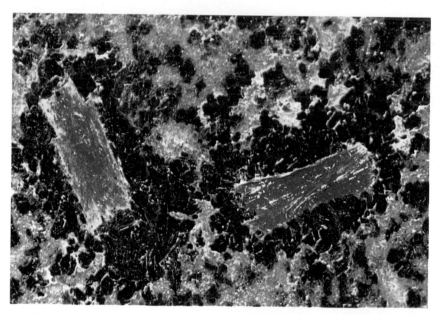

Rubies in igneous rock from Zambia.

surface you stand a very good chance of destroying it; it is better to put up with carrying a large piece of rock for a while than to end up with nothing. The only minerals likely to be of interest in hard sedimentary rocks would probably occur in veins running across the rock. The collector should take out a section of the vein and examine it at home for individual mineral specimens.

The minerals which can be collected from soft, fine grained sedimentary rocks are those which have been reproduced by diagenesis,

A mineral vein in sedimentary rock exposed by road cutting for the new harbour at Roscoff, Brittany, France.

Sedimentary rocks often contain nodules which, when cracked open, reveal mineralised interiors. *Left:* a septarian nodule from Hurricane, Utah. *Right:* a thunder egg from Madras, Oregon.

like the large crystals of selenite (often up to two inches across) found in the Gault clay in the Weald of Kent. It is normally possible to remove such specimens from the clay in the field, particularly at coastal exposures where running water will frequently have separated the minerals from the clay.

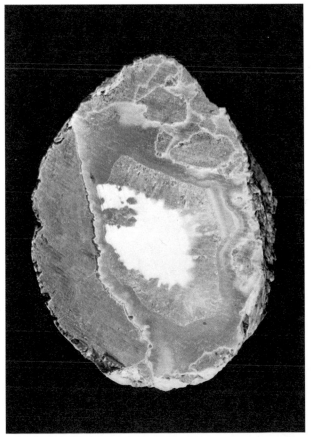

Fossil collecting is generally similar to mineral collecting, though even more careful observation is necessary. Some luck is also involved, for though an area may be known to contain fossils, they may be very unevenly distributed. For the removal of fossils from hard sedimentary rocks, the procedure is similar to that for removing mineral specimens from hard igneous or metamorphic rocks. The rock surrounding the fossil should be extracted in one piece, and the specimen removed and cleaned up later at home. It is important to note that when you are collecting from hard sedimentary rocks your chisel should always be directed away from the fossil which is to be removed; this avoids damaging the fossil should the chisel slip, and reduces the possibility of a piece of rock splitting off along with a piece of the fossil. Large numbers of fossil brachiopods, gastropods, tribolites and echinoids are found in the Permian rocks of the Supai formation in eastern Arizona. Fossils preserved in soft sedimentary rocks such as clays are often in a fairly soft condition themselves, and great care is needed when removing them. They should be dug out gently, using a knife and a small trowel.

Rock collecting from weathered surfaces is relatively easy, since such surfaces are usually surrounded by a lot of debris, much of it of specimen size. Samples of rock are easy to remove from a weathered surface; even though the specimen may have a weathered surface, fresh rock can be exposed by breaking it open. Spoil heaps usually consist of specimen-sized pieces of rock. Those on the surface may be deeply weathered but specimens from deeper down will be in an unweathered condition.

Weathered surfaces obscure any interesting minerals contained in the rock, and the minerals themselves are often weathered or altered. To obtain a specimen of the mineral, remove the weathered debris and treat the underlying rock as a fresh face. Spoil heaps frequently contain many interesting mineral specimens, as the rocks have been broken open in the mining process and the minerals exposed. An afternoon spent scouring a spoil heap for mineral specimens is usually very profitable to the collector.

A weathered rock surface, the man-made exposure of Old Delabole Slate Quarry, with a scree containing specimen size samples.

Bornite from Pima County, Arizona, showing a weathered tarnish on the surface of the mineral.

Loose rock at Shap Granite Quarry, Westmorland.

Fossils are easier to see on a weathered face than they are on a fresh face because the fossil and the rock containing it react differently to the weathering processes and the fossil frequently stands out in relief. Such fossils are often found in limestones. In spoil heaps from quarries or mines using sedimentary rocks (such as cement works) nearly perfect fossils are frequently found. The weathering process separates the fossils from their parent rock, and the process is often accelerated when the fossil is thrown on to the heap. A careful search of a spoil heap (particularly the lower slopes) often produces fossils which can be added to a collection without the trouble of removing them from solid rock.

Inevitably, you are more likely to find typical specimens than exceptional ones. In the case of rocks, the specimens can only be typical. The only variation in quality of specimens depends on the

You may find a specimen of bismuth like the one (left) from Cornwall, but you are more likely to find one like that below, from Whitby, Yorkshire.

care with which they are extracted or selected. With minerals, small misformed crystals are much more common than two-inch long perfectly formed ones. You may be able to start collecting exceptional specimens from the outset if you are fortunate to live in an area known for the quality of its minerals, such as the Boulder County area of Colorado, where 67 different vein forming minerals have been identified, or the Harding Mine at Dixon, New Mexico, an area of pegmatites which yield fine crystals of muscovite, microlite, lapidolite, and spodumene. Otherwise, you should build up a collection of typical specimens and augment it with any better specimens you may find subsequently. The situation is the same for the collector of fossils: the one-inch slightly flattened and broken brachiopod is much more common than the eight-inch flawless brachiopod. Again, some areas are richer in fine fossil specimens than others: the collector with access to the Croixan series of mountains running across south west Montana and north west Wyoming, for example, should be able to build up a collection of fine specimens of fossil brachiopods and arthropods. Less fortunate collectors should begin by collecting whatever specimens they can find, and improve the collection with better examples as they find them. If you find anything that appears really exceptional or unusual, take it to a museum and show it to an expert there; it will not be taken from you if you want to keep it, but should anyone else want to study it at a later date, the museum will have a record of its whereabouts.

The cliff at Aust, Gloucestershire, which contains many fine fossils, particularly in the Rhaetic Bone Bed.

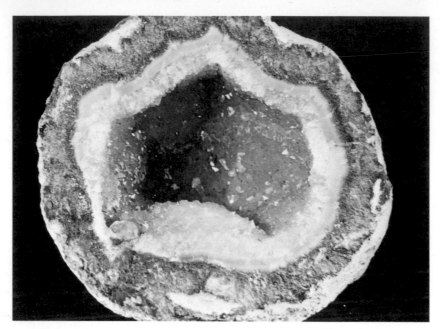

A fine geode from Durango, Mexico. If you find anything like this, you may consider yourself lucky.

There are several points for the collector to bear in mind when seeking access to an exposure. In addition to the need to get permission from the owner, there is the problem of actually getting to the site. If there is a road or track passing nearby then access is easy, but if the exposure is isolated, as is often the case in upland or coastal areas, you may have to travel overland to get there. You are likely to be travelling over someone's land, so remember a few basic rules: keep to paths, and avoid cutting across fields which have crops in them; close gates behind you; do not frighten any animals in the fields; do not leave litter behind you. The simple rules, known in Britain as the Country Code, are the basis of peaceful co-existence between the farmer or landowner and visitors to the countryside.

If you find that the exposure is fenced off, do not disregard the fencing: it will have been put there for a purpose. Possibly the ground is unsafe. If you are physically barred from the exposure in this way, try to find out why. If the ground is unsafe or the rock face is dangerous, there may be a sign telling you so. It may be that the fence is simply there to keep animals away from the site. If this appears to be so, and the ground looks safe, that is, without obvious cracks or holes, you can proceed.

Rock faces are potentially dangerous. Caves and mine workings have their obvious hazards, as do flooded gravel pits. Working quarries need to be approached sensibly: respect any warning notices, and make sure you know what time blasting occurs in the quarry. If a quarryman tells you that a particular face is dangerous, then approach it with extra care. Coastal exposures, particularly those with high cliffs, need to be treated with respect. Find out the times of the tides to minimize the risk of being cut off when collecting in some inaccessible area. Be careful when seeking specimens in a crumbling cliff face: violent digging in an attempt to remove a specimen can bring down the rocks above you. Avoid areas where the cliffs overhang or are undercut.

If you are going to visit exposures alone, particularly in coastal or mountainous areas, tell someone where you are going and when you expect to be back. For expeditions into really remote or inaccessible areas, you should not travel alone; always take at least one companion and make sure you are properly equipped.

When you are at the exposure, treat it with respect. Do not hammer it unnecessarily. If you come across a particularly fine specimen in a rock but find difficulty in removing it, do not continue trying as you may well damage it, while a better equipped or more skilful collector might be able to remove it quite easily. If you are visiting one of the classic geological exposures, do not hammer excessively; better still do not hammer at all. Such sites are used extensively for research, and your indiscriminate hammering may destroy something of great value. It is much better to leave these sites alone and find other sites with similar rock and mineral specimens from which to take your specimens.

Do not throw rocks around at exposures: there may be other people around in danger of being hit. Do not let rocks roll down a slope or face when you have removed and discarded them: there may be someone else further down the slope. When hammering a hard rock, face be very careful, since the slivers that break off are often razor sharp and can glance off with considerable speed; wear a pair of cheap goggles, or cover the rock with a cloth or a thick layer of newspaper before hitting it with your hammer. A little forethought, and the application of these few basic rules, makes collecting a much safer business.

POLISHING AND CUTTING

Exceptionally fine rock and mineral specimens, for example large, well-formed crystals, are usually displayed in their natural state. Ordinary specimens can be treated by cutting and polishing to make them suitable for display or for use in jewellery. Attractive small, irregular shaped specimens can be given a high polish by hand or by tumbling them in a tumbling machine. Gemstones, pebbles and rock fragments may be cut, ground and polished to form cabochons, which are normally smooth, flat-backed domes. Facet cutting is usually reserved for gemstones: the surface is cut in a series of planes which are designed to refract and reflect light to maximum effect, enhancing the brilliancy of the stone. All these techniques can be applied only to specimens of sufficient hardness (above 3 on Moh's scale of hardness); soft sedimentary rocks such as shales and clays will not take a polish. On the other hand, very hard specimens need a great deal of work to give them a perfect polish.

The surface of the specimen is smoothed and polished by grinding it with another material. This material obviously needs to be harder than the specimen which is to be treated. Diamond, at the top of Moh's scale with a hardness of 10, is the ideal material to use – but it is expensive. Silicon carbide (carborundum) is made commercially by heating silicon dioxide with carbon in an electric furnace at a temperature of 2000°C; it is extremely hard, standing at approximately

9.5 on Moh's scale, and can therefore be used to grind and polish most rock and mineral specimens. Despite its closeness to it on Moh's scale, diamond is many times harder than silicon carbide – the scale indicates only relative hardness. Some hard gemstones, such as ruby, sapphire, emerald, and topaz, can be worked only with diamond-impregnated tools.

Silicon carbide is sold as a silver coloured grit, in various grades, which correspond to the grades of sandpaper. The grades are measured by the number of holes to the square inch in the mesh through which the grit was graded. Grades 60 and 80 are very coarse, 220 is coarse, 400 is fine, and from 600 to 1200 are very fine. Similar grades are available on impregnated grinding wheels, and on sandpaper.

Some softer rocks (less than hardness 6 on Moh's scale) can be ground by hand, but the process is slow and laborious. A rounded, water-worn pebble can be given a gloss by hand, using sandpaper. The stone is rubbed against the paper, which is laid flat on a soft surface such as foam rubber or newspaper. Coarse paper (220) is used first, and then progressively finer grades (400 and 600) until the surface is smooth and without scratches. The process is completed by polishing the stone on wet felt or leather with tin oxide or cerium oxide polishing powder. It is important to wash the pebble and your hands thoroughly between each stage : the whole effort can be ruined by a stray particle of silicon carbide grit finding its way into the polishing stage.

Flat surfaces can be given a high polish by hand. The only equipment needed is a flat steel plate, one foot square and at least $\frac{1}{4}$ inch thick, a piece of plate glass of similar size, silicon carbon grit in grades 120, 240, and 600, a tin of metal polish and a piece of soft felt. The steel plate is wetted and covered with a thin layer of 120 grade grit, and the specimen is rubbed over it, with the face to be polished downwards. The direction of rubbing should be varied – a figure of eight motion achieves this and allows a rhythm to be set up. More water and grit should be added as needed. When the surface is flat and free from irregularities it should be washed thoroughly, along with the steel plate. The plate is wetted again, and covered with a layer of 240 grade grit; the specimen is rubbed over it until its surface has a smooth matt finish. Again the specimen and the plate should be washed thoroughly. Next, the glass plate is wetted and covered with a thin layer of 600 grade silicon carbide powder; the specimen is rubbed over it until a fine-smooth surface is obtained. The surface should feel silky to touch. Before the final polishing stage, the specimen should be washed thoroughly, and the working area carefully cleared up : all traces of the grinding grits should be removed. The surface of the specimen can then be polished by buffing it with metal polish on a wad of felt.

Polishing stones by hand is hard work; the effort can be eliminated by the use of a simple tumbling machine. This machine simulates the action of waves and rivers in nature, tumbling and buffeting sharp-edged pebbles against each other until they become rounded and smooth. It consists of a tough plastic or moulded rubber barrel (or metal barrel with a rubber lining) fitted with a watertight cap. It is mounted on rollers which are driven by a small electric motor.

A simple tumbling machine.

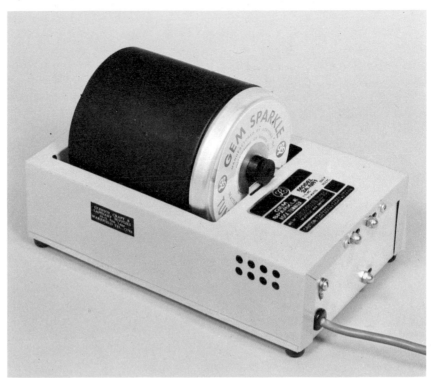

The tumbler barrel may be any size from a pint upwards – a pint barrel will hold about a pound of fairly small specimens. The specimens are placed in the barrel with some silicon carbide grit and water and the barrel is rotated for periods of up to four weeks for each stage of the grinding and polishing process. Thus, when buying a machine you would be well advised to look for one which, apart from being efficient, is constructed to minimise the noise output. Fortunately, some of the least expensive, simply constructed machines are capable of producing excellent results.

The first stage in the tumbling process is the selection of the specimens. They should all be of a similar size and hardness. Material of hardness 5.50 or less is liable to be crumbled to powder. Flakey, chipped or cracked specimens should be left out. The quantity of specimens to be polished will depend on the size of the tumbler barrel: a one quart barrel, as is envisaged here, holds about 2lbs. The specimens should be washed and placed in the barrel (they should $\frac{2}{3}$ fill it), and 2oz. of grade 80 silicon carbide grit added. Water, specimens should be washed and placed in the barrel (they should two-thirds fill it), and 2oz of grade 80 silicon carbide grit added. Water, sufficient to cover the specimens, is then added. The lid is fitted, and checked to ensure that it is secure and free from leaks. The barrel is placed on the rollers of the machine, and tumbled for seven to ten days, depending on the original hardness of the specimens. The machine should be stopped each day, and the contents examined. This allows the release of any gas pressure that may have built up as a result of the grinding process, which can be dangerous if allowed to accumulate. More water or grit should be added as needed. When the specimens have lost their surface irregularities and discolourations they should be washed thoroughly, along with the barrel, to remove all traces of the coarse grit. This should not be done in a sink, since an accumulation of grit can block drains. The stones should be washed in a colander over a bucket or bowl, and the barrel rinsed into the same container. The mixture of grit and water can then be filtered through thick layers of newspaper, and the residue thrown away.

For the second stage grind, the specimens are returned to the barrel, along with 2oz of 220 grade silicon carbide grit and sufficient water to cover them. The barrel is tumbled for seven days, and the contents checked each day. At the end of this period the specimens should be completely smooth to the touch. They and the barrel should be washed thoroughly again, and the process repeated using 2oz of 400 grade silicon carbide grit. At the end of seven days the specimens should feel silky to the touch, and should look bright and colourful. A small magnifying glass is useful for checking that all the flaws and scratches have been removed. Before polishing the specimens and the barrel should be thoroughly washed, and the whole working area cleaned. Silicon carbide grit is so clinging and pervasive, and it is so essential to keep the polishing operation free from any trace of it, that it is a worthwhile investment to buy a second tumbler barrel, and use it exclusively for polishing. The specimens are placed in this barrel with care, to avoid scratching them, and 2oz of tin or cerium oxide polishing powder added, along with sufficient water to cover them. A small quantity of buffer material, such as cork fragments or plastic granules, should also be added; this helps cushion the revolving specimens. The barrel is then tumbled for two days without stopping. If after this period the specimens have a high gloss surface, the process is complete. If not, they should be tumbled for two further days. They should finally be washed in a mild detergent. When dry, they should have a high polish on all surfaces.

Tumbled stones.

A lapping saw.

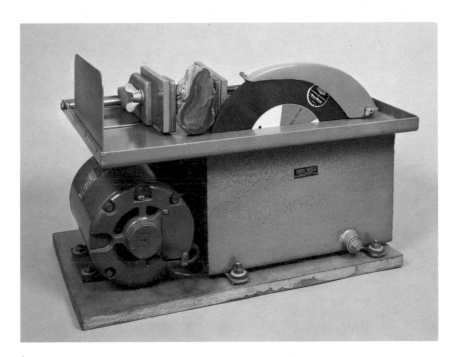

Further work with rock and mineral specimens, such as making them into cabochons for use in jewellery, involves the use of a lapping saw. This is a circular saw with a diameter of six to eight inches, which has its edge impregnated with small diamonds. The edge of the blade does not have teeth and is not sharp to touch: the blade does not cut through rock in the normal way, but rather grinds it. It is in effect a very thin grindstone. It may be mounted either vertically or horizontally. In use, the blade rotates very rapidly, and a constant supply of lubrication is necessary. The lubricant also keeps the blade cool at the point of friction between it and the specimen which is being cut. It runs steadily over the blade from a tank built into the machine. The type of coolant used should be that specified by the manufacturer: water is frequently recommended, though some lapping saws need a light machine oil. The manufacturer's instructions regarding the blade should be read with great care, since some blades are designed to be run in a reverse direction at some point in their working lives, while others must never be reversed. The lapping saw is used to cut irregular specimens into regular shapes (slabbing), and to trim off excess material before grinding a specimen into a cabochon or facetted form. It can also be used to produce specific shapes which can then be smoothed and polished in the tumbler, so that the general outline made by the saw cuts remains.

Lapping saws are sometimes part of lapidary machines which use the same small electric motor to drive a series of grinding wheels. Machines designed solely for grinding and polishing are also made. The grinding wheels, which may be horizontal or vertical, are usually six to eight inches in diameter and half to one inch thick. They are made of different grades of silicon carbide, the most popular being 100 and 220. The sanding and polishing discs are similar to the sanding discs used with household electric drills, and are impregnated with silicon carbide of grades 400 and 600 respectively. As with the diamond

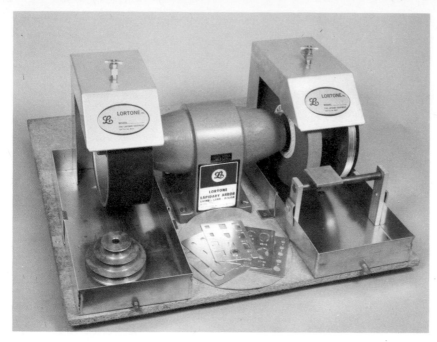

A lapidary machine.

lapping saw, the grinding wheels and sanding/polishing discs require a constant stream of coolant when in use. A drip feed arrangement is normally incorporated in the design, along with a splash guard to protect the motor. The buffing wheel, which is used for polishing, is normally made of hard felt, kept dry and impregnated with tin oxide powder, or of perspex, scored and grooved and covered with a paste of tin oxide powder. Leather can also be used.

For drilling holes in mineral specimens, for example for use in a necklace, a diamond drill is used. This is a specialised tool – a

Diamond drills.

diamond-tipped bit cannot be used in an ordinary home power tool. Purpose-built machines, running at speeds of up to 9000 r.p.m. off a twelve volt battery, are widely available. A stand for the drill helps prevent breaking the expensive diamond bits. The method of operation will be set out fully in the manufacturer's instructions, which should be followed carefully. Very delicate drilling operations are carried out using a different type of drill, which consists of a fine metal tube which is carefully raised and lowered on to the specimen. The specimen is in a container with water and silicon carbide grit. The rotating tube is lowered on to the specimen for a few seconds, and then lifted, to allow water to cool the bottom of the hole and to deposit more grit. The process is repeated until the hole is finished.

The cabochon is one of the simplest shapes in jewellery. Simple versions can be made by slicing symmetrically shaped pebbles on the lapping saw, and then finishing them off on the grinding and polishing machine. However this method will rarely allow the stone to be used in one of the range of fittings made for use with cabochons. It is usual to start with an unpolished pebble which is then cut and ground to a specified size. The required shape is marked on the flat surface which is to be the base of the cabochon. The easiest way to do this is to use a plastic template – these are available stamped out in a variety of shapes which correspond in size to the range of available cabochon mounts and fittings. The specimen is then ground down to the shape that has been marked, using the 120 grade silicon carbide grinding wheel. The base should then be smoothed by holding it lightly against the side of the grinding wheel to remove any scratches or saw marks. The side of the grinding wheel should never be used for any heavy grinding. The base is completed by creating a slight bevel around its edge, which is done by passing it across the grinding wheel at a slight angle. The stone is now ready for dopping – the process of attaching a handle so that the stone can be more easily worked. The equipment needed is a length of wooden dowel about five inches long and between a quarter and three-quarters of an inch thick, and some dopping wax, which is sealing wax containing a little powdered shellac. A small amount of the wax is heated in an old saucepan until it melts, and one end of the dopping stick is dipped into it until it is thickly covered with hot wax. It is then twirled to spread the wax evenly, and then placed firmly, wax end down, on a flat metal surface. The wax will flatten out as it cools, leaving a conical, flat-surfaced bed of wax at the end of the stick. The specimen to be ground is heated gently in a low oven, until it is hot enough to melt the dopping wax. The waxed end of the dopping stick is heated until the wax is hot and just melting, and then is brought firmly together with the flat base of the hot specimen. The specimen is adjusted so that it is centred over the stick, and the cooling wax is moulded beneath it to provide a firm seat. It is then allowed to cool and harden.

The specimen is now ready for grinding on the 120 grade grinding wheel. It is held by the dopping stick, with one hand near the specimen and the other at the end of the stick, and brought into contact with the wheel at an angle of roughly 45 degrees. The dopping stick is slowly rotated, so that a bevel is produced around the side of the specimen. The angle at which the specimen is held to the wheel is increased, and another bevel cut. This process is continued until a rough dome shape, consisting of a series of bevels, is produced. The specimen must be rotated continuously during this process, to prevent any flat areas forming. The roughly shaped specimen is returned to the grinding wheel and rocked gently backwards and forwards, so that the angles and irregularities between the successive bevels are gradually eliminated, leaving a continuous smooth dome.

The coarse grinding will have left a surface with some scratches on it. These are removed on the 220 grade grinding wheel, after the specimen has been thoroughly washed in clean water. Grinding on the fine wheel requires quite a delicate touch : the stick should be rotated rapidly and kept moving across the wheel to prevent the formation of any flat areas. When the surface is smooth, the specimen should be washed again. It is now ready for sanding, which is done on a sanding sheet attached to the rubber-faced disc on the machine. Using 320 or 400 grade silicon carbide sanding discs, the specimen is rolled and moved quickly and lightly across the spinning disc until all the scratches caused by the fine grinding are removed, and the surface is flawless. Water from a plastic bottle should be applied to the disc during the operation. The cabochon should now have a smooth matt finish, and is ready for polishing.

Cabochon stones.

Before polishing, both the dopped stone and your hands should be thoroughly washed, to ensure that no stray silicon carbide grit gets into the final process and ruins it. The polishing is done with the felt buffing wheel, which is coated with a paste made of tin (or cerium) oxide polishing powder and water. The cabochon is rotated across the face of the spinning pad for a few minutes, using firm pressure. The result should be a mirror finish on the smooth domed surface. The cabochon can be removed from the dopping stick by gently heating the wax, or by placing them in the freezer compartment of a refrigerator for a few minutes, which contracts the wax and allows the stone to drop off.

Faceting is a more complicated technique than cabochon cutting. Until quite recently, it was practised only by professional lapidaries, since its use on diamonds and precious gems requires a considerable knowledge of the principles of the refraction of light and of mathematics. Special cuts have been evolved, such as the 'brilliant' cut for diamonds, which are suited to the original crystal form, and which enhance the stone's brilliancy. These specialist techniques are beyond the reach of the amateur, but semi-precious stones can be faceted successfully using quite simple equipment.

The equipment consists of a horizontal grinding wheel, which is usually made of copper impregnated with diamonds. This type of wheel is expensive, but necessary, because most minerals which can be faceted have a hardness greater than 7. Two grades of wheel are commonly used, 400 grade and 800 grade; silicon carbide grit wheels of grades 320 and 600 can be used, but they tend to wear out rapidly when used with very hard minerals. The wheel is lubricated constantly while in use, usually with water from a drip-feed device.

Because faceting requires that the stone is held at an exact angle to the grinding wheel, the dopping stick cannot be held in the hand as in cabochon cutting. Instead it is held in a device known as a faceting head, which is attached to a vertical bar (the mast) on the side of the grinding wheel unit. The faceting head is an angled bar, the upper part of which is attached to a toothed gearwheel. This is an index gear, which allows the faceting head to be moved through any number

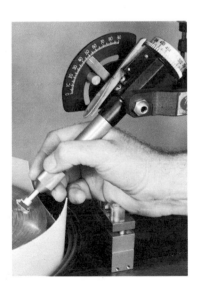

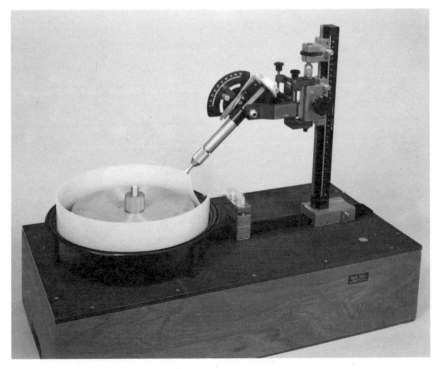

A faceting machine, and (above) the head in use.

217

of positions, depending on how many facets are to be cut. The lower end of the faceting head has a drill bit chuck, into which the dopping stick carrying the specimen is fitted. At the top end of the faceting head there is a calibrated quadrant head, which gives an exact reading of the angle at which the lower end is being held against the grinding wheel. It can be set to pre-determine the angle.

A wide variety of facet cuts are possible. There are several books on faceting written for the amateur which give precise instructions regarding procedure, and which contain indispensable charts indicating the angles of the cut and the points on the index gear which must be used for each particular type of faceted stone. For example, with an index gear which has 64 teeth (some have 32 or 48), the charts reveal that faces cut at settings 0, 8, 16, 24, 32, 40, 48, and 56 will give a symmetrical stone with eight facets. It is important to remember that opposite faces should be cut alternately; thus in the above example the order would be 0, 32, 48, 16, 24, 56, 8, 40. When the angle of cut and the required number of faces have been determined, the machine is set up appropriately and the grinding and polishing proceeds as described for cabochon cutting.

Polishing faceted stones can be quite difficult. All the cutting of all the faces should be completed before any of them is polished.

Faceted stones.

A mixture of tin oxide polishing powder and water on a felt buffer is used. Firm pressure should be applied, and the buffer kept moist. Each facet should take only ten to fifteen seconds to polish. The greatest problem is scratches, which are caused by grit or hard dust getting on the buffer, or by a small piece breaking off from a corner of the specimen. The completed faceted stone should be carefully examined under light from a clear (not pearly or frosted) bulb; it should have a polish that is flat, without scratches, and which extends over the whole of each facet. Such a perfect result usually takes a few attempts to achieve.

Rock and mineral specimens which have been tumbled or cut and polished can be used or presented in a number of ways. Bright tumbled pebbles can be displayed in glass jars or in dishes. Small irregular-shaped specimens which have been tumbled and highly polished are the basis of baroque jewellery. There are an enormous number of jewellery fittings, known as findings, which can be used for making necklaces, bracelets, pendants, or cuff links. The polished specimens are nowadays attached to the mounts with epoxy resin. Larger specimens can be used as paperweights.

Cabochons can be set in any kind of jewellery mount designed for a flat surface. These include rings, cuff links, pendants, and bracelets. Special fittings made for use with cabochons have a raised edge which is folded over the stone after it has been glued in position. There are many catalogues of cabochon fittings in a wide variety of sizes and styles.

Faceted specimens can be simply displayed against a black velvet background, or they can be incorporated in jewellery. The most common use is in rings. However, ring settings designed for faceted stones are not widely available, so it is worth designing your faceted stone so that it will fit a cabochon ring mount. This is done by grinding a flat base on the stone which fits the mount.

A selection of settings for stones.

Bibliography

Barber, Janet   *Pebbles as a Hobby*   1972

Bennison, G. M. & Wright, A. E.   *The Geological History of the British Isles*   1967

Boegel, H.   *Collectors Guide to Minerals and Gemstones*   1971

Bottley, E. P.   *Rocks and Minerals*   1969

Calder, N.   *Restless Earth : report on the new geology*   1972

Casanova, R.   *Fossil Collecting*   1960

Deeson, A. F. L. (ed.)   *The Collector's Encyclopedia of Rocks and Minerals*   1973

Delair, J. B.   *Collecting Rocks and Fossils*   1967

Eiby, G. A.   *Earthquakes*   1967

Evans, I. O.   *Rocks, Minerals and Gemstones*   1972

Fenton, C. L. & M. A.   *The Rock Book*   1952

Fletcher, E.   *Rock and Gem polishing*   1973

Franck, A. E. & Metz, R.   *Minerals and Precious Stones*   1973

Gaskell, T. F.   *Physics of the Earth*   1970

Gass, I. G., Smith, P. J., & Wilson, R. C. L.   *Understanding the Earth*   1971

Harland, H. B.   *Earth, Rocks, Minerals, and Fossils*   1960

Holmes, A.   *Principles of Physical Geology*   1965

Hurlbut, C. S.   *Minerals and Man*   1972

Mason, B. & Berry, L. G.   *Elements of Mineralogy*   1968

Olson, D. F.   *Stone grinding and polishing*   1973

Pough, F. H.   *Field guide to rocks and minerals*   1970

Read, H. H. (ed.)   *Rutley's Elements of Mineralogy*   1962

Scarfe, H.   *Cutting and setting stones*   1972

Rogers, C.   *Rocks and Minerals*   1973

Tarling, D. H. & A. P.   *Continental Drift*   1971

Warring, R.   *Rock collecting and making semi-precious jewellery : cutting and polishing gemstones*   1972

Wegener, A.   *The Origins of Continents and Oceans*   1966

Wilcoxson, K.   *Volcanoes*   1967

Zin, H. S. & Shaffer, P. R.   *Rocks and minerals – a guide to familiar minerals, gems, ores, and rocks*   1965

Books, guides, maps, and sources of information of use to the collector:
The British Regional Geology Handbooks

These are indispensable to the serious collector. They contain an introduction to the area with a guide to research and physical features; an analysis of the rocks in the area, period by period; a description of the structure of the area; a summary of the economic products of the area; and a list of maps and specialist publications. They do not give any specific localities, but they do give detailed descriptions of successions in various areas. The series, published by HMSO, covers areas :

> Northern England
> London and the Thames Valley
> Central England

East Yorkshire and Lincolnshire
The Wealden District
South-west England
East Anglia and adjoining areas
South Wales
North Wales
Pennines and adjacent areas
Bristol and Gloucester district
The Hampshire Basin and adjoining areas
Grampian Highlands
Northern Highlands
South of Scotland
Midland Valley of Scotland
Tertiary Volcanic Districts

The Geological Society of America

This society publishes guide books, maps, and memoirs which give detailed reports on annual field trips organised by the Society, and which explain the geology of interesting areas of the United States.

The Geologists' Association Centenary Guides

Published by the Geologists' Association in England, this series of approximately 40 guides covers areas of special interest in the British Isles, including such areas as the Lake District, Dartmoor, and the Yorkshire Coast. They list specific exposures and give details of what can be found there, and maps showing where each exposure is.

Proceedings of the Geologists' Association

The journal of the Geologists' Association is published four times a year, and often contains reports of field meetings which normally give details of exposures, successions, and specimens worth collecting.

Magazines

Gems (The British Lapidary Magazine), 29 Ludgate Hill, London E.C.4 : this gives details of exposures in localities in Britain and throughout the world. The magazine also publishes special guides such as *Finding Britain's Gems* and *A Map of Gemstone Sites in the British Isles.*

The Lapidary Journal of the United States, P.O. Box 80937-E, San Diego, California 92138, U.S.A. : this is essentially the American equivalent of *Gems.* Similar publications include :

Gems and Minerals, P.O. Box 687, Mentone, California 92359, U.S.A.

Rocks and Minerals, Box 29, Peekskill, New York, U.S.A.

Canadian Rockhound, P.O. Box 191, Station A, Vancouver 1, British Columbia, Canada.

Rockhound, 24–9 Trellick Tower, 5 Golborne Road, London, W.10, England.

Maps

One inch and six inch geological maps are produced by the Institute of Geological Sciences in England. Very good geological maps are produced by the U.S. Department of the Interior. The Geological Society of America also produces its own maps of areas of special geological interest.

MINERAL
IDENTIFICATION

Before setting out, the collector should find out as much as he can about the area he is to visit, since the nature of the geological environment is a good guide to the probable nature of the minerals to be found there. Thus an area of igneous rocks is certain to be made up of rocks formed from the major silicate minerals, and is likely to contain oxides and silicates as accessory minerals (see pp 99—104). The successful collector is one who knows what to look for at each exposure.

In the tables that follow, the minerals are classified according to their chemical composition. The silicates are the largest group, and the other major groups are the elements, the oxides, the hydroxides, the sulphides, the sulphates, the carbonates, phosphates, and the chlorides. The less common mineral, the tellurides, arsenides, vanadates, etc., are treated as separate groups. The chemical tests on pp 113—116 should give some idea of the elements contained in a specimen (a list of chemical symbols for all the elements appears on p 69), and in many cases the tests with acids will establish which chemical group the specimen belongs to. Physical features which will help confirm the identity of the mineral – colour, lustre, streak, fracture, cleavage, hardness, specific gravity (see pp 104—111) – are also included in the tables.

The following tables are reproduced from *The Collector's Encyclopedia of Rocks and Minerals* edited by A. F. L. Deeson (published in Britain by David & Charles, and in America by Clarkson N. Potter).

MINERAL	FORMULA	SYSTEM	HABIT	COLOUR	LUSTRE
ELEMENTS					
Antimony	Sb	Hexagonal	Tabular crystals	Tin-white	Metallic
Arsenic	As	Hexagonal	Massive	Tin-white	Metallic
Bismuth	Bi	Hexagonal	Massive	Silver-white	Metallic
Copper	Cu	Cubic	Massive	Red	Metallic
Diamond	C	Cubic	Octahedral crystals	Variable	Adamantine
Gold	Au	Cubic	Massive	Yellow	Metallic
Graphite	C	Hexagonal	Tabular crystals	Greyish-black	Metallic to dull
Iron	Fe	Cubic	Massive	Grey or black	Metallic
Platinum	Pt	Cubic	Grains	Whitish-grey to dark grey	Metallic
Silver	Ag	Cubic	Cubic crystals	Silver-white	Metallic
Sulphur	S_8	Orthorhombic	Tabular crystals	Yellow	Resinous to greasy
Tellurium	Te	Hexagonal	Prismatic or acicular crystals	Tin-white	Metallic
OXIDES					
Anatase	TiO_2	Tetragonal	Pyramidal crystals	Shades of brown	Metallic adamantine
Arsenolite	As_2O_3	Cubic	Octahedral crystals	White	—
Baddeleyite	ZrO_2	Monoclinic	Prismatic crystals	Variable	Greasy to vitreous
Bauxite	$Al_2O_3.2H_2O$	Amorphous	Massive	White or grey	Dull
Bismite	Bi_2O_3	Monoclinic	Massive	Yellow or green	subadamantine to dull
Brannerite	UTi_2O_6	Triclinic	Grains	Black	—
Brookite	TiO_2	Orthorhombic	Tabular crystals	Yellowish-brown to black	Metallic adamantine
Cassiterite	SnO_2	Tetragonal	Prismatic crystals	Yellowish-brown to brownish-black	Metallic adamantine
Chromite	$FeCr_2O_4$	Cubic	Massive	Black	Metallic
Columbite	$(Fe, Mn)(Nb, Ta)_2O_6$	Orthorhombic	Prismatic crystals	Black to brownish-black	Submetallic to dull gre
Corundum	Al_2O_3	Hexagonal	Pyramidal crystals	Variable	Adamantine to vitreou
Cuprite	Cu_2O	Cubic	Octahedral crystals	Red or black	Adamantine to earthy
Diaspore	$AlO.OH$	Orthorhombic	Acicular crystals	Variable	Pearly to vitreous
Franklinite	$(Zn, Mn, Fe^{2+})(Fe^{3+}, Mn^{3+})_2O_4$	Cubic	Octahedral crystals	Black	Metallic
Goethite	$FeO.OH$	Orthorhombic	Platy crystals	Black or brown	Adamantine; metallic to dull
Hausmannite	Mn_3O_4	Tetragonal	Pyramidal crystals	Brownish-black	Submetallic
Hematite	Fe_2O_3	Hexagonal	Tabular crystals	Steel-grey to red	Metallic to dull
Ilmenite	$FeTiO_3$	Hexagonal	Tabular crystals	Black	Metallic
Limonite	$FeO(OH).nH_2O$	Amorphous	Massive	Brown, black or yellow	Silky to dull
Magnetite	Fe_3O_4	Cubic	Octahedral crystals	Black	Metallic

TREAK	FRACTURE	CLEAVAGE	HARDNESS	SG	REACTION TO ACIDS OR H$_2$O
rey	Uneven	Perfect in one direction	3.0–3.5	6.6–6.72	—
in-white	Uneven	Perfect in one direction	3.5	5.63–5.78	—
lver-white	Brittle	Perfect in one direction	2.0–2.5	9.7–9.8	Soluble in concentrated HNO$_3$
ed	Hackly	None	2.5–3.0	8.5–9.0	Dissolves in HNO$_3$
sh-grey	Conchoidal	Perfect in three directions	10	3.5–3.53	Insoluble in acids
ellow	Uneven	None	2.5–3.0	19.3	Insoluble in HCl
lack or dark grey	—	Perfect basal	1.0–2.0	2.09–2.23	—
rey	Hackly	Poor	4.0	7.3–7.9	Easily soluble in HCl
rey	Hackly	None	4.0–4.5	14.0–19.0	Soluble in hot H$_2$SO$_4$
ilver-white	Hackly	None	2.5–3.0	10.1–11.1	Soluble in HNO$_3$
hite	Conchoidal to uneven	Poor	1.5–2.5	2.07	—
rey	—	Perfect in one direction	2.0–2.5	6.1–6.3	Soluble in hot concentrated H$_2$SO$_4$
lourless or pale yellow	Subconchoidal	Perfect in one direction	5.0–6.5	3.9	—
	Conchoidal	Perfect in one direction	1.5	3.87	—
hite to brownish-white	Subconchoidal to uneven	Perfect in one direction	6.5	5.4–6.02	—
lourless	Earthy	None	1.0–3.0	2.55	—
eyish-yellow	Uneven to earthy	None	4.5	8.64–9.22	Soluble in concentrated HNO$_3$
rk greenish brown	Conchoidal	None	4.5	4.5–5.43	Decomposes in hot concentrated H$_2$SO$_4$
lourless or greyish- een	Subconchoidal to uneven	Indistinct	5.5–6.0	4.14	—
	Subconchoidal to uneven	Imperfect	6.0–7.0	6.99	—
own	Uneven	None	5.5	4.5	Insoluble in acids
ddish-brown to ownish-black	Conchoidal	Poor	3.5–4.0	5.4–6.4	—
hite	Uneven to conchoidal	None	9.0	4.0	Insoluble in acids
ownish-red	Conchoidal to uneven	Poor	3.5–4.0	6.14	Soluble in HCl
hite	Conchoidal	Good in one direction	6.5–7.0	3.4–3.5	Insoluble in acids
ack to brownish-black	Conchoidal	Indistinct	5.5–6.5	5.07–5.22	—
ownish-yellow to low	Uneven	Perfect in one direction	5.0–5.5	3.4–4.3	—
estnut-brown	Uneven	Good basal	5.5	4.84	Soluble in hot HCl with the evolution of chlorine
ddish-brown	Subconchoidal to uneven	None	5.0–6.0	5.26	Soluble in concentrated HCl
ack	Conchoidal to subconchoidal	None	5.0–6.0	4.75	Slowly soluble in HCl
own or yellow	Conchoidal to earthy	None	5.0–5.5	3.6–4.0	—
ack	Uneven	None	6.0	5.2	—

225

MINERAL	FORMULA	SYSTEM	HABIT	COLOUR	LUSTRE
Manganite	$MnO(OH)$	Monoclinic	Prismatic crystals	Grey or black	Submetallic
Martite	Fe_2O_3	Hexagonal	Octahedral crystals	Black	Dull to submetallic
Massicot	PbO	Orthorhombic	Massive	Yellow	Dull to greasy
Minium	Pb_3O_4	Amorphous	Massive	Shades of red	Greasy to dull
Molybdite	MoO_3	Orthorhombic	Crusts	Yellow	Silky to earthy
Periclase	MgO	Cubic	Grains	Colourless to greyish white	Vitreous
Perovskite	$CaTiO_3$	Cubic/monoclinic	Cubic crystals	Black, brown or red	Metallic adamantine
Psilomelane	$(Ba,Mn)Mn_4O_8(OH)_2$	Orthorhombic	Massive	Black	Submetallic
Pyrochlore	$(Ca,Na,Ce)(Nb,Ti,Ta)_2(O,OH,F)_7$	Cubic	Octahedral crystals	Brown or black	Vitreous to resinous
Pyrolusite	MnO_2	Tetragonal	Massive	Grey	Metallic
Quartz	SiO_2	Hexagonal	Prismatic crystals	Variable	Vitreous
Ramsdellite	MnO_2	Orthorhombic	Tabular crystals	Grey to black	Metallic
Rutile	TiO_2	Tetragonal	Prismatic or acicular crystals	Variable	Metallic adamantine
Senarmontite	Sb_2O_3	Cubic	Octahedral crystals	Colourless or greyish-white	Resinous
Spinel	$MgAl_2O_4$	Cubic	Octahedral crystals	Variable	Vitreous
Tantalite	$(Fe,Mn)(Ta,Nb)_2O_6$	Orthorhombic	Prismatic or tabular crystals	Brownish-black to black	Submetallic to subresinous
Tapiolite	$FeTa_2O_6$	Tetragonal	Prismatic crystals	Black	Subadamantine to submetallic
Tellurite	TeO_2	Orthorhombic	Acicular crystals	White	Subadamantine
Tenorite	CuO	Monoclinic	Elongated tabular crystals	Grey or black	Metallic
Thorianite	ThO_2	Cubic	Cubic crystals	Dark grey to black	Submetallic
Trevorite	$NiFe_2O_4$	Cubic	Massive	Black or brownish-black	Metallic
Uraninite	UO_2	Cubic	Octahedral crystals	Black	Greasy to submetallic
Valentinite	Sb_2O_3	Orthorhombic	Prismatic or tabular crystals	Colourless or white	Adamantine
Woodruffite	$(Zn,Mn^{2+})_2Mn_5{}^{4+}O_{12}.4H_2O$	Uncertain	Massive	Black	Dull
Zincite	ZnO	Hexagonal	Massive	Orangish-yellow to red	Subadamantine
HYDROXIDES					
Brucite	$Mg(OH)_2$	Hexagonal	Tabular crystals	White (often tinted)	Waxy to vitreous
Gibbsite	$Al(OH)_3$	Monoclinic	Tabular crystals	White (often tinted)	Pearly to vitreous
SULPHIDES					
Aikinite	$PbCuBiS_3$	Orthorhombic	Prismatic or acicular crystals	Greyish-black	Metallic

REAK	FRACTURE	CLEAVACE	HARDNESS	SG	REACTION TO ACIDS OR H$_2$O
ddish-brown	Uneven	Perfect in two directions	4·0	4·2–4·4	Soluble in HCl with the evolution of chlorine
ddish or purplish-brown	Conchoidal	—	6·0–7·0	4·8	—
llow	—	Imperfect	2·0	9·6	Decomposes in H$_2$SO$_4$ with the precipitation of lead sulphate
angish-yellow	—	None	2·5	9·0	Soluble in HCl with the evolution of chlorine
	None	Good in one direction	1·0–2·0	4·5	—
ite	Irregular	Perfect in one direction	5·5	3·56	Easily soluble in HCl
lourless or grey	Uneven	Indistinct	5·5	4·0	Decomposes in hot H$_2$SO$_4$
ownish-black to black	—	—	5·0–6·0	4·7	Soluble in HCl with the evolution of chlorine
ht brown to lowish-brown	Subconchoidal to uneven	Indistinct	5·0–5·5	4·2–4·5	Slowly soluble in H$_2$SO$_4$
ack to bluish-black	Uneven	Perfect in one direction	6·0 6·5	5·0	---
	Conchoidal	None	7·0	2·6	Insoluble in acids
ack	—	Good in two directions	3·0	4·7	—
le brown to black	Conchoidal to uneven	Good in one direction	6·0–6·5	4·23	Insoluble in acids
hite	Uneven	Poor	2·0–2·5	5·5	Easily soluble in HCl
ite	Conchoidal	None	7·8–8·0	3·55	—
rk red to black	Subconchoidal to uneven	Good in one direction	6·0	7·95	Partially decomposes when evaporated with concentrated H$_2$SO$_4$
own to brownish-black	Uneven to subconchoidal	None	6·0–6·5	7·9	—
	—	Perfect in one direction	2·0	5·9	Easily soluble in HCl
	Conchoidal to uneven	Poor	3·5	5·8–6·4	Easily soluble in HCl
ey to greenish-grey	Uneven to subconchoidal	Poor	6·5	9·7	Soluble in H$_2$SO$_4$ with the evolution of hydrogen
own	—	Poor	5·0	5·2	Soluble with difficulty in HCl
ownish-black to ve-green	Uneven to conchoidal	—	5·0–6·0	10·8	Slowly attacked by HCl
ite	—	Perfect in one direction	2·5–3·0	5·76	Soluble in HCl
ownish-black	Conchoidal	—	4·5	3·71	
angish-yellow	Conchoidal	Perfect in one direction	4·0	5·7	Soluble in HCl
ite	None	Perfect in one direction	2·5	2·39	—
ite	Tough	Perfect in one direction	2·5–3·5	2·3 2 4	—
yish-black	Uneven	Indistinct	2·0–2·5	7·07	Decomposes in HNO$_3$ with the precipitation of sulphur and lead sulphide

MINERAL	FORMULA	SYSTEM	HABIT	COLOUR	LUSTRE
Alabandite	MnS	Cubic	Massive	Black	Submetallic
Argentite	Ag_2S	Cubic	Cubic crystals	Dark grey	Metallic
Arsenopyrite	$FeAsS$	Monoclinic	Prismatic crystals	Silver-white	Metallic
Bismuthinite	Bi_2S_3	Orthorhombic	Acicular crystals	Grey	Metallic
Blende	ZnS	Cubic	Tetragonal crystals	Variable	Resinous to adamanti
Bornite	Cu_5FeS_4	Cubic	Cubic crystals	Red or brown	Metallic
Boulangerite	$Pb_5Sb_4S_{11}$	Monoclinic	Prismatic crystals	Bluish-grey	Metallic
Bravoite	$(Ni,Fe)S_2$	Cubic	Cubic crystals	Grey	Metallic
Chalcocite	Cu_2S	Orthorhombic	Prismatic or tabular crystals	Blackish-grey	Metallic
Chalcopyrite	$CuFeS_2$	Tetragonal	Tetrahedral crystals	Yellow	Metallic
Cinnabar	HgS	Hexagonal	Tabular or prismatic crystals	Red	Adamantine to metall
Covelline	CuS	Hexagonal	Massive	Indigo-blue	Submetallic to resinou
Enargite	Cu_3AsS_4	Orthorhombic	Prismatic crystals	Greyish-black or black	Metallic
Galena	PbS	Cubic	Cubic crystals	Grey	Metallic
Germanite	$Cu_3(Ge,Ga,Fe,Zn)(As,S)_4$	Cubic	Detrital masses	Dark reddish-grey	Metallic
Greenockite	CdS	Hexagonal	Pyramidal crystals	Shades of yellow	Adamantine to resinou
Jamesonite	$Pb_4FeSb_6S_{14}$	Monoclinic	Acicular crystals	Greyish-black	Metallic
Marcasite	FeS_2	Orthorhombic	Tabular crystals	Pale bronze-yellow	Metallic
Matildite	$AgBiS_2$	Orthorhombic	Massive	Black or grey	Metallic
Millerite	NiS	Hexagonal	Capillary crystals	Brassy-yellow	Metallic
Molybdenite	MoS_2	Hexagonal	Tabular crystals	Grey	Metallic
Nagyagite	$Pb_5Au(Te,Sb)_4S_{5\ 8}$	Monoclinic	Tabular crystals	Blackish-grey	Metallic
Orpiment	As_2S_3	Monoclinic	Prismatic crystals	Lemon-yellow	Pearly
Parkerite	$Ni_3(Bi,Pb)_2S_2$	Monoclinic	Platy crystals	Bronze	Metallic
Pentlandite	$(Fe,Ni)_9S_8$	Cubic	Massive	Bronze-yellow	Metallic
Polybasite	$Ag_{16}Sb_2S_{11}$	Monoclinic	Tabular crystals	Black	Metallic
Proustite	Ag_3AsS_3	Hexagonal	Prismatic crystals	Scarlet-vermilion	Adamantine
Pyargyrite	Ag_3SbS_3	Hexagonal	Prismatic crystals	Dark red	Adamantine
Pyrargyrite	Ag_3SbS_3	Hexagonal	Prismatic crystals	Black or red	Metallic adamantine
Pyrite	FeS_2	Cubic	Cubic crystals	Pale brassy-yellow	Metallic

STREAK	FRACTURE	CLEAVAGE	HARDNESS	SG	REACTION TO ACIDS OR H_2O
Green	Uneven	Perfect in one direction	3.5–4.0	4.0	Soluble in HCl with the evolution of hydrogen sulphide
Silver-grey	Subconchoidal	Poor	2.0–2.5	7.3	—
Dark greyish-black	Uneven	Good in one direction	5.5–6.0	6.07	—
Grey	None	Perfect in one direction	2.0	6.4	—
Brown or white	Conchoidal	Perfect in one direction	3.5–4.0	3.9–4.1	Soluble in HCl with the evolution of hydrogen sulphide
Pale greyish-black	Conchoidal to uneven	Poor	3.0	5.07	Soluble in HNO_3 with the precipitation of sulphur
Brownish-grey to brown	Brittle	Good in one direction	2.5–3.0	5.7–6.3	Soluble in hot HCl with the evolution of hydrogen sulphide
Grey	Conchoidal to uneven	Perfect in one direction	5.5–6.0	4.62	Soluble in hot HNO_3 with the evolution of hydrogen sulphide
Blackish-grey	Conchoidal	Indistinct	2.5–3.0	5.5–5.8	—
Greenish-black	Uneven	Indistinct	3.5–4.0	4.1–4.3	Soluble in HNO_3 with the separation of sulphur
Scarlet	Uneven	Perfect in one direction	2.0–2.5	8.09	—
Grey or black	Uneven	Perfect in one direction	1.5–2.0	4.6–4.7	—
Greyish-black	Uneven	Perfect in two directions	3.0	4.4–4.5	Soluble in aqua regia
Grey	Subconchoidal	Perfect in one direction	2.5–2.75	7.58	—
Dark grey or black	Brittle	None	4.0	4.46–4.6	Soluble in HNO_3
Orangish-yellow to brick-red	Conchoidal	Good in one direction	3.0–3.5	5.0	Soluble in concentrated HCl with the evolution of hydrogen sulphide
Greyish-black	—	Good basal	2.5	5.63	Decomposes in HNO_3 with the separation of antimony oxide and lead sulphate
Greyish-black	Uneven	Indistinct	6.0–6.5	4.9	Soluble in HNO_3
Pale grey	Uneven	None	2.5	6.9	Soluble in HNO_3 with the precipitation of sulphur
Greenish-black	Uneven	Perfect in two directions	3.0–3.5	5.5	—
Bluish-grey	None	Perfect in one direction	1.0–1.5	4.62–4.73	Decomposes in HNO_3 with the separation of molybdenum oxide
Blackish-grey	—	Perfect in one direction	1.0–1.5	7.4	Soluble in HNO_3 with a residue of gold
Pale lemon-yellow	Irregular	Perfect in one direction	1.5–2.0	3.5	Soluble in H_2SO_4
Black	—	Perfect in one direction	3.0	8.74	—
Bronze-brown	Conchoidal	None	3.5–4.0	4.6–5.0	—
Black	Uneven	Poor	2.0–3.0	6.1	Decomposes in HNO_3
Vermilion	Conchoidal to uneven	Good in one direction	2.0–2.5	5.6	Decomposes in HNO_3 with the separation of sulphur
Purplish-red	Conchoidal to uneven	Visible in one direction	2.5	5.8	Decomposes in HNO_3 with the separation of silver and antimony oxide
Red	Conchoidal	Good in one direction	2.0–3.0	5.8	Decomposes in HNO_3
Greenish-black to brownish-black	Conchoidal to uneven	Indistinct	6.0–6.5	5.0	Insoluble in HCl

MINERAL	FORMULA	SYSTEM	HABIT	COLOUR	LUSTRE
Pyrrhotite	FeS	Hexagonal	Tabular or platy crystals	Bronze-yellow to brown	Metallic
Realgar	As_4S_4	Monoclinic	Prismatic crystals	Red to orangish-yellow	Resinous to greasy
Stannite	Cu_2FeSnS_4	Tetragonal	Massive	Grey or black	Metallic
Stephanite	Ag_5SbS_4	Orthorhombic	Prismatic or tabular crystals	Black	Metallic
Stibnite	Sb_2S_3	Orthorhombic	Prismatic or acicular crystals	Grey	Metallic
Teallite	$PbSnS_2$	Orthorhombic	Tabular crystals	Greyish-black	Metallic
Tennantite	Cu_3AsS_3	Cubic	Tetragonal crystals	Grey or black	Metallic
Tetradymite	Bi_2Te_2S	Hexagonal	Massive	Pale grey	Metallic
Tetrahedrite	Cu_3SbS_3	Cubic	Tetragonal crystals	Grey or black	Metallic
Ullmannite	$NiSbS$	Cubic	Cubic crystals	Grey to silver-white	Metallic
Wurtzite	ZnS	Hexagonal	Pyramidal or prismatic crystals	Brownish-black	Resinous
SULPHATES					
Alum	$KAl(SO_4)_2.12H_2O$	Cubic	Massive	Colourless or white	Vitreous
Aluminite	$Al_2SO_4(OH)_4.7H_2O$	Monoclinic	Massive	White	Earthy
Alunite	$KAl_3(SO_4)_2(OH)_6$	Hexagonal	Rhombohedral crystals	White	Vitreous
Alunogene	$Al_2(SO_4)_3.18H_2O$	Triclinic	Crusts	Colourless or white	Vitreous or silky
Anglesite	$PbSO_4$	Orthorhombic	Tabular crystals	Colourless or white	Adamantine to resinous
Anhydrite	$CaSO_4$	Orthorhombic	Massive	Colourless or blue	Vitreous to pearly
Antlerite	$Cu_3(SO_4)(OH)_4$	Orthorhombic	Tabular or prismatic crystals	Shades of green	Vitreous
Aphthitalite	$NaKSO_4$	Hexagonal	Tabular crystals	Variable	Vitreous to resinous
Barytes	$BaSO_4$	Orthorhombic	Platy crystals	Variable	Vitreous
Brochantite	$Cu_4SO_4(OH)_6$	Monoclinic	Prismatic or acicular crystals	Shades of green	Vitreous
Celestine	$SrSO_4$	Orthorhombic	Tabular crystals	Variable	Vitreous
Chalcanthite	$CuSO_4.5H_2O$	Triclinic	Prismatic crystals	Sky-blue	Vitreous
Glauberite	$Na_2Ca(SO_4)_2$	Monoclinic	Tabular or prismatic crystals	Variable	Vitreous to waxy
Gypsum	$CaSO_4.2H_2O$	Monoclinic	Tabular or prismatic crystals	Variable	Subvitreous to pearly
Jarosite	$KFe_3(SO_4)_2OH_6$	Hexagonal	Tabular crystals	Yellow to dark brown	Subadamantine to vitreous
Langbeinite	$K_2Mg_2(SO_4)_2$	Cubic	Massive	Colourless	Vitreous
Linarite	$PbCu(SO_4)(OH)_2$	Monoclinic	Tabular crystals	Azure-blue	Vitreous
Mascagnite	$(NH_4)_2SO_4$	Orthorhombic	Crusts	Colourless or grey	Vitreous
Melanterite	$FeSO_4.7H_2O$	Monoclinic	Prismatic crystals	Green	Vitreous

STREAK	FRACTURE	CLEAVAGE	HARDNESS	SG	REACTION TO ACIDS OR H_2O
Dark greyish-black	Uneven to subconchoidal	None	3·5–4·5	4·58–4·65	Decomposes in HCl with the evolution of hydrogen sulphide
Red to orangish yellow	Conchoidal	Good in one direction	1·5–2·0	3·56	Decomposes in HNO_3
Black	Uneven	Indistinct	4·0	4·3–4·5	Decomposes in HNO_3 with the separation of sulphur and tin oxide
Black	Subconchoidal to uneven	Imperfect	2·0–2·5	6·25	Decomposes in HNO_3 with the separation of sulphur and antimony oxide
Grey	Subconchoidal	Perfect in one direction	2·0	4·63	Soluble in HCl
Black	—	Perfect basal	1·5	6·36	Easily decomposes in hot concentrated H_2SO_4
Black or brown	Subconchoidal to uneven	None	3·7–4·5	4·6–5·0	Decomposes in HNO_3 with the separation of sulphur
Pale grey	—	Perfect in one direction	1·5–2·0	7·4	—
Black, brown or cherry-red	Subconchoidal to uneven	None	3·0–3·7	4·8–5·1	Decomposes in HNO_3 with the separation of sulphur and antimony oxide
Greyish-black	Uneven	Perfect basal	5·0–5·5	6·65	Decomposes in HNO_3
Brown	—	Visible in one direction	3·5–4·0	3·98	Soluble in HCl with the evolution of hydrogen sulphide
Colourless	Conchoidal	Poor	2·0–2·5	1·8	—
Colourless	Earthy	None	1·0–2·0	1·66	—
White	Uneven	Good in one direction	3·5–4·0	2·6–2·9	Slowly soluble in H_2SO_4
—	—	Perfect in one direction	1·5–2·0	1·77	Soluble in water
Colourless	Conchoidal	Good in one direction	2·5–3·0	6·38	—
White to greyish-white	Uneven to splintery	Perfect in one direction	3·5	2·98	—
Pale green	Uneven	Good in one direction	3·5–4·0	3·9	Soluble in HCl
Variable	Conchoidal to uneven	Poor	3·0	2·65–2·70	Soluble in water
White	Uneven	Perfect in two directions	3·0–3·5	4·5	—
Pale green	Uneven to conchoidal	Perfect in one direction	3·5–4·0	3·97	—
White	Uneven	Perfect in one direction	3·3–5·0	3·97	—
Colourless	Conchoidal	Imperfect	2·5	2·28	—
White	Conchoidal	Perfect in one direction	2·5–3·0	2·75–2·85	—
White	Conchoidal	Good in two directions	2·0	2·3	Slightly soluble in water
Pale yellow	Uneven to conchoidal	Good basal	2·5–3·5	2·9–3·26	Soluble in HCl
Colourless	Conchoidal	None	3·5–4·0	2·83	Slowly soluble in water
Pale blue	Conchoidal	Perfect in one direction	2·5	5·33–5·35	Soluble in HNO_3 with the precipitation of lead sulphate
Colourless	Uneven	Good in one direction	2·0–2·5	1·77	Soluble in water
Colourless	Conchoidal	Perfect in one direction	2·0	1·9	Soluble in water

MINERAL	FORMULA	SYSTEM	HABIT	COLOUR	LUSTRE
Mirabilite	$Na_2SO_4.10H_2O$	Monoclinic	Prismatic or tabular crystals	Colourless or white	Vitreous
Natroalunite	$NaAl_3(SO_4)_4(OH)_6$	Hexagonal	Tabular crystals	White	Vitreous
Plumbojarosite	$PbFe_6(SO_4)_4(OH)_{12}$	Hexagonal	Crusts	Shades of brown	Dull
Polyhalite	$K_2MgCa_2(SO_4)_4.2H_2O$	Triclinic	Massive	Colourless or white	Vitreous
Syngenite	$K_2Ca(SO_4)_2.H_2O$	Monoclinic	Tabular or prismatic crystals	Colourless	Vitreous
Thenardite	Na_2SO_4	Orthorhombic	Tabular crystals	Colourless (often tinted)	Vitreous
CARBONATES					
Alstonite	$BaCa(CO_3)_2$	Orthorhombic	Pyramidal crystals	Colourless or white (often tinted)	Vitreous
Ancylite	$(Sr,Ca)_3(Ce,La)_4$ $(CO_3)_7(OH)_4.3H_2O$	Orthorhombic	Prismatic crystals	Variable	Vitreous
Ankerite	$Ca(Mn,Mg,Fe)$ $(CO_3)_2$	Hexagonal	Rhombohedral crystals	Yellowish-brown to brown	Vitreous to pearly
Aragonite	$CaCO_3$	Orthorhombic	Prismatic crystals	Colourless or white	Vitreous
Aurichalcite	$(Zn,Cu)_5(OH)_6(CO_3)_2$	Orthorhombic	Crusts	Pale greenish-blue	Pearly
Azurite	$Cu_3(CO_3)_2(OH)_2$	Monoclinic	Prismatic crystals	Deep azure-blue	Vitreous
Bismutite	$Bi_2CO_3.H_2O$	Tetragonal	Crusts	White, grey or yellow	Vitreous to pearly
Calcite	$CaCO_3$	Hexagonal	Tabular or acicular crystals	Colourless (often tinted)	Vitreous
Cerussite	$PbCO_3$	Orthorhombic	Prismatic crystals	Colourless (often tinted)	Adamantine
Chalybite	$FeCO_3$	Hexagonal	Rhombohedral crystals	Variable	Pearly to vitreous
Dolomite	$CaMg(CO_3)_2$	Hexagonal	Rhombohedral crystals	Variable	Vitreous
Gay-lussite	$Na_2Ca(CO_3)_2.5H_2O$	Monoclinic	Prismatic crystals	Colourless or white	Vitreous
Lansfordite	$MgCO_3.5H_2O$	Monoclinic	Prismatic crystals	Colourless or white	Vitreous
Magnesite	$MgCO_3$	Hexagonal	Massive	Colourless or white	Vitreous
Malachite	$Cu_2CO_3(OH)_2$	Monoclinic	Massive	Shades of green	Silky
Nesquehonite	$MgCO_3.3H_2O$	Orthorhombic	Prismatic crystals	Colourless to white	Vitreous
Phosgenite	$Pb_2CO_3Cl_2$	Tetragonal	Prismatic or tabular crystals	White to brown	Adamantine
Rhodochrosite	$MnCO_3$	Hexagonal	Massive	Shades of pink and red	Vitreous
Shortite	$Na_2Ca_2(CO_3)_3$	Orthorhombic	Tabular or prismatic crystals	Colourless or pale yellow	Vitreous
Smithsonite	$ZnCO_3$	Hexagonal	Massive	Greyish-white to dark grey	Vitreous
Strontianite	$SrCO_3$	Orthorhombic	Prismatic or acicular crystals	Colourless or grey	Vitreous
Trona	$Na_3H(CO_3)_2.2H_2O$	Monoclinic	Massive	Colourless or grey to white	Vitreous
Witherite	$BaCO_3$	Orthorhombic	Pyramidal crystals	Colourless or white	Vitreous
Zaratite	$Ni_3CO_3(OH)_4.4H_2O$	Cubic	Massive	Emerald-green	Vitreous to greasy

STREAK	FRACTURE	CLEAVAGE	HARDNESS	SG	REACTION TO ACIDS OR H_2O
hite	Conchoidal	Perfect in one direction	1·5–2·0	1·5	Easily soluble in water
hite	Conchoidal	Good in one direction	3·5–4·0	2·6–2·9	Slowly soluble in H_2SO_4
le brown	None	Poor	1·0	3·6	Slowly soluble in HCl
	Splintery	Perfect in one direction	3·5	2·78	Decomposes in water with the separation of gypsum
lourless	Conchoidal	Perfect in two directions	2·5	2·6	Decomposes in water with the separation of gypsum
	Uneven	Perfect in one direction	2·5–3·0	2·6	—
hite	Uneven	Imperfect	4·0–4·5	3·7	Soluble in HCl
hite	Splintery	None	4·0–4·5	3·95	Soluble in HCl with the evolution of carbon dioxide
lourless	Subconchoidal	Perfect in one direction	3·5–4·0	3·02	—
lourless	Subconchoidal	Good in one direction	3·5–4·0	2·9–3·0	Soluble with effervescence in HCl
	None	Perfect basal	2·0	3·5–3·6	Soluble with effervescence in HCl
ue	Conchoidal	Perfect in one direction	3·5–4·0	3·7–3·8	Soluble with effervescence in HCl
ey	None	Good basal	2·5–3·5	6·1–7·7	Soluble with effervescence in HCl
hite to grey	Conchoidal	Good in two directions	3·0	2·7	Soluble with effervescence in HCl
lourless or white	Conchoidal	Good in two directions	3·0–3·5	6·55	Soluble with effervescence in HCl
hite	Uneven	Perfect in two directions	3·5–4·5	3·7–3·9	Effervesces in hot HCl
hite to grey	Conchoidal to subconchoidal	Perfect in two directions	3·5–4·0	2·9	Soluble with effervescence in warm HCl
lourless or greyish ite	Conchoidal	Perfect in one direction	2·5–3·0	1·99	Easily soluble with effervescence in HCl
hite	Uneven	Good in two directions	2·5	1·7	Soluble in HCl
hite	Conchoidal	Perfect in one direction	3·5–4·0	3·0–3·5	Soluble with effervescence in HCl
le green	Irregular	Good basal	3·5–4·0	3·9–4·0	Soluble with effervescence in HCl
	Splintery	Perfect in one direction	2·5	1·85	Easily soluble with effervescence in HCl
hite	Conchoidal	Good in two directions	2·0–3·0	6·1	Soluble with effervescence in HNO_3
hite	Uneven to conchoidal	Perfect in one direction	3·5–4·0	3·7	Soluble with effervescence in warm HCl
	Conchoidal	Good in one direction	3·0	2·6	Decomposes in water with the separation of calcium carbonate
ite	Uneven to subconchoidal	Good in one direction	4·0–4·5	4·43	Soluble with effervescence in HCl
	Uneven	Good in one direction	3·5	3·75	Soluble with effervescence in HCl
	Uneven to subconchoidal	Perfect in one direction	2·5–3·0	2·14	Soluble in water
ite	Uneven	Good in one direction	3·0–3·5	4·3	Soluble with effervescence in HCl
en	Conchoidal	—	3·5	2·57–2·69	Soluble with effervescence when heated in HCl

MINERAL	FORMULA	SYSTEM	HABIT	COLOUR	LUSTRE
PHOSPHATES					
Amblygonite	$(Li, Na)AlPO_4(F,OH)$	Triclinic	Prismatic crystals	White	Vitreous to greasy
Apatite	$Ca_5(PO_4)_3(F,Cl,OH)$	Hexagonal	Prismatic or pyramidal crystals	Variable	Vitreous to subresinou
Autunite	$Ca(UO_2)_2(PO_4)_2 \cdot 10-12H_2O$	Tetragonal	Platy crystals	Yellow	Pearly to vitreous
Beraunite	$Fe^{2+}Fe^{3+}(PO_4)_3(OH)_5 \cdot 3H_2O$	Monoclinic	Tabular crystals	Shades of red	Vitreous
Beryllonite	$NaBePO_4$	Monoclinic	Tabular or prismatic crystals	White to pale yellow	Vitreous
Evansite	$Al_3PO_4(OH)_6 \cdot 6H_2O$	Amorphous	Massive	Colourless or white (often tinted)	Vitreous to resinous
Lithiophilite	$LiMn(PO_4)$	Orthorhombic	Massive	Salmon	Vitreous
Mimetite	$Pb_5(AsO_4,PO_4)Cl$	Hexagonal	Acicular crystals	Colourless, yellow or brown	Resinous
Monazite	$(Ce,La,Yt,Th)(PO_4)$	Monoclinic	Prismatic crystals	Yellow, white or brown	Waxy to resinous
Plumbogummite	$PbAl_3(PO_4)_2(OH)_5 \cdot H_2O$	Hexagonal	Massive	Greyish-white to yellow	Dull to resinous
Pseudomalachite	$Cu_5(PO_4)_2(OH)_4 \cdot H_2O$	Monoclinic	Massive	Shades of green	Vitreous
Purpurite	$(Mn,Fe)PO_4$	Orthorhombic	Prismatic crystals	Reddish-purple	Satiny
Pyromorphite	$Pb_5(PO_4)_3Cl$	Hexagonal	Prismatic crystals	Green, yellow or brown	Resinous to subadamantine
Scoralite	$(Fe,Mg)Al_2(PO_4)_2(OH)_2$	Monoclinic	Pyramidal crystals	Shades of blue	Vitreous
Sicklerite	$(Li, Mn, Fe)PO_4$	Orthorhombic	Massive	Yellowish-brown to dark brown	Dull
Strengite	$FePO_4 \cdot 2H_2O$	Orthorhombic	Tabular crystals	Colourless, red or violet	Vitreous
Torbernite	$Cu(UO_2)_2(PO_4)_2 \cdot 12H_2O$	Tetragonal	Tabular crystals	Shades of green	Vitreous to subadamar
Triphylite	$Li(Fe,Mn)PO_4$	Orthorhombic	Massive	Brownish-grey to greenish-grey	Vitreous to subadamantine
Turquoise	$CuAl_6(PO_4)_4(OH)_8 \cdot 5H_2O$	Triclinic	Massive	Shades of blue and green	Vitreous to waxy
Variscite	$AlPO_4 \cdot 2H_2O$	Orthorhombic	Massive	Green	Vitreous to waxy
Vivianite	$Fe_3(PO_4)_2 \cdot 8H_2O$	Monoclinic	Prismatic crystals	Colourless	Vitreous to dull
Wardite	$Na_4aAl_{12}(PO_4)_8(OH)_{18} \cdot 6H_2O$	Tetragonal	Pyramidal crystals	Colourless or shades of green	Vitreous
Wavellite	$Al_6(PO_4)_4(OH)_6 \cdot 9H_2O$	Orthorhombic	Massive	Greenish-white, green or yellow	Vitreous
Xenotime	$YtPO_4$	Tetragonal	Prismatic crystals	Brown, red or yellow	Vitreous
CHLORIDES					
Atacamite	$Cu_2Cl(OH)_3$	Orthorhombic	Prismatic or tabular crystals	Shades of green	Adamantine
Calomel	Hg_2Cl_2	Tetragonal	Tabular or prismatic crystals	Variable	Adamantine
Carnallite	$KMgCl_3 \cdot 6H_2O$	Orthorhombic	Pyramidal crystals	Colourless to milky-white	Greasy to dull

STREAK	FRACTURE	CLEAVAGE	HARDNESS	SG	REACTION TO ACIDS OR H_2O
...lourless	Uneven to subconchoidal	Perfect in one direction	5·5–6·0	3·11	
...hite	Conchoidal to uneven	Poor	5·0	3·17–3·23	Soluble in HCl
...llow	None	Perfect in two directions	2·0–2·5	3·1	—
...llow to olive	—	Good in one direction	3·5–4·0	2·8–2·9	Readily soluble in HCl
...hite	Conchoidal	Perfect in one direction	5·5–6·0	2·81	—
...hite	Conchoidal	None	3·0–4·0	1·8–2·2	Easily soluble in HCl
...eyish-white	Uneven	Perfect in one direction	4·4	3·5–3·58	Soluble in HCl
...hite	Uneven	Indistinct	3·5–4·0	7·0	—
...ite	Conchoidal to uneven	Good in two directions	5·0–5·5	4·6–5·4	Slowly decomposes in HCl
...lourless or white	Uneven	None	4·5–5·0	4·0	Soluble in hot HCl
...rk green	Splintery	Good in one direction	4·5–5·0	4·35	Soluble in HCl
...ddish-purple	Uneven	Good in one direction	4·0–4·5	3·3·	Easily soluble in HCl
...ite	Uneven	Indistinct	3·5–4·0	7·0	Soluble in HNO_3
...ite	Uneven	Indistinct	5·5–6·0	3·38	Slowly soluble in hot HCl
...e yellowish-brown to ...wn		Good in one direction	4·0	3·2–3·4	Soluble in HCl
...te	Conchoidal	Good in one direction	3·5	2·87	Soluble in HCl
...e green		Perfect basal	2·0–2·5	3·22	Soluble in HCl
...ourless to greyish-...te	Uneven to subconchoidal	Good in one direction	4·0–5·0	3·55	Soluble in HCl
...te to pale green	Conchoidal to smooth	Perfect basal	5·0–6·0	2·6–2·85	Soluble with difficulty in HCl
...te	Uneven to splintery	Good in one direction	3·5–4·5	2·57	
...ourless or bluish-...te	Fibrous	Perfect in one direction	1·5–2·0	2·68	Easily soluble in HCl
	—	Perfect basal	5·0	2·87	Soluble with difficulty in HCl
...te	Uneven to subconchoidal	Perfect in one direction	3·25–4·0	2·36	Easily soluble in HCl
...e brown, pale red or ...e yellow	Uneven to splintery	Good in one direction	4·0–5·0	4·4–5·1	—
...le-green	Conchoidal	Perfect in one direction	3·0–3·5	3·76	—
...e yellowish-white	Conchoidal	Good in one direction	1·5	7·15	—
...ourless	Conchoidal	None	2·5	1·6	Soluble in water

MINERAL	FORMULA	SYSTEM	HABIT	COLOUR	LUSTRE
Halite	$NaCl$	Cubic	Cubic crystals	Variable	Vitreous
Sal Ammoniac	NH_4Cl	Cubic	Trapezohedral crystals	Colourless or white	Vitreous
Sylvine	KCl	Cubic	Cubic crystals	Colourless or white	Vitreous
Vanadinite	$Pb_5(VO_4)_3Cl$	Hexagonal	Prismatic crystals	Shades of red and yellow	Subresinous to subadamantine
NITRATES					
Nitratine	$NaNO_3$	Hexagonal	Massive	Colourless or white	Vitreous
Nitre	KNO_3	Orthorhombic	Crusts	Colourless or white	Vitreous
BORATES					
Borax	$Na_2B_4O_7.10H_2O$	Monoclinic	Prismatic or tabular crystals	Variable	Vitreous
Colemanite	$Ca_2B_6O_{11}.5H_2O$	Monoclinic	Prismatic crystals	Variable	Vitreous to adamantine
Ulexite	$NaCaB_5O_8.8H_2O$	Triclinic	Capillary or acicular crystals	Colourless or white	Vitreous to silky
ARSENATES					
Adamite	$Zn_2(OH)AsO_4$	Orthorhombic	Prismatic crystals	Variable	Vitreous
Annabergite	$(Ni,Co)_3(AsO_4)_2.8H_2O$	Monoclinic	Crusts	Pale apple-green	Silky to vitreous
Chalcophyllite	$Cu_{18}Al_2(AsO_4)_3(SO_4)_3(OH)_{27}.33H_2O$	Hexagonal	Tabular crystals	Shades of green	Vitreous to subadamantine
Clinoclase	$Cu_3AsO_4(OH)_3$	Monoclinic	Tabular crystals	Greenish-black to greenish-blue	Vitreous to pearly
Erythrite	$(Co,Ni)_3(AsO_4)_2.8H_2O$	Monoclinic	Prismatic to acicular crystals	Crimson to peach-red	Vitreous to pearly
Liroconite	$Cu_2Al(AsO_4)(OH)_4.4H_2O$	Monoclinic	Acicular crystals	Sky-blue to green	Vitreous
Olivenite	$Cu_2(AsO_4)(OH)$	Orthorhombic	Prismatic or acicular crystals	Olive-green to brown	Adamantine to vitreous
Pharmacolite	$CaHAsO_4.2H_2O$	Monoclinic	Massive	White to grey	Vitreous
Roselite	$Ca_2(Co,Mg)(AsO_4)_2.2H_2O$	Monoclinic	Prismatic crystals	Pink to dark red	Vitreous
Scorodite	$FeAsO_4.2H_2O$	Orthorhombic	Pyramidal or tabular crystals	Leek-green to brown	Vitreous to subadamantine
ARSENIDES					
Algodonite	Cu_6As	Hexagonal	Massive	Grey to silver-white	Metallic
Niccolite	$NiAs$	Hexagonal	Massive	Pale copper-red	Metallic
Smaltite	$CoAs_2$	Cubic	Cubic crystals	Tin-white to silver-grey	Metallic
Sperrylite	$PtAs_2$	Cubic	Cubic crystals	Tin-white	Metallic
TELLURIDES					
Altaite	$PbTe$	Cubic	Massive	Tin-white	Metallic
Calaverite	$(AuTe)_2$	Monoclinic	Bladed crystals	Brass-yellow to silver-white	Metallic
Petzite	$(Ag,Au)_2Te$	Cubic	Massive	Steel-grey to black	Metallic

TREAK	FRACTURE	CLEAVAGE	HARDNESS	SG	REACTION TO ACIDS OR H2O
olourless or white	Conchoidal	Perfect basal	2·0	2·2	Soluble in water
	Conchoidal	Visible in one direction	1·5–2·0	1·53	Soluble in water
hite	Uneven	Perfect basal	2·0	2·0	Soluble in water
hite to yellow	Uneven to conchoidal	—	2·75–3·0	6·88	Soluble in HCl with the precipitation of lead chloride
olourless	Conchoidal	Perfect in one direction	1·5–2·0	2·24–2·29	Easily soluble in water
olourless or white	Subconchoidal	Perfect in one direction	2·0	2·2	Easily soluble in water
hite	Conchoidal	Good in one direction	2·0–2·5	1·7	Soluble in water
hite	Uneven to subconchoidal	Perfect in one direction	4·5	2·4	Soluble in HCl
	Uneven	Perfect in one direction	2·5	2·0	Decomposes in hot water
	Uneven	Good in two directions	3·5	4·3–4·4	—
	None	Poor	2·5–3·0	3·0	—
ale green	—	Perfect in one direction	2·0	2·65	—
uish-green	Uneven	Perfect in one direction	2·5–3·0	4·33–4·38	—
ale shades of red	—	Perfect in one direction	1·5–2·5	2·9	—
ky-blue to green	Uneven	Indistinct	2·0–2·5	2·9–3·0	Soluble in HNO_3
ive-green to brown	Conchoidal	Indistinct	3·0	4·4	Soluble in HCl
	Uneven	Perfect in one direction	2·0–2·5	2·53–2·73	Readily soluble in HCl
ed	—	Perfect in one direction	3·5	3·5–7·34	Easily soluble in HCl
	Subconchoidal	Indistinct	3·5–4·0	3·28	Soluble in HCl
	Subconchoidal	None	4·0	8·38	Soluble in HNO_3
le brownish-black	Brittle	None	5·0–5·5	7·8	Soluble in H_2SO_4
	Conchoidal to uneven	Good in two directions	5·5	6·5	Soluble in HNO_3
ack	Conchoidal	Poor	6·0–7·0	10·58	—
	Subconchoidal	Pertect in one direction	3·0	8·15	—
llowish to greenish-grey	Subconchoidal to uneven	None	2·5–3·0	9·24	Decomposes in HNO_3 with residue of gold powder
	Subconchoidal	Good in one direction	2·5–3·0	8·7–9·02	Decomposes in HNO_3 with the separation of gold

MINERAL	FORMULA	SYSTEM	HABIT	COLOUR	LUSTRE
Sylvanite	$AgAuTe_4$	Monoclinic	Prismatic or tabular crystals	Steel-grey to silver-white	Metallic
VANADATES					
Carnotite	$K_2(UO_2)_2(VO_4)_2.3H_2O$	Orthorhombic	Platy crystals	Canary-yellow	Dull to earthy
Descloizite	$Pb(Zn,Cu)VO_4OH$	Orthorhombic	Pyramidal or prismatic crystals	Variable	Greasy
Mottramite	$Pb(Cu,Zn)VO_4OH$	Orthorhombic	Prismatic crystals	Brownish-red to blackish-brown	Greasy
Tyuyamunite	$Ca(UO_2)_2(VO_4)_2.10H_2O$	Orthorhombic	Scaly crystals	Yellow to greenish-yellow	Adamantine to waxy
TUNGSTATES					
Scheelite	$CaWO_4$	Tetragonal	Octahedral crystals	Colourless or white	Vitreous
Stolzite	$PbWO_4$	Tetragonal	Tabular crystals	Reddish-brown to brown	Resinous to subadamantine
Tungstite	H_2WO_4	Orthorhombic	Acicular crystals	Yellow or yellowish-green	Resinous to earthy
Wolframite	$(Fe,Mn)WO_4$	Monoclinic	Prismatic crystals	Dark grey, brownish-black or black	Submetallic to metallic
MOLYBDATES					
Powellite	$CaMoO_4$	Tetragonal	Pyramidal or tabular crystals	Variable	Subadamantine
Wulfenite	$PbMoO_4$	Tetragonal	Tabular crystals	Orangish-yellow to yellow	Resinous to adamantine
ANTIMONIDE					
Allemontite	$AsSb$	Hexagonal	Massive	Tin-white to reddish-grey	Metallic
FLUORIDE					
Fluorite	CaF_2	Cubic	Cubic crystals	Variable	Vitreous
SELENIDE					
Tiemannite	$HgSe$	Cubic	Tetragonal crystals	Steel-grey to blackish-grey	Metallic
SILICATES					
Actinolite	$Ca_2(Mg,Fe)_5Si_8O_{22}(OH)_2$	Monoclinic	Prismatic crystals	Green	Vitreous
Aegirine	$NaFe(Si_2O_6)$	Monoclinic	Prismatic crystals	Green	Vitreous
Aenigmatite	$Na_2Fe_5TiSi_6O_{20}$	Triclinic	Prismatic crystals	Black	Vitreous
Afwillite	$Ca_3(SiO_3.OH)_2 2H_2O$	Monoclinic	Prismatic crystals	Colourless	Vitreous
Akermanite	$Ca_2(MgSi_2O_7)$	Tetragonal	Tabular crystals	Variable	—
Albite	$NaAlSi_3O_8$	Triclinic	Tabular crystals	White (often tinted)	Vitreous
Allanite	$(Ca,Ce,La,Na)_2(Al,Fe,Be,Mn,Mg)_3(SiO_4)_3(OH)$	Monoclinic	Tabular crystals	Black to dark brown	Submetallic to resinous
Alleghanyite	$Mn_5Si_2O_8(OH)_2$	Monoclinic	Bladed crystals	Pink to brown	Vitreous to resinous
Allophane	$Al_2SiO_5.5H_2O$	Amorphous	Massive	Variable	Vitreous to subresinous

STREAK	FRACTURE	CLEAVAGE	HARDNESS	SG	REACTION TO ACIDS OR H_2O
Steel-grey to silver-white	Uneven	Perfect in one direction	1.5–2.0	8.16	Decomposes in HNO_3 with the separation of gold
	Crumbly	Good in one direction	1.0–2.0	4.1	Soluble in HCl
Variable	Subconchoidal to uneven	None	3.0–3.5	6.2	Easily soluble in HCl
Orange to brownish-red	Conchoidal	None	3.0–3.5	5.9	Easily soluble in HCl
	—	Perfect basal	2.0	3.67–4.35	Soluble in HCl
White	Uneven to subconchoidal	Good in one direction	4.5–5.0	6.1	Decomposes in HCl leaving a residue of hydrous tungstic oxide
Colourless	Conchoidal to uneven	Imperfect	2.5–3.0	7.9–8.3	Decomposes in HCl with the separation of yellow tungstic acid
	—	Perfect basal	2.5	5.5	—
Reddish-brown, brownish-black or black	Uneven	Perfect in one direction	4.0–4.5	7.4	Decomposes in hot concentrated HCl
	Uneven	Indistinct	3.5–4.0	4.23	Decomposes in HCl
White	Subconchoidal to uneven	Good in one direction	2.7–3.0	6.5–7.0	Soluble in concentrated HCl
Grey	None	Perfect in one direction	3.0–4.0	6.3	—
White	Conchoidal	Perfect in one direction	4.0	3.0–3.3	—
Black	Uneven to conchoidal	None	2.5	8.19	—
	Subconchoidal to uneven	Good in two directions	5.0–6.0	2.9–3.3	Insoluble in acids
	Uneven	Good in two directions	6.0–6.5	3.4–3.5	—
Reddish-brown	Uneven	Perfect in two directions	5.5	3.8–3.85	Partially decomposes in HCl
White	Conchoidal	Perfect in one direction	4.0	2.6	—
	None	Indistinct	5.0–6.0	2.9	Gelatinises with HCl
Colourless	Uneven to conchoidal	Perfect in one direction	6.0–6.5	2.62–2.65	—
Grey	Uneven to subconchoidal	Poor	5.5–6.0	3.5–4.2	Gelatinises with HCl
	Conchoidal	None	5.5	4.0	Decomposes in HCl
Colourless	Conchoidal	None	3.0	1.85–1.89	Gelatinises with HCl

MINERAL	FORMULA	SYSTEM	HABIT	COLOUR	LUSTRE
Almandine	$Fe_3Al_2Si_3O_{12}$	Cubic	Cubic crystals	Dark red	Vitreous
Analcite	$NaAlSi_2O_6.H_2O$	Cubic	Cubic crystals	Colourless or white (often tinted)	Vitreous
Andalusite	Al_2SiO_5	Orthorhombic	Prismatic crystals	Variable	Vitreous
Andesine	Plagioclase *feldspar* (50–70 per cent *albite*, 50–30 per cent *anorthite*)	Triclinic	Massive	Variable	Subvitreous to pearly
Andradite	$Ca_3Fe_2Si_3O_{12}$	Cubic	Cubic crystals	Variable	Vitreous
Anorthite	$CaAl_2Si_2O_8$	Triclinic	Prismatic or tabular crystals	Colourless, white or greenish-grey	Vitreous to pearly
Anthophyllite	$(Mg,Fe)_7Si_8O_{22}(OH)_2$	Orthorhombic	Massive	Brown	Vitreous
Apophyllite	$KCa_4Si_8O_{20}(F,OH).8H_2O$	Tetragonal	Prismatic crystals	White or grey (often tinted)	Vitreous to pearly
Astrophyllite	$(K,Na)_2(Fe^{2+},Mn)_4 TiSi_4O_{14}(OH)_2$	Triclinic	Bladed crystals	Bronze-yellow to gold yellow	Submetallic to pearly
Augite	$(Ca,Mg,Fe,Al)_2(Al,Si)_2O_6$	Monoclinic	Prismatic crystals	Black to greenish-black	Vitreous to resinous
Axinite	$Ca_2(Mn, Fe)Al_2BSi_4O_{15}OH$	Triclinic	Acicular crystals	Variable	Vitreous
Babingtonite	$Ca_2Fe^{2+}Fe^{3+}Si_5O_{14}(OH)(OH)$	Triclinic	Prismatic crystals	Black or greenish-black	Vitreous
Benitoite	$BaTiSi_3O_9$	Hexagonal	Tabular crystals	Blue or white	Vitreous
Bertrandite	$Be_4Si_2O_7(OH)_2$	Orthorhombic	Tabular crystals	Colourless or pinky-white	Vitreous to pearly
Beryl	$Be_3Al_2Si_6O_{18}$	Hexagonal	Prismatic crystals	Variable	Vitreous
Biotite	$K_2(Mg,Fe)_{4-6}(Si,Al)_8O_{20}(OH)_4$	Monoclinic	Tabular or prismatic crystals	Green to black	Pearly
Brewsterite	$(Sr,Ba)Al_2Si_6O_{16}.5H_2O$	Monoclinic	Prismatic crystals	White	Vitreous
Bytownite	Plagioclase *feldspar* (10–30 per cent *albite*, 90–70 per cent *anorthite*)	Triclinic	Massive	Variable	Vitreous to pearly
Cancrinite	$c\ 4(NaAlSiO_4).CaCO_3.H_2O$	Hexagonal	Massive	Yellow, white or red	Subvitreous to pearly
Celsian	$BaAl_2Si_2O_8$	Monoclinic	Massive	Colourless	Greasy
Chabazite	$(Ca,Na,K)_7Al_{12}(Al,Si)_2Si_{26}O_{80}.40H_2O$	Hexagonal	Rhombohedral crystals	Variable	Vitreous
Chlorite	$c\ (Mg,Fe)_5Al(AlSi_3)O_{10}(OH)_8$	Monoclinic	Tabular crystals	Shades of green	Pearly
Chloritoid	$(Mg,Fe)_2Al_4Si_2O_{10}(OH)_4$	Monoclinic	Massive	Variable	Pearly
Chrysocolla	$CuSiO_3.2H_2O$	Amorphous	Massive	Shades of green and blue	Vitreous
Chrysotile	$Mg_3Si_2O_5(OH)_4$	Monoclinic	Fibrous masses	Shades of green and brown	Silky
Clinochlore	$(Mg,Fe^{2+},Al)_6(Si,Al)_4O_{10}(OH)_8$	Monoclinic	Tabular or prismatic crystals	Variable	Pearly
Cordierite	$(Mg,Fe)_2Al_4Si_5O_{18}$	Orthorhombic	Prismatic crystals	Shades of blue	Vitreous to dull
Danburite	$CaB_2Si_2O_8$	Orthorhombic	Tetrahedral crystals	Shades of yellow	Vitreous

TREAK	FRACTURE	CLEAVAGE	HARDNESS	SG	REACTION TO ACIDS OR H_2O
hite	Conchoidal to uneven	None	7·5	3·95–4·25	—
hite	Subconchoidal	Poor	5·0–5·5	2·22–2·29	Gelatinises in HCl
olourless	Subconchoidal to uneven	Good in one direction	7·5	3·16–3·2	Insoluble in acids
	None	Perfect in one direction	5·0–6·0	2·68–2·69	—
hite	Conchoidal to uneven	None	7·5	3·8–3·9	—
hite	Uneven	Good in two directions	6·0–6·5	2·7	Decomposes in HCl with the separation of gelatinous silica
	None	Perfect in one direction	5·5–6·0	2·9–3·4	Insoluble in HCl
hite	Uneven	Perfect in one direction	4·5–5·0	2·3–2·5	Decomposes in HCl with the separation of silica
	None	Perfect in one direction	3·0	3·4–3·5	Decomposes in HCl with the separation of scaly silica
hite to grey or eyish-green	Uneven to conchoidal	Good in one direction	5·0–6·0	3·2–3·5	Insoluble in HCl
olourless	Conchoidal	Good in one direction	6·5–7·0	3·27	—
	Conchoidal	Good in two directions	5·5–6·0	3·4	Insoluble in HCl
	Conchoidal	Poor	6·0–6·5	3·6	—
	Flaky	Perfect basal	6·0–7·0	2·6	Insoluble in HCl
hite	Conchoidal	Poor	7·5–8·0	2·6	—
olourless	None	Perfect basal	2·5–3·0	2·7–3·1	Decomposes in H_2SO_4 leaving residue of scaly silica
	Uneven	Perfect in one direction	5·0	2·45	—
	Uneven	Perfect in one direction	6·0	2·72	—
olourless	Uneven	Perfect in one direction	5·0–6·0	2·4–2·5	Effervesces in HCl
	Conchoidal to uneven	Perfect in one direction	6·0–6·5	3·37	Insoluble in acids
hite	Uneven	Poor	4·0–5·0	2·1–2·2	Decomposes in HCl with the separation of silica
ale green	Earthy	Perfect basal	1·5–2·5	2·65–2·94	—
olourless	Scaly	Perfect basal	6·5	3·52–3·57	Decomposes in H_2SO_4
hite	Conchoidal	None	2·0–4·0	2·0–2·24	—
hite	Fibrous	None	2·55	2·2	—
olourless or greenish-hite	Earthy	Perfect in one direction	2·0–2·25	2·65–2·78	Decomposes in H_2SO_4
hite	Uneven	Good in one direction	7·0–7·5	2·6–2·7	—
hite	Conchoidal to uneven	None	7·0	2·9–3·0	—

MINERAL	FORMULA	SYSTEM	HABIT	COLOUR	LUSTRE
Datolite	$CaBSiO_4OH$	Monoclinic	Tabular, pyramidal or prismatic crystals	Variable	Vitreous to greasy
Diopside	$MgCaSi_2O_6$	Monoclinic	Prismatic crystals	Variable	Vitreous
Dioptase	$CuSiO_2(OH)_2$	Hexagonal	Prismatic crystals	Shades of green	Vitreous
Edingtonite	$BaAl_2Si_3O_{10}.4H_2O$	Tetragonal	Massive	White, greyish-white or pink	Vitreous
Enstatite	$MgSiO_3$	Orthorhombic	Prismatic crystals	Variable	Vitreous to silky
Epidote	$Ca_2(Al,Fe)_3 (SiO_4)_3(OH)$	Monoclinic	Prismatic crystals	Shades of green and brown	Vitreous to pearly
Fayalite	Fe_2SiO_4	Orthorhombic	Tabular crystals	Yellow	Metallic to resinous
Forsterite	Mg_2SiO_4	Orthorhombic	Tabular crystals	Variable	Vitreous
Glaucophane	$Na_2(Mg,Fe)_3 Al_2Si_8O_{22}(OH)_2$	Monoclinic	Prismatic crystals	Shades of blue	Vitreous to pearly
Gmelinite	$(Na_2,Ca)Al_2Si_4O_{12}. 6H_2O$	Hexagonal	Rhombohedral crystals	Colourless, white (often tinted) or red	Vitreous
Grossular	$Ca_3Al_2Si_3O_{12}$	Cubic	Cubic crystals	Greenish-white to olive-green	Vitreous
Harmotome	$BaAl_2Si_6O_{16}.6H_2O$	Monoclinic	Prismatic crystals	Variable	Vitreous
Hemimorphite	$Zn_4Si_2O_7(OH)_2.H_2O$	Orthorhombic	Pyramidal crystals	White	Vitreous to adamantir
Hornblende	$(Ca,Mg,Fe,Na,Al)_{7-8} (Al,Si)_8O_{22}(OH)_2$	Monoclinic	Prismatic crystals	Black or greenish-black	Vitreous
Humite	$Mg_7Si_3O_{12}(F,OH)_2$	Orthorhombic	Pyramidal crystals	White, yellow or brown	Vitreous to resinous
Idocrase	$Ca_{10}(Mg,Fe^{2+},Fe^{3+})_2 Al_4Si_9O_{34}(OH)_4$	Tetragonal	Prismatic crystals	Brown to green	Vitreous
Jadeite	$NaAlSi_2O_6$	Monoclinic	Massive	Shades of green and white	Subvitreous to pearly
Kaolinite	$Al_2Si_2O_5(OH)_4$	Monoclinic	Massive	White or grey	Pearly to dull
Kyanite	Al_2SiO_5	Triclinic	Bladed crystals	Blue or white	Vitreous to pearly
Labradorite	Plagioclase *feldspar* (30–50 per cent *albite*, 70–50 per cent *anorthite*)	Triclinic	Massive	Greyish-brown	Vitreous
Laumontite	$CaO.Al_2O_34SiO_2.4H_2O$	Monoclinic	Prismatic crystals	White	Vitreous
Lazurite	$Na_{4-5}Al_3Si_7O_{12}S$	Cubic	Massive	Azure-blue	Vitreous
Lepidolite	$K_2Li_3Al_4Si_7O_{21}(OH,F)_3$	Monoclinic	Aggregates	Lilac	Pearly
Leucite	$KAlSi_2O_6$	Tetragonal	Pseudocubic crystals	Grey, white or colourless	Dull
Levynite	$CaAl_2Si_3O_{10}.5H_2O$	Orthorhombic	Massive	White or greyish-green	Vitreous
Margarite	$CaAl_4Si_2O_{10}(OH)_2$	Monoclinic	Aggregates	White, violet or grey	Pearly
Melilite	$Ca_2MgSi_2O_7$	Tetragonal	Tabular crystals	White or pale yellow	Vitreous
Mesolite	$Na_2Ca_2(Al_2Si_3O_{10})_3. 8H_2O$	Monoclinic	Acicular crystals	White to grey	Vitreous
Microcline	$KAlSi_3O_8$	Triclinic	Prismatic crystals	White to pale yellow	Vitreous
Milarite	$K_2Ca_4Be_4Al_2Si_{24}O_{60}. H_2O$	Hexagonal	Prismatic crystals	Colourless to pale green	Vitreous
Monticellite	$MgCaSiO_4$	Orthorhombic	Prismatic crystals	Colourless or grey	Vitreous
Muscovite	$KAl_2Si_3O_{10}(OH)_2$	Monoclinic	Tabular crystals	Colourless or white	Pearly

REAK	FRACTURE	CLEAVAGE	HARDNESS	SG	REACTION TO ACIDS OR H$_2$O
ite	Conchoidal to uneven	None	5·0–5·5	2·9–3·0	Gelatinises with HCl
ite or grey	Uneven	Perfect in one direction	5·5	3·2–3·38	—
en	Conchoidal to uneven	Perfect in one direction	5·0	3·3	Gelatinises with HCl
ite	Subconchoidal to uneven	Perfect in one direction	4·0–4·5	2·7	Gelatinises with HCl
ourless or grey	Uneven	Perfect in one direction	5·5–6·0	3·2–3·9	Insoluble in HCl
ourless or grey	Uneven	Perfect basal	6·0–7·0	3·4–3·5	—
ourless	Conchoidal	Good in one direction	6·5	4·0–4·14	Gelatinises with HCl
ourless	Subconchoidal to uneven	Distinct in one direction	6·0–7·0	3·21–3·33	Decomposes in HCl with the separation of gelatinous silica
yish-blue	Subconchoidal to uneven	Perfect in one direction	6·0–6·5	3·1–3·11	—
	Uneven	Good in one direction	4·5	2·04–2·17	Decomposes in HCl with the separation of silica
te	Subconchoidal to uneven	None	7·5	3·5	—
te	Uneven to subconchoidal	Good in one direction	4·5	2·44–2·5	Decomposes in HCl
te	Uneven to subconchoidal	Perfect in one direction	4·5–5·0	3·4–3·5	Gelatinises in acetic acid
	Subconchoidal to uneven	Perfect in two directions	5·0–6·0	3·0–3·4	—
	Subconchoidal to uneven	Good in one direction	6·0–6·5	3·1–3·2	Gelatinises with HCl
te	Subconchoidal to uneven	Indistinct	6·5	3·35–3·45	Partially decomposes in HCl
ourless	Splintery	Good in two directions	6·5–7·0	3·33–3·35	—
	—	Perfect basal	2·0–2·5	2·6–2·63	—
ourless	—	Perfect in one direction	5·0–7·25	3·56–3·67	—
	Conchoidal	Good in two directions	5·0–6·0	2·71	Decomposes with difficulty in HCl
ourless	Uneven	Good in three directions	3·5–4·0	2·25–2·36	Gelatinises in HCl
e	Uneven	Indistinct	5·0–5·5	2·38–2·45	Decomposes in HCl to give gelatinous silica and hydrogen sulphide
te	None	Perfect basal	2·5–4·0	2·8–2·9	Reacts slowly with HCl
ourless	Conchoidal	Indistinct	5·5–6·0	2·4–2·5	Soluble in HCl
	Subconchoidal	Indistinct	1·0–1·5	2·1	Gelatinises with HCl
	None	Perfect basal	3·5–4·5	4·0	Slowly decomposes in boiling HCl
	Conchoidal	Good in one direction	5·0	2·9–3·1	Gelatinises with HCl
	—	Perfect in one direction	5·0	2·2–2·4	Gelatinises with HCl
	Uneven	Poor	6·0–6·5	2·55	—
	Conchoidal	Indistinct	5·5–6·0	2·55–2·59	Decomposes in HCl
urless	Uneven	Good in one direction	5·0–5·5	3·03–3·25	Soluble in HCl
urless	None	Perfect basal	2·0–2·5	2·76–3·0	—

243

MINERAL	FORMULA	SYSTEM	HABIT	COLOUR	LUSTRE
Natrolite	$Na_2Al_2Si_3O_{10}.2H_2O$	Orthorhombic	Prismatic crystals	Colourless or white	Vitreous
Nepheline	$NaAlSiO_4$	Hexagonal	Prismatic crystals	Colourless, white or yellow	Vitreous to greasy
Nosean	$Na_8Al_6Si_6O_{24}SO_4$	Cubic	Cubic crystals	Grey, blue or brown	Subvitreous
Oligoclase	Plagioclase *feldspar* (70–90 per cent *albite*, 30–10 per cent *anorthite*)	Triclinic	Massive	White, green or red	Vitreous
Orthoclase	$KAlSi_3O_8$	Monoclinic	Prismatic or tabular crystals	White, pink, yellow or brown	Vitreous
Pectolite	$NaCa_2Si_3O_8OH$	Monoclinic	Acicular crystals	Whitish-grey	Silky
Petalite	$LiAl(Si_2O_5)_2$	Monoclinic	Massive	Colourless, white or grey	Vitreous
Phenacite	Be_2SiO_4	Orthorhombic	Lenticular crystals	Colourless, yellow or pale red	Vitreous
Phillipsite	$(Ca,Na,K)_3(Al_3Si_5O_{16}).6H_2O$	Monoclinic	Aggregates	White	Vitreous
Phlogopite	$KMg_3AlSi_3O_{10}(OH)_2$	Monoclinic	Tabular crystals	Yellowish-brown to brownish-red	Pearly
Piemontite	$Ca_2(Al,Fe,Mn)_3Si_3O_{12}OH$	Monoclinic	Prismatic crystals	Reddish-brown to reddish-black	Vitreous
Pollucite	$(Ca,Na)AlSi_2O_6.nH_2O$	Cubic	Cubic crystals	Colourless	Vitreous
Prehnite	$Ca_2Al_2Si_3O_{10}(OH)_2$	Orthorhombic	Massive	White, grey or light green	Vitreous
Pyrope	$Mg_3l_2Si_3O_{12}$	Cubic	Fragments	Deep crimson-red	Vitreous
Pyrophyllite	$Al_2Si_4O_{10}(OH)_2$	Monoclinic	Massive	Variable	Pearly to dull
Rhodonite	$MnSiO_3$	Triclinic	Tabular or prismatic crystals	Pink to grey	Vitreous
Riebeckite	$Na_2Fe_3^{2+}Fe_2^{3+}Si_8O_{22}(OH)_2$	Monoclinic	Prismatic crystals	Blue or bluish-black	Vitreous
Roepperite	$(Fe,Mn,Zn)_2SiO_4$	Orthorhombic	Massive	Yellow	Vitreous
Roscoelite	$K(V,Al)_3Si_3O_{10}(OH)_2$	Monoclinic	Scales	Clove-brown to greenish-brown	Pearly
Schorlomite	$Ca_3(Fe,Ti)_2(Si,Ti)_3O_{12}$	Cubic	Massive	Black	Vitreous
Scolecite	$CaAl_2Si_3O_{10}.3H_2O$	Monoclinic	Prismatic crystals	White	Vitreous to silky
Serpentine	$Mg_3Si_2O_5(OH)_4$	Monoclinic	Massive	Variable	Subresinous to greasy
Sillimanite	Al_2SiO_3	Orthorhombic	Elongate crystals	Variable	Vitreous
Sodalite	$Na_4Al_3Si_3O_{12}Cl$	Cubic	Cubic crystals	Grey or white (often tinted)	Vitreous
Spessartite	$Mn_3Al_2Si_3O_{12}$	Cubic	Cubic crystals	Shades of red	Vitreous
Sphene	$CaTiSiO_5$	Monoclinic	Prismatic crystals	Variable	Adamantine to resinous
Spodumene	$LiAlSi_2O_6$	Monoclinic	Prismatic crystals	Variable	Vitreous
Staurolite	$(Fe,Mg)_4Al_{18}Si_8O_{46}(OH)_2$	Monoclinic	Prismatic crystals	Shades of brown	Subvitreous
Stilbite	$NaCa_2Al_5Si_{13}O_{36}.14H_2O$	Monoclinic	Tabular crystals	White	Vitreous
Talc	$Mg_3Si_4O_{10}(OH)_2$	Monoclinic	Massive	White (often tinted)	Pearly
Tephroite	Mn_2SiO_4	Orthorhombic	Massive	Shades of red and grey	Vitreous to greasy

STREAK	FRACTURE	CLEAVAGE	HARDNESS	SG	REACTION TO ACIDS OR H_2O
White	Uneven	Perfect in one direction	5.0–5.5	2.2–2.25	Gelatinises with HCl
—	Subconchoidal	Good in one direction	5.5–6.0	2.55–2.65	Gelatinises with HCl
Variable	Uneven	Poor	5.5	2.25–2.46	Gelatinises with HCl
—	Conchoidal to uneven	Perfect in one direction	6.0–7.0	2.65–2.67	Unaffected by acids
—	Conchoidal	Good in two directions	6.0	2.6	Unaffected by acids
White	Uneven	Perfect in two directions	5.0	2.68–2.78	Decomposes in HCl with the separation of silica
Colourless	Conchoidal	Perfect in one direction	6.0–6.5	2.39–2.46	Unaffected by acids
—	Conchoidal	Good in one direction	7.5–8.0	2.97–3.0	—
Colourless	Uneven	Good in two directions	4.0–4.5	2.2	Gelatinises with HCl
—	None	Perfect basal	2.5–3.0	2.78–2.85	Decomposes in H_2SO_4 with the separation of silica
Red	Uneven	Perfect in one direction	6.5	3.4	Unaffected by acids
Colourless	Conchoidal	Poor	6.5	2.9	Slowly decomposes in HCl with the separation of silica
Colourless	Uneven	Good in one direction	6.0–6.5	2.8–2.95	Decomposes slowly in HCl
Dark red	Conchoidal	None	7.5	3.7	Gelatinises in HCl
Variable	Uneven	Perfect basal	1.0–2.0	2.8–2.9	Partially decomposes in H_2SO_4
White	Conchoidal to uneven	Perfect in two directions	5.5–6.0	3.5–3.7	Slightly affected by HCl
—	—	Perfect in two directions	4.0	3.43	—
Yellow to reddish-grey	—	Good in two directions	5.5–6.0	4.0	Gelatinises in HCl
—	None	Perfect basal	1.0–2.0	2.92–2.94	—
Greyish-black	Conchoidal	None	7.0–7.5	3.81–3.88	Gelatinises with HCl
—	—	Good in one direction	5.0–5.5	2.16–2.4	Gelatinises with HCl
Variable	Conchoidal to splintery	Poor	2.5–4.0	2.5–2.65	—
Colourless	Uneven	Perfect in one direction	6.0–7.0	3.23–3.24	—
Colourless	Conchoidal to uneven	Good in two directions	5.5–6.0	2.14–2.3	Decomposes in HCl with the separation of gelatinous silica
White	Subconchoidal	None	7.0–7.5	4.15–4.27	—
White	Subconchoidal	Good in two directions	5.0–5.5	3.4–3.56	Decomposes in H_2SO_4
White	Uneven to subconchoidal	Perfect in one direction	6.5–7.0	3.13–3.2	—
Colourless or grey	Subconchoidal	Good in one direction	7.0–7.5	3.65–3.75	—
Colourless	Uneven	Perfect in one direction	3.5–4.0	2.09	Decomposes in HCl
White	None	Perfect basal	1.0	2.7–2.8	—
Pale grey	Subconchoidal	Good in two directions	5.5–6.0	4.0–4.12	Gelatinises in HCl

245

MINERAL	FORMULA	SYSTEM	HABIT	COLOUR	LUSTRE
Thomsonite	$NaCa_2Al_5Si_5O_{20}.6H_2O$	Orthorhombic	Massive	White	Vitreous to pearly
Thorite	$ThSiO_4$	Tetragonal	Prismatic or pyramidal crystals	Brownish-yellow to black	Vitreous to resinous
Topaz	$Al_2SiO_4(OH,F)_2$	Orthorhombic	Prismatic crystals	Yellow or white (often tinted)	Vitreous
Tourmaline	$(Na,Ca)(Li,Mg,Fe^{2+} Al)_3(Al,Fe^{3+})_6 B_3Si_6O_{27}(O,OH,F)_4$	Hexagonal	Prismatic or acicular crystals	Black (often tinted)	Vitreous to resinous
Tremolite	$Ca_2Mg_5Si_8O_{22}(OH)_2$	Monoclinic	Bladed crystals	White to dark grey	Vitreous
Uranophane	$Ca(UO_2)_2Si_2O_7.6H_2O$	Orthorhombic	Acicular crystals	Yellow	Vitreous
Uvarovite	$Ca_3Cr_2Si_3O_{12}$	Cubic	Cubic crystals	Emerald-green	Vitreous
Willemite	Zn_2SiO_4	Hexagonal	Prismatic crystals	White or greenish-yellow	Vitreous to resinous
Wollastonite	$CaSiO_3$	Monoclinic	Tabular crystals	White	Vitreous
Zinnwaldite	$K_2(Li,Fe,Al)_6 (Si,Al)_8O_{20}(F,OH)_4$	Monoclinic	Tabular crystals	Pale violet, yellow or brown	Pearly
Zircon	$ZrSiO_4$	Tetragonal	Prismatic crystals	Colourless (often tinted)	Adamantine
Zoisite	$Ca_2Al_3Si_3O_{12}OH$	Orthorhombic	Prismatic crystals	Variable	Vitreous

STREAK	FRACTURE	CLEAVAGE	HARDNESS	SG	REACTION TO ACIDS OR H_2O
Colourless	Uneven to subconchoidal	Perfect in one direction	5·0–5·5	2·3–2·4	Gelatinises in HCl
Pale orange to dark brown	Conchoidal	Good in one direction	4·5–5·0	5·4	Gelatinises with HCl
Colourless	Subconchoidal to uneven	Perfect in one direction	8·0	3·4–3·65	Partially decomposes in H_2SO_4
Colourless	Subconchoidal to uneven	Poor	7·0–7·5	2·98–3·2	Unaffected by acids
—	Subconchoidal to uneven	Perfect in one direction	5·0–6·0	2·9–3·2	—
—	None	Poor	2·0–3·0	3·81–3·9	Soluble in warm HCl with the separation of silica
Greenish-white	Subconchoidal to uneven	None	7·5	3·42	—
Colourless	Conchoidal to uneven	Poor	5·5	3·89–4·18	Gelatinises in HCl
White	Uneven	Perfect in one direction	4·5–5·0	2·8–2·9	Decomposes in HCl with the separation of silica
—	None	Perfect basal	2·5–3·0	2·62–3·2	—
Colourless	Conchoidal	Poor	7·5	4·68–4·7	—
Colourless	Uneven to subconchoidal	Perfect in one direction	6·0–6·5	3·25–3·37	—

Glossary

accessory minerals   minerals present in small quantities in a rock.

allochems   the granular parts of a limestone aggregate.

ammonite   a fossil cephalopod with a whorled, chambered shell.

archeocyathids   cup shaped fossil organisms intermediate between sponges and corals.

arkoses   sandstones which contain feldspar grains and some other minerals, usually micas, along with the quartz.

arthropods   animals with jointed feet and segmented bodies in the form of an external shell, including insects, spiders and crustaceans.

atomic number   the number of protons in the nucleus of one atom of an element.

atomic weight   the relative mass of one atom of an element or isotope (on the basis of carbon having an atomic weight of exactly 12).

batholith   a large mass of igneous rock which has been pushed up to the surface from the interior of the earth.

belemnite   a fossil cephalopod with an internal skeleton shaped like a tapered cylinder, similar to that found in cuttlefish.

binary star   a double star

brachiopod   fossil marine animals with a hinged shell which opens to release a flexible stalk and two coiled appendages for collecting food.

breccia   rock consisting of angular fragments.

bysmalith   a small mass of igneous rock which has been pushed up to the surface from the interior of the earth.

Cainozoic   the division of geological time from 70 million years ago until the present day.

Cambrian   the division of geological time from 600 million years ago until 530 million years ago.

cataclasis   the mechanical destruction of the grains making up a rock.

cephalopods   free swimming marine molluscs characterised by a head with arms or tentacles attached to it.

chert   sedimentary rocks containing very fine bands of silica crystals.

chordates   animals with internal skeletons made of bone or cartilage, including the vertebrates and man.

clastic rocks   sedimentary rocks formed from broken pieces of older rocks.

conchoidal fracture   a fracture in the form of a curved, concentrically ribbed surface resembling the lines of growth on a shell.

Cretaceous   the division of geological time from 135 million years ago until 64 million years ago.

crinoid   a marine animal consisting of a stem bearing a cup with arms attached.

cryptocrystalline   a crystal structure in which the crystals are too small to be distinguished by the naked eye.

Devonian   the division of geological time from 395 million years ago until 345 million years ago.

diatoms   small, unicellular algae.

echinoderms   marine animals with sharp pointed spines, including sea urchins.

echinoid   a fossil echinoderm with a spherical, spiny shell.

eurypterid   a large scorpion-like fossil marine animal.

extrusive rocks   rocks which have flowed out on to the earth's surface and cooled there.

felsic   term derived from *fel*dspar and *si*lica, and used to describe light coloured silicate minerals such as quartz and feldspar.

ferro-magnesian particles   particles of minerals consisting largely of iron and magnesium.

goniatite   a free-swimming fossil shell-fish.

granitisation   the formation of granitic rocks by partial melting with little overall movement of the melted material.

graptolite   a fossil chordate which formed branched, cup-shaped colonies.

groundmass   the fine-grained mass of rock which encloses phenocrysts.

holocrystalline rocks   rocks consisting entirely of crystals.

holohyaline rocks   rocks consisting entirely of glass.

hyalocrystalline rocks   rocks which are part glassy and part crystalline.

hypabyssal rocks   intrusive igneous rocks forming thin sheets or layers near the earth's surface.

intrusive rocks   igneous rocks which have solidified before reaching the surface.

ion   an atom which has lost or gained an electron and become charged.

isomorphs   substances which crystallize in the same form and form solid solutions.

isotope   a variant of an element with identical chemical properties but a different atomic weight due to the different number of neutrons in the nucleus.

Jurassic   the division of geological time from 196 million years ago until 135 million years ago.

laccolith   a dome or arch shaped intrusion of igneous rock.

leucocratic rocks   rocks consisting mainly of light coloured minerals.

lithification   the process by which loose sedimentary rock is converted into a massive rock by recrystallisation under extreme pressure.

lopolith   a saucer shaped intrusion of igneous rock.

Low Velocity Zone   a layer of melted and partially melted rocks lying between 50 and 250 kilometres beneath the earth's crust.

mafic   a term used to describe minerals containing iron and magnesium minerals only.

magma   rock in a hot, mobile, liquid state.

melanocratic rocks   rocks consisting mainly of dark coloured mafic minerals.

mesocratic rocks   igneous rocks consisting of approximately equal amounts of light and dark minerals.

Mesozoic   the 'age of the reptiles', the division of geological time from 225 million years ago until 70 million years ago.

metamorphic aureole   the zone around an igneous rock in which metamorphism has taken place.

metamorphic rocks   rocks which have been changed in mineral content as a result of high temperature and pressure.

monomict   a rock consisting of grains of a single mineral.

moraine   accumulations of material transported and deposited by glaciers.

oligomict   a rock consisting of grains with one mineral predominant.

ophitic   texture of rock in which large grains of pyroxene enclose a number of small tabular plagioclase crystals.

Ordovician   the division of geological time from 500 million years ago until 435 million years ago.

paleomagnetism   magnetism retained in rocks containing iron minerals.

Paleozoic   the division of geological time from 600 million years ago until 225 million years ago.

pegmatites   rocks consisting of large grains, often with large well formed crystals.

Permian   the division of time from 270 million years ago until 225 million years ago.

phacolith   a body of igneous rock which was intruded and deformed as a resulting of folding.

phenoclast   a large fragment of rock within the groundmass of a sedimentary rock.

phenocryst   large crystals set in the finer-grained groundmass of a porphyritic igneous rock.

photosynthesis   the process by which plants break down carbon dioxide under sunlight and release oxygen.

plate tectonics   a theory which describes the earth's crust as a series of rigid plates of cool rock which are moved about by the action of heat rising from the interior.

plutonic rocks   igneous rocks forming large intrusive bodies.

polymict   a rock consisting of grains of various minerals.

polymorph   a substance which exists in two or more physical forms having the same chemical composition.

Pre-Cambrian   the division of geological time from the formation of the earth until 600 million years ago.

protosun   the primitive sun, before it reached its present state of equilibrium.

pyroclasts   fragments of magma, mineral crystals, and glass expelled from volcanoes.

pyroclastic igneous rocks   rocks formed from material expelled from volcanoes.

Quaternary   the division of geological time from one million years ago until the present day.

radiolarians   small single-celled marine animals, consisting of silicic body capsule with spikes.

seismic waves   shockwaves produced in the rocks of the earth as a result of earthquakes.

seismograph   instrument for recording seismic waves.

Silurian   the division of geological time from 440 million years ago until 400 million years ago.

specific gravity   the relative density of a material, measured as the ratio of its weight in air to the weight of an equal volume of water.

spectrometer   instrument for analysing atoms by observing the spectrum of the light they radiate when heated.

stratigraphy   the study of the layered rocks exposed at the earth's surface.

supernova   a catastrophic explosion in a star which results in its losing a large part of its mass.

Tertiary   the division of geological time from 64 million years ago until one million years ago.

tetrahedra   triangular pyramids, with sides consisting of four equilateral triangles.

thermonuclear reaction   a reaction in which atoms of hydrogen fuse to form helium atoms, with the release of energy.

Triassic   the division of geological time from 225 million years ago until 195 million years ago.

trilobite   an extinct marine arthropod with a curved shell enclosing its body and numerous legs.

turbidity current   currents carrying suspensions of small rocks and mud which flow under the sea, from the edge of the continental shelf to deeper water.

ndex

ACKNOWLEDGMENTS

Aerofilms Ltd.   53, 60, 149, 154, 155(a), 163(b), 164

Ardea Photographics   38(a)

Serge Berton/Camera Press   161

Canadian High Commission   45

J. Allen Cash   58, 59(b), 156, 124(b)

Michele da Silva/Camera Press   34, 119

D. Elson   39(f)

Georg Gerster/John Hillelson Agency   24

Ormond Gigli/Camera Press   159(a)

Elisabeth Hodson/Camera Press   18

Angelo Hornak   211, 212, 213, 214(a), (b), 216, 217(a), (b), 218, 219

Institute of Geological Sciences   5, 29(a), (b), 32(a), (b), 38(b), 39(a), (b), (d), (e), 40, 41, 49, 50(a), (b), 51(a), 52(b), 54(a), (b), 56, 57, 59(a), 61, 62, 63(a), (b), 64, 123(a), 137(a), (b), (c), 142, 148, 150(d), 151, 191(c), 201(a), 207

Leicestershire County Council   44

J. Messerschmidt/Camera Press   165(a)

J. R. Middleton   123(b)

NASA   25

Josephine Nelson/Camera Press   156

S. Penn   129(a), 198(a), 205(b)

Photori   12

Fritz Prenzel/Camera Press   160

I. D. Sutton   31(b)

Swiss National Tourist Office   Cover

US Department of the Interior   26

US Geological Survey   35, 124(a), 193

A. C. Waltham   26, 27, 31(a), 33, 39(c), 52(a), 143, 146, 155(b), 162, 191(a), (b), 198(b), 200

Government of Western Australia   159(b)

All other photographs in this book were taken by Ian Cameron.

The authors are grateful to John Turner of Glenjoy Lapidary Supplies, Sun Street, Wakefield, for his assistance in taking the photographs on pp. 211–219.